Paul Howard. Twenties. Non-smoker. Athletic. Works out regularly. GSOH. Loaded. Likes: tantric cooking and teppanyaki sex. Dislikes: racism, cruelty to animals, war, famine, children suffering, ketchup. Marital status: pending. Star sign: Capricorn, *née* Aquarius. Compatible with water sign when Jupiter is in the cusp of blahdy blahdy blah. WLTM girls aged 16–30 with a view to friendship. Yeah, roysh!

The Curious Incident of the Dog in the Nightdress

ROSS O'CARROLL-KELLY
[as told to PAUL HOWARD]

Illustrated by Alan Clarke

PENGUIN
IRELAND

PENGUIN IRELAND

Published by the Penguin Group
Penguin Ireland, 25 St Stephen's Green, Dublin 2, Ireland
(a division of Penguin Books Ltd)
Penguin Books Ltd, 80 Strand, London WC2R ORL, England
Penguin Group (USA) Inc., 375 Hudson Street, New York, New York 10014, USA
Penguin Group (Australia), 250 Camberwell Road,
Camberwell, Victoria 3124, Australia (a division of Pearson Australia Group Pty Ltd)
Penguin Group (Canada), 90 Eglinton Avenue East, Suite 700, Toronto, Ontario, Canada M4P 2Y3
(a division of Pearson Penguin Canada Inc.)
Penguin Books India Pvt Ltd, 11 Community Centre,
Panchsheel Park, New Delhi – 110 017, India
Penguin Group (NZ), cnr Airborne and Rosedale Roads, Albany,
Auckland 1310, New Zealand (a division of Pearson New Zealand Ltd)
Penguin Books (South Africa) (Pty) Ltd, 24 Sturdee Avenue,
Rosebank, Johannesburg 2196, South Africa

Penguin Books Ltd, Registered Offices: 80 Strand, London WC2R ORL, England

www.penguin.com

First published 2005

1

Copyright © Paul Howard, 2005
Illustration copyright © Alan Clarke, 2005

The moral right of the author has been asserted

Set in 13.75/16.25 pt Monotype Garamond
Typeset by Rowland Phototypesetting Ltd, Bury St Edmunds, Suffolk
Printed in Great Britain by Clays Ltd, St Ives plc

A CIP catalogue record for this book is available from the British Library

ISBN-13 978-0-184-48808-5
ISBN-10 1-844-88089-3

To Paul Wallace, Alan Kelly and Jenny Lowe

HC-O'H and Associates,
Baggotrath Lane,
Dublin 2

Our ref: U/FOFF
11 September 1997

<u>WITHOUT PREJUDICE</u>

Dear Ms Masters,
Re: Paternity of your unborn child

I act on behalf of Mr Charles O'Carroll-Kelly in the above matter.
I respond to your correspondence with my client and your unsub-
stantiated claim that his son, Mr Ross O'Carroll-Kelly, is the father
of your unborn child.

I enclose a cheque in the amount of £50,000 (fifty thousand
pounds). This once-off payment is made purely in recognition of
your difficult circumstances and does not represent an admission
of liability on the part of my client's son.

It is made subject to the following conditions:

- No consent is given to register Mr Ross O'Carroll-Kelly as the
  father of the child;
- Neither you nor any member of your family will attempt to
  contact Mr Ross O'Carroll-Kelly now or at any time in the future;
- Mr Ross O'Carroll-Kelly will remain without knowledge of this
  settlement;
- No proceedings seeking a Declaration of Parenthood will be
  taken at any time.

This is in full and final settlement of all discussions to date. We do not expect to receive any correspondence from you in the future.

Yours sincerely,

HENNESSY COGHLAN-O'HARA

Contents

RESIDENTS' BOR, BERKELEY COURT, PRETTY MUCH TROUSERED

I hold up my empty glass, which the borman takes as a signal that I want another drink, we're talking straight JD here and it has to be said, roysh, the goy gives good measures. Christian goes, 'Take it easy, Young Skywalker,' but I just, like, ignore him, though fair focks to him, roysh, it's not everyone would spend their Christmas Eve like this.

Lauren's here as well. I hear her kissing Christian and then there's, like, total silence and I can tell that the two of them are, like, talking about me with their eyes. Another JD disappears down the old Gregory. I hear Lauren go, 'Ross, do you not think you've had enough?' and though he doesn't say anything, roysh, I can tell that Christian's just looking at her, going, Do not even *go* there?

I reach back and grab Lauren by the orm and pull her close to the bor. I go, 'Yes, Lauren, I *have* had enough. But tonight I've decided to have *more* than enough,' and she doesn't say anything, roysh, and I end up going, 'My marriage has just broken up. Think that entitles me to get mullered.'

She rubs the back of my neck and it makes me want to go to sleep.

22:58.04
RESIDENTS' BOR, BERKELEY COURT, BASICALLY LOCKED NOW

I blame the Brothers. I mean, what the fock were they thinking? It's like one of those school trips to Amsterdam that always crack me up. These teachers bring, like, eighty or ninety kids to the sex-and-drug capital of the world and then, like, act shocked when the kids get on the old doobey-doobey-do and go looking for their Nat King. What the fock did they think was going to happen?

Well, it was pretty much the same deal with the Urban Plunge. 'An exchange programme with a difference,' is what Brother Augustus called it, roysh, and he wasn't wrong. They sent us all out to live in Pram Springs for two weeks and a bunch of focking Antos came to live in our gaffs in Foxrock and Dalkey and, like, Ballsbridge and shit?

My eyes are getting seriously heavy now. And my head. It feels, like, too heavy for my neck to hold it up.

I remember, roysh, being served *spoice booorger an' chips wi' cuddy sorce* for the fourth day in a row, then ringing the school and going, 'Just what the *fock* are we supposed to be learning from this?' and Brother Augustus just goes, 'Humility.'

Anto had this sister, Tina, who was, like, bet-down. I mean, the focking tide wouldn't take her out.

RESIDENTS' BOR, BERKELEY COURT, SERIOUSLY HAMMERED

Fionn's at my elbow. What does that four-eyed focker want? *I've just been talking to Sorcha.* That's what he goes. He's like, 'I've just been talking to Sorcha,' and I go, 'How is she?' hating myself for sounding so basically pathetic. Fionn goes, 'She's not good,' but he's actually talking to Christian and Lauren, roysh, obviously having decided that I'm too focking mullered to have a conversation. Fionn goes, 'How's he?' and sort of, like, nods in my direction, and Christian's like, 'See for yourself.'

I order another and I hear Fionn tutting to himself, yeah, like *he's* Betty focking Ford. Lauren goes, 'So what happened to all the food?' and Fionn goes, 'Well, you know how much Sorcha hates the idea of good food going to waste. She got, like, Claire, Aoife, and Amie with an ie to gather it up and drop it to one of the Simon hostels. I mean, that's SO her, isn't it?' and at that moment in time, roysh, I hate Fionn's guts because he's always had the big-time hots for her and I know he's going to try and, like, use this to get in there.

I'm sitting there thinking about all those, like, junkies, stoners and focking soap-dodgers eating our poached loin of Wicklow venison and roast monkfish tail with Pernod butter sauce. The whole Dublin homeless community will be out in focking hives tomorrow.

I laugh out loud.

It must be out loud because Fionn turns around to the borman and goes, 'I can't believe you're still serving him,' and the borman just, like, shrugs and focks off down the other end of the bor.

I'm like, 'Well, she couldn't be *that* upset then,' and Fionn, like, pushes his glasses up on his nose and goes, 'What are you talking about, Ross?' and I'm there, 'Just saying, if she's doing the whole focking Bob Geldof thing, she couldn't be that upset,' and Fionn goes, '*Couldn't be that upset?* She finds out at her wedding reception that the man she just married has a secret love-child . . .'

I'm feeling a bit Moby and I think I'm going to vom.

'. . . and *a skobie* love-child at that.' I look over my left shoulder and it's, like, Oisinn, who's arrived in with JP. It was actually Oisinn who went, '*And a skobie love-child at that,*' and I'm just like, 'With mates like you goys . . .'

23:59.12
RESIDENTS' BOR, BERKELEY COURT, OFF MY FOCKING TROLLEY

Maaa-aaa-aaa-aaa! Maa-aaa-aaa-aaa! I'm thinking about Tina's laugh. She had a laugh like focking machine-gunfire. *Maaa-aaa-aaa-aaa!* I have to say, roysh, that Sorcha's not the only one who's surprised I got her up the Damien.

I told the goys at the time, roysh, that it was revenge. Her brother, as in the creamer I swapped houses with – turns out that Anto was his *actual* name – he was as happy as a dog with two mickeys out on Brighton Road, robbing everything that wasn't hammered to the focking floor, even the Boehm porcelain figurine the old dear was given for her work with the Ban Poor People from the National Gallery campaign. Rattling his sister was payback. At least, that's the story I told the goys when I got back to school.

I open my guts. Focking chemical warfare. Must be the wild mushroom and sherry soup – the only thing any of us got to actually eat at the reception. Or maybe it's the JD.

The borman's fixing a new bottle to the optic. He's settling in for a long night.

Oisinn goes, 'I actually remember that time. We were in, like, transition year,' and JP's like, 'Older woman and everything,' and Oisinn's there, 'The goy was a ledge,' and JP goes, 'But what are the chances of *her* working in the actual same hotel where Ross was having his reception?' and there's, like, total silence for a few seconds, then Fionn goes, 'Well, if x is the number of waitressing jobs available in the city at any given time and y is the—' and I turn around and go, 'Fionn, we all know you did Honours maths, what do you want, a focking round of applause?' and that shuts him up.

Oisinn sort of, like, sniffs the air and goes, 'Who opened their lunch?'

00:12.28
RESIDENTS' BOR, BERKELEY COURT, SERIOUSLY STOCIOUS
Erika's delighted, according to Fionn.

Lauren goes, 'I can't understand why Sorcha stays friends with that girl,' and Fionn's like, 'Hey, aren't you and Christian supposed to be at the Concert Hall tonight?' and Lauren goes, 'We had tickets for the NSO's Carols by Candlelight,' and Christian goes, 'We couldn't leave him on his own.' I wish people would stop talking about me like I'm not here.

00:54.19
RESIDENTS' BOR, BERKELEY COURT, THE MOST PISSED I'VE EVER BEEN
At least JP and Oisinn aren't treating me like I need to be

basically babysat. They've, like, pulled up a couple of stools and they're knocking back the old hill-billy idiot juice as well now. JP's telling us about some new development of two-bedroom townhouses he's flogging out in Bogsville – Camolin, I think he called it. He's like, 'Half-an-hour's drive from Dublin City Centre . . . that is, if you happen to drive a Westland WG-25 Sharpeye,' and behind me I hear the sound of high-fiving going on.

Tina was a dog basically and I'm being hord on dogs there. Her boat wasn't up to much and she'd no top tens as such. I mean, *I'd* bigger pecs. It was like hopping Action Man. She did have nice pins, though, I'd have to say. Brown and, I suppose, shapely. She'd a good Peter Pan, too. I think I'd been in the gaff about a week before I even met her. She was in, like, Santa Ponsa when I arrived.

01:19.07

RESIDENTS' BOR, BERKELEY COURT, PRETTY MUCH HORRENDUFIED

I have to drop the kids off at the pool. I've been bursting for an hour, but I didn't, like, trust my legs. It's got to the stage where I've no choice, though, because the smell is Pádraig focking Pearse, so I stagger to the jacks and go into Trap One. I don't feel like I'm going to vom anymore, but I feel majorly dizzy.

I stuff, like, reams and reams of bog roll into the can. Don't know why, roysh. Just one of those things you do when you're horrendufied. Then I stagger back out. From, like, way across the lobby, roysh, I can hear Christian going, 'She loves him. She'll come round,' and Fionn's shaking his head going, 'Not this time.'

6

RESIDENTS' BOR, BERKELEY COURT, ACTUALLY HORRENDUFIED

I think I've drunk myself sober. I can actually feel a hang-over coming on, so I decide to redouble my efforts at the bor. It's, like, doubles all the way now.

So there I was, roysh, in the kitchen one night, listening to Tina's old man banging on about how much bread he still owed the Credit Union since the Wurdled Cup – '*I folleyed Jackie's Army all over de wurdled, never any trouble ourra anyone*' – when in she walks, reeking of *Charlie Red*. She's like, 'Howiya?'

Now we're talking big-time CHV here, but I could tell straight away, roysh, that she had a bit of a thing for yours truly. I was there, 'Hey,' and she was like, 'Howiya?'

The taxi-driver brought her luggage into the kitchen. Four focking cases. I was like, 'How long were you gone – a year?' and she went, 'Only one of dem's clothes. Tree of dem's cigarettes,' and I sort of, like, nodded and went, 'So isn't that, like, smuggling?' and they all – even the taxi-driver – cracked their holes laughing. Tina went, 'It's mad the way dee talk, isn't it? It's like anudder language,' and the four of them looked at me like I was a seal with a new trick.

Tina went, 'Me mate's brudder-in-law sells dem. On O'Connell Bridge. I do bring dem back wi' me. Dat's how I'm able to go away tree times a year,' and honestly, roysh, she was pure Council House Vermin and I'd no basic interest, so I just went, 'Yeah, whatever. I'm wrecked. I'm going to hit the old Margaret Thatcher,' and they all cracked their holes laughing again and as I was heading up the stairs, roysh, I heard the old dear go, 'Your pooer brudder's after gettin' some class of an allergy, whatever der feedin' him out dayer.'

So I hopped into the sack, roysh, and I was asleep maybe ten minutes when – surprise, sur-focking-prise – the bedroom door opens and in comes Tina, clearly gagging for me. Took a few seconds for the old mince pies to adjust to the light, roysh, then I saw she was wearing this, like, nightdress, and it was, like, pink, roysh, and it showed off her Peter Pan really well. She copped me checking out her legs. She was there, 'I never really boorn in de sun, look,' and she storted, like, pulling various parts of the nightdress up and down to show me her colour.

02:19.06

RESIDENTS' BOR, BERKELEY COURT, UNBELIEVABLY HORRENDUFIED

I can hear Fionn going, 'He *must* have known. How could he *not* have known?' and Christian, fair focks to him, roysh, he's sticking up for me because I'm too hammered to. He's like, 'I'm his best friend, Fionn. If he'd known, I'd have known as well,' and Fionn's there, 'I'm just saying, I find it hard to believe –' and Christian's like, 'You *heard* his old man, Fionn. He paid her to disappear,' and Fionn goes, 'I'm just saying . . .' and Lauren's, like, rubbing the back of Christian's neck now, trying to, like, calm him down.

You don't need me to join up the dots for you. I ended up scoring her. Well, *she* scored *me*, is more like it. I mean, I was only, like, sixteen and she was a very old nineteen, definitely been around the old block more than once. It was my first score – first of many, without trying to sound too bigheaded – and the goys are roysh, when I went back to school, I was a ledge, a *total* ledge.

My eyes won't focus. Everything's, like, moving, like when your Savalas is focked and the picture keeps moving

8

up and up. That's what it's like. I remember when it was over, Tina rolled out of the sack, felt around on the floor for the nightdress and was like, 'Me fella'll moorder me if he finds out 'bout dis,' and off she went, back to her room.

03:04.40
RESIDENTS' BOR, BERKELEY COURT, PRETTY MUCH BLIND

Oisinn's telling JP a joke. It's, like, this refugee goes into an off-licence, roysh, and he goes, 'I wonder if you could recommend a good port?' and the goy in the off-licence goes, 'Rosslare. Now fock off back to where you came from,' and we all crack our holes laughing, roysh, but then all of a sudden I stort thinking about Sorcha, standing there, her Brendan Grace even whiter than her dress. And the tears in her eyes and her face frozen in this, like, smile – the botox – and her telling me that she never, *ever* wanted to see me again.

Christian goes, 'Ross, you can't stay here,' and I look at him and then I look around the bor. I'm there, 'It's the Berkeley Court, Christian. What's wrong with it?' and he goes, 'It's, like, Christmas, my young Jedi friend. It's a time for –' and I'm there, 'I *have* no family. Not anymore. My old pair are dead to me.'

He's like, 'You also have a –' and straight away, roysh, I cut him off, going, 'Don't say it, Christian. Do *not* even go there.'

There's, like, total silence again, roysh, and no one says anything for ages until Fionn – big focking Biggles goggles on him – goes,

'Ross O'Carroll-Kelly, you've really focked things up this time.'

9

1. D. I. V. O. R. C. E.

I wake up at three o'clock on Christmas afternoon. I look at my phone and I've got, like, two missed calls and two basic voice messages. I dial 171 and I hear, 'Merry Christmas, Kicker!' and I'm thinking, he's either very focking brave or very focking stupid. He's there going, 'You're probably sat there in that hotel worrying your little head off about my leg. Well, you can stop your fretting right now, young man. That salad fork managed to miss all the major arteries and so forth. And you can stop worrying about the police as well. I won't be pressing charges, have no fear of that. No need for you to go on the run, or become a, quote-unquote, fugitive.'

Eleven o'clock in the morning and he's already on the focking cognac, the tool. He goes, 'We were wondering, your mother and I, whether you were coming home for Christmas dinner. A hotel's no place to spend the big day. We were hoping perhaps you'd calmed down by now. Lots of strong emotions expressed on the day, anger and so forth. I spoke to Sorcha's father, Ross, and the girl's heartbroken, with a capital H. Can't imagine what it must have been like, finding out a secret like that at her wedding reception of all places.'

He's there, 'I know it was as much of a shock to you, Ross, to find out you had a . . . well, whatever. We did it to protect you. You had your whole life and rugby career ahead of you. We didn't want to see you dragged down in the mire by some . . . well, the only word I can think of, Ross, is hussy. We weren't to know she'd be serving the food at the reception. I mean, what's the Berkeley Court coming to that they would hire somebody from that class?' He's like, 'Anyway, Kicker, dinner's at three. Just wanted to let you know that your mother and I are happy to have you back.'

What a tosser.

The other message is from the Paradise Cove hotel in Mauritius, wanting to know where the fock we are, which puts paid to the rumour that Sorcha ended up going on the honeymoon with Fionn, my *so-called* friend, who has very kindly offered himself to her as a shoulder to cry on, roysh, obviously trying to get in there while she's, like, vulnerable. He had the actual cheek, roysh, to ring me up the day after the wedding, the goggled-eyed freak, and go, 'This is *really* awkward for me, because you're both my friends. I want you to know that I'm here for *both* of you. If there's any message you want me to pass on to her, I will,' but I said fock-all to him, roysh, wouldn't give him the pleasure. I'll talk to her myself when she storts, like, answering her phone again.

The kid, for what it's worth, is called Ronan, or Rohnin, after that focking tool out of Boyzone because apparently 'No Matter What' was, like, *our* song, even though we were only together for, like, ten minutes, which, incidentally, was a record for me that lasted three years. Other bits that I've been able to piece together are that Tina's old man rang the gaff when he found out his daughter was up the Damien, told the whole story to my old dear, and Hennessy, the old man's solicitor, was sent out to Knackeragua with fifty thousand bills in a briefcase and a contract that Tina had to sign, promising never to contact me. Like Knob Features said, what were the chances she'd be working in *that* hotel on *that* day?

The phone beside the bed rings. It's, like, reception. The bird goes, 'There's a package here for you, Mr O'Carroll-Kelly.' I throw on my beige Dockers, my light-blue Ralph and my Dubes and head down to reception. Turns out it's from, like, Christian, roysh, basically a food parcel. He's unbelievable, he really is. I could tell, roysh, he really wanted to ask me out to his gaff for Christmas dinner, but of course he couldn't, what with the whole history between me and his old dear. His old pair are giving it another go now, roysh, like the cheeks of my orse: back together after a whole load of shit.

Inside the parcel, roysh, there's a turkey, ham and stuffing sandwich, we're talking toasted, a couple of cans of Coke, a flask of coffee, a piece of Christmas cake and a couple of, like, mince pies and I feel this, like, wet on my face, roysh, and I realize that I'm, like, crying. The bird at reception is staring at me and I don't want her to think I'm a steamer, so I turn around and as I'm walking away, roysh, she goes, 'Merry Christmas, Sir,' but I don't, like, answer her.

I hop into the old Golf GTI – we're talking black, *with* alloys – and I drive out to Killiney and end up eating my

Christmas dinner sitting in the cor pork opposite the Dorsh station, just to be near Sorcha's gaff. I must have tried her number, like, fifty times but she's not answering. She'll be watching 'EastEnders' now. Phil Mitchell's going to kick seven shades out of Dirty Den tonight. I watch the clock until I know it's over, then I ring her mobile from the payphone outside the station. She doesn't recognize the number, so she answers it.

The second she hears it's me, she's straight on the offensive. She's like, '*Thirty-seven* missed calls? Are you *out* of your mind?' and I'm like, 'As a matter of fact, I am. It's Christmas Day and I want to be with my wife.'

She's not in the best of form, it has to be said. She goes, 'Which wife would this be?' and straight away I'm there, 'The one who promised to love, honour and obey me just three days ago.' She goes, 'HELLO? We left that bit out of the ceremony, *remember?*' I'm like, 'Well, the one who promised me, 'til death do us port,' and she goes, 'Were you even *listening* during the service, Ross? Or were you too busy looking around for other girls to impregnate?' which is way harsh, it has to be said.

Then the waterworks come on. She goes, 'You *ruined* what should have been the happiest day of my life. You've done a lot of shitty things in your time, but this was easily the worst,' and without thinking, roysh, I end up going, 'Yeah, roysh, what about the time I was with your sister?' which, luckily for me, she doesn't hear, roysh, because she's, like, blowing her nose.

She goes, 'So, have you seen him yet?' and I'm like, 'Who?' and she's there, 'OH! MY! GOD! HELLO? Your *son*,' as if I'm supposed to be, like, psychic or something. I go, 'Sorcha, please. This shit happened *years* ago. Before

14

we even knew each other. I only found out about it the same time as you. It's not my fault,' and she's there giving it, 'It *is* your fault, Ross. You've spent the last seven years of your life having indiscriminate sex wherever you could get it. Now you're reaping what you've sown. *Literally*.'

I go, 'Sorcha, can I remind you that we're still married,' and she's there, 'Daddy says I can get an annulment,' and I'm like, 'Don't change the subject,' and there's this, like, silence on the line, roysh, then she goes, 'OH MY GOD! You don't know what an annulment is, do you?' and I don't answer. She goes, 'It's something that you get from the Vatican to have your marriage declared null and void when you find out that it's based on a lie.'

I actually thought it was some kind of surgical procedure, like a tummy-tuck or some shit. I tell her that I still love her and she tells me not to make her laugh and then the pips go and I've no more change.

The Berkeley Court is supposed to do a shit-hot buffet breakfast, though I'll never know, roysh. It's usually well over by the time I get up at, like, three o'clock in the afternoon. Brekky for me is basically a jor of, like, jelly beans out of the minibor, we're talking seven or eight bills a pop here. Not that I give a fock. All of this is going on the old man's credit cord, the dickhead. He's too scared *not* to pay in case he never sees me again, and that's SO got to be worth milking. My only real care in the world at the moment is how to avoid the ones that taste like focking Germoline.

*

15

I meet Erika coming out of French Connection, looking incredible, as usual, we're talking Denise Richards, except with airbags as standard. She's, like, delighted to see me, which can mean only one thing, roysh – she's got something really bitchy to say to me. She goes, 'How are you coping?' and of course I end up falling straight into the trap, roysh – it's the big brown eyes, the hum of *Issey Miyake* – and I go, 'Actually, not too good. How's Sorcha doing? Same as me, I'd say?' and she's like, 'Actually, she's great. Seeing quite a lot of Fionn. Every time I call to the house, he's there. In her room.' I am seriously going to smash every pane of glass in that focker's face.

I'm there, 'He's just being there for her, as, like, a friend and shit? I mean, they go way back. They represented Dublin together in the All-Ireland Irish debating championships,' and she sort of, like, rubs the top of my orm, roysh, and goes, 'Sure, Ross. Whatever works for *you.*'

I just, like, change the subject. I nod at her shopping bags and go, 'Buy anything nice?' and she's there, 'A fabulous dress in BTs. The Hunt Ball is tomorrow night.' I make the mistake of going, 'Need a date?' and she's like, 'With one of Sorcha Lalor's cast-offs? I don't *think* so,' and I'm there, 'Fair enough.' Her loss. She goes, 'The goy I'm going with is *actually* a stockbroker. Drives a BMW 5 Series, automatic. Owns, like, eight houses,' and I'm there, 'Cool,' and she goes, 'Yes, it is rather. What are *you* doing here anyway?' I go, 'Here?' and she's like, 'Yes, Ross, *here*. Outside the Powerscourt Townhouse Shopping Centre, where your *wife*, or whatever she is to you, just happens to work?' I'm there, 'I basically have to see her. Is she, like, in the shop?' and Erika goes, 'She's in Paris, Ross. Supposedly picking up some new designs for the spring,' and then, roysh, her eyes become little slits and she gives me this, like, evil smile and goes, 'Fionn's gone with her,' and I can feel my face go all, like, hot, roysh, like I'm embarrassed or something, but I'm not, roysh, I'm basically focking angry.

I just turn around, roysh, and stort walking back towards Grafton Street. Erika goes, 'ROSS!' and I turn around, roysh, and she goes, 'Did you know there's a video of the wedding reception doing the rounds? *Oh my God!* It's, like, SO funny. It's like something from "Emmerdale".'

Oisinn turns around to me and goes, 'You alroysh, Major?' which is what the goys have been calling me ever since I took up permanent residence in Room 404 of the Berkeley Court, and I think it's basically got something to do with, like, 'Fawlty Towers'. I go, 'Hey, I'm easy like Sunday morning, dude,' and he's like, 'You sure?' and I'm there, 'Why wouldn't I be? I'm surrounded by beautiful young ladies. I just hope there's enough of me to go around,' and he high-fives me, roysh, and then puts another pint of Ken in front of me.

I get chatting to Sophie and Chloë, as in Sorcha's friends, roysh, who just happen to be in Ron Black's. I make a point of *not* asking how she is, roysh, just so it goes back to her that I'm, like, getting on with my life and, like, living the dream. Chloë's saying that her points have gone – OH! MY! GOD! – *way* off the board today because she had, like, a Quarter Pounder with cheese and fries in town and that's, like, twenty-three points, which is, like, five more than she's supposed to have in the *whole* day.

Sophie goes, '*Oh my God*, that's not even counting the

packet of M & Ms you had for breakfast. That's, like *seven* points,' and Chloë goes, 'HELLO? It's, like, five. And I had, like, points saved up from yesterday anyway,' and Sophie's there, 'Not five, though,' and Chloë gives her a filthy and says she's going outside for a cigarette and when she's gone, roysh, Sophie goes, 'OH MY GOD, we went to see Aoife today, in, like, hospital. I know she's, like, sick and everything but – OH MY GOD! – she is, like, SO, thin. The *bitch*.'

I turn around to Christian and ask him how the job-hunting's going. He goes, 'I got one. Storted work this morning. In, like, Forbidden Planet,' and I'm like, 'Forbidden Planet? As in the shop where all the focking nerds hang out?' totally forgetting, of course, that Christian spends half his life in there. I'm like, 'Hey, no offence, dude,' and Lauren goes, 'It's only while you're waiting for George Lucas to discover you, isn't it, sweetheart?' and I'm there thinking how great the two of them are together, and how shocking it is that she's *actually* Hennessy's daughter.

I go, 'Yeah, how's the script coming along?' and Christian's like, 'Ah, only so-so,' and Lauren's there, 'Don't listen to him, Ross. It's incredible. I know the goy's gone on the record saying there isn't going to be a *Star Wars* seven, eight and nine, but when he reads this he is *definitely* going to think again,' and I look at Christian and I think how much more confidence he has since he met her.

She turns around to me and she goes, 'How are *you* doing, Ross?' and I'm there, 'Let's just say I'm back in the morket place. You know me, Lauren. I think it's pretty much accepted that I'm a love cat . . . and tonight I'm back on the prowl. Big-time.' But of course Lauren has no time for that kind of shit, roysh, she goes, 'Oh, quit with that macho crap, Ross. This is me and Christian you're talking to,' and then she looks over my shoulder and goes, 'I take it you're talking about Chloë and Sophie?' who everyone knows, roysh, aren't exactly Lauren's cup of tea.

She's there, 'They're shallow people, Ross.' She's a straight shooter, there's no doubt about that. She's like, 'Come on, going off with Sorcha's friends? You're better than that,' and Christian's, like, nodding his head. He goes, 'Have you spoken to her, Ross?' and I'm like, 'I've tried. She's more interested in Fionn these days, from what I hear,' and he goes, 'That's *total* bullshit. You two are meant to be together – you know it and she knows it. Just be patient, young padwan. Don't do anything that'll make the situation worse,' and I end up having to go, 'Yeah, I know you're talking basic sense.'

So of course, typical me, roysh, I'm full of good intentions, but what happens? I hit the can – I have to drop anchor in Porcelain Bay – and on the way back I end up bumping into, like Maolíosa, who's, like, repeating second year Social Science in Trinity, nipped her a couple of times in, like, Reynord's and once in the Ice Bor last summer, we're talking Jolene Blalock here, except with blonde hair. So we get chatting, roysh, and, not blowing my own trumpet or anything, but I can pretty much tell straight away that she fancies another shot at the title.

The only thing is, roysh, she storts boring me focking senseless, telling me she SO wants to travel when she finishes college and would – *Oh my God!* – SO love to do the whole Australia thing when she graduates, which will be a major miracle at this rate because she is going to *have* to get her finger out in a major way if she's going to pass her summer exams, blah blah blah, the usual bullshit you get from nineteen- and twenty-year-olds, but of course the stud muffin here's cracking on to be totally interested.

I get a text message and it's from, like, JP, who I notice has just arrived in, obviously straight from work, wearing a tin of fruit that must have cost at least a thousand bills and it's pretty obvious he's coining it in selling those gaffs in Camolin, in other words focking Bogsville. I read the message and it's like, **HE SHOOTS! HE SCORES!** and I look over, roysh, and him and Oisinn give me the thumbs-up and of course now I've totally forgotten Christian and Lauren's advice and I'm playing the big-time Jack the Lad.

Maolíosa asks me who the text was from, roysh, because I did the usual trick for making birds jealous, which is you read it and then, like, halfway through you just stort smiling to yourself. Then when she asked who it was from, roysh, I just went, 'Oh, it's, em . . . no one,' and then stared off into space with this, like, half-smile on my boat. Birds are, like, SO easy to read, roysh. To try to make *me* jealous, she storts, like, banging on then about her ex, some dude called Eanna, who she says is *such* a dickhead and who – *Oh my God!* – SO thinks he's *it*.

So I'm there, trying to sound all concerned about her, roysh, going, 'You've just got to move on,' making my move early. There's a goy at the other end of the bor and he's giving us loads, staring straight at us basically, and I'm wondering who he is. Maolíosa goes, 'It's, like, difficult to put that kind of hurt behind you,' and I slip the old hand onto her knee, roysh – cool as a polar bear's knob-end – and I go, 'It *does* get better, Babes. Believe me. I had a marriage that broke up.'

I look back at the goy and he's still, like, staring at us.

Might just be that he fancies me. I decide it's best to ignore him, roysh, not give him any ideas.

She goes, 'A *marriage?* OH MY GOD! I had *literally* no idea. I am SO sorry,' and slowly, roysh, my left hand sets off on an expedition up the side of her skirt – how does JP put it? – trekking the uplands of her tights. I go, 'Let me be your guide. It gets better, believe me. Time is a great healer.' She goes, 'How long has it been for you?' and I'm like, 'Two weeks. Nearly,' and she suddenly pulls away from me, like I'm some kind of freak, roysh, and I'm storting thinking that I might have actually blown this.

Then all of a sudden, roysh, the goy who's been, like, staring at me suddenly whips out this camera and, like, takes a photograph of me. Of course, at first, roysh, I think nothing of it. There's rumours doing the rounds that Blackrock, of all teams, are about to ask me to play for them next season. I mean, they're basically focking dreaming, roysh, but there's bound to be interest in the story, that's a fact of life. But the next thing, roysh, Lauren arrives over. She's like, 'Ross, that goy . . .' and I'm like, 'Hey, it's fine, the papers are always going to be interested in me,' and Lauren goes, 'He's a private detective, Ross. He used to do work for my dad. Surveillance mostly,' and I'm storting to feel Moby Dick all of a sudden. She goes, 'Ross, cheating husbands were his speciality,' and I'm just like, 'Oh, *fock!*' and Christian's there, 'Come on, there's still time to catch him,' and the three of us end up pegging it out of Ron Black's and I see him straight away, roysh, getting into a silver Peugeot 206 opposite Bleu.

He's actually storting the engine when Lauren stands in front of the cor and makes this, like, motion to the goy to turn it off. He opens the door and goes, 'What the fu—'

and then he's like, '*Lauren*? Hey, Lauren, how are you?' and Lauren's like, 'I'm fine, Martin,' and he's like, 'Hey, I was sorry to hear about your dad. I'm sure they can't prove anything. He'll be out for the summer, you mark my words.'

Lauren sort of, like, shrugs her shoulders, roysh, then goes, 'That guy you just took a picture of . . . he's a friend of mine,' and the goy looks at me, roysh, and goes, 'Oh, *shit!*' I'm there, 'Who hired you?' and he looks at Lauren and goes, 'You know I can't divulge that,' and I go, 'Edmund Lalor?' as in Sorcha's old man. He looks at me and goes, 'Look, it's just another job to me. I was told to get pictures of you in, shall we say, *compromising* positions,' in other words with my hand up some bird's skirt.

Lauren – cool as fish's fart – goes, 'But you're not going to give him that film, are you, Martin? You're going to give it to us,' and suddenly the goy's got a face on him like a focking poodle shitting a peach stone. He's going, 'Lauren, *please* don't ask me to do that,' and she goes, 'That time you broke into that accountant's office. You were arrested on the premises, Martin, with a torch, a crowbar and a confidential file in your hand, and it was my dad who got you off. He even got you an apology from the Gordaí. Come on, Martin, you owe me this,' and I'm looking at the goy, roysh, and he's, like, humming and hawing and, like, basically wrestling with his conscience and eventually, roysh, he whips out his camera, tips the film into his hand and, like, hands it to me and I just, like, crush it under one of my Dubes.

Lauren goes, 'Thanks, Martin,' and the goy's like, 'I can tell him I decided not to take the job – conflict of interest or something,' and then he turns to me, roysh, and he's there, 'This guy really hates you. Don't know what you did, but you'd better watch your back,' and then he gets into his cor and heads off down Dawson Street.

I turn around to Lauren and I go, 'Hey, thanks,' and she looks at me and just, like, shakes her head and goes, 'What were you doing with that girl anyway?' and Christian's like, 'Lauren's roysh, Ross. You've got to sort this thing out,' and they go back into Ron Black's, roysh, and I end up sitting down on the step outside SamSara, whipping out the old Theobald Wolfe and, like, belling Sorcha. She answers on the third ring and straight away she's giving me the Ice Queen act. She's like, 'What do *you* want?' It is half-eleven, I suppose. I'm there, 'What do *I* want? An explanation would be nice. There was a goy in Ron Black's tonight taking photographs of me,' and she goes, 'Maybe *Hello!* are doing a special feature on you and your latest . . . conquest,' and I'm there, 'Don't give me that. Your old man hired a private dick to follow me around.'

She goes, 'My father is a family law barrister, remember? So he knows what he's talking about. Evidence of infidelity will copperfasten my case for an annulment,' and I'm there, 'So it's dirty tricks now, is it?' and she's like, 'I take it you were *in flagrante* with some little slapper tonight, then?' interested all of a sudden in what I'm getting up to, a sure sign that she actually still wants me.

I go, 'How's Fionn?' and she's there, '*Meaning?*' and I'm like, 'Did you have a nice time in Paris? Romantic, was it?' She goes, 'HELLO? *We* didn't go to Paris, Ross. *I* went to Paris. Fionn went to the Ardennes, if you must know. He's still there. He's doing his PhD on Arthur Rimbaud, *if* you must know,' like I'm supposed to know who the fock that is.

She goes, 'You hurt me, Ross,' and she just, like, bursts into tears and I don't know what it is, roysh, but I suddenly

23

stort talking, I don't know, straight from the hort. I'm like, 'I know you're basically hurting, Babes. And I know it's going to be pretty much impossible to put what we had back together. But do you think we could try?' and I swear to God, roysh, the girl's weakening, because she goes, 'I miss you, Ross,' but then, roysh, for no reason she suddenly storts losing it, going, 'You ruined my life. You ruined the happiest day of my life. Do you know what people are calling me?' and I'm like, 'Whoa, one mood at a time, Babes,' and then I hear her old dear in the background going, 'Hang up, Sorcha. I *told* you not to speak to him. *Hang up!*' but before she does, roysh, she goes, 'They're calling me Britney, Ross. Her wedding was a joke, too. But at least she made it beyond the reception.'

The old Jack and Jill is proving to be a bit of an issue with the management of the hotel, roysh, we're talking four measly Ks and they're, like, on to me practically every day, roysh, giving it, 'Your credit card won't swipe, Sir,' and of course I'm there, 'No shit, Sherlock,' because the thing is maxed to the focking gills. But Friday night, roysh, one of the birds at reception – a ringer for Keira Knightley, except taller – she phones the room and tells me that the management are offering me an ultimatum, roysh, and of course I, like, misheard her and thought I was getting, like, a massage or some shit.

I end up going, 'So, do you come to the room for that, or do I have to go to the health centre?' but she thinks I'm being Jack the Lad, roysh, and she just, like, blanks me, and I have to say, fair focks to her, roysh, because she wants me bad, but all she does is just remind me again how much dosh I owe, roysh, and it's actually five-and-a-half Ks now. Probably what pushed them over the edge, roysh, was last Saturday afternoon when I had all the goys over – we're talking Christian, we're talking JP, we're talking Oisinn. We went on the total lash and the fockers put about eight hundred lids worth of booze on my tab, not to mention nosebag and focking cigars.

I go, 'It'll be paid. Don't you worry your pretty little head about that,' but she's in no form to be sweet-talked, roysh, and she just goes, 'You have until midday tomorrow to settle your account. Thank you, Sir,' and she hangs up. So I'm left lying there on the Margaret, watching 'Coronation Street' of all things, and I'm thinking that Gail looks like your face when you look at, like, your reflection in the back of a spoon. Basically bored off my tits, roysh, I head over to the little shelf in the room where they keep, like, the kettle and the cups and saucers and the little miniature packets of Bourbon Creams – there was none this morning, which was the first sign that the management were losing the rag with me – and I grab the teaspoon to, like, test my theory. Like I said, I was bored off my tits. Anyway, roysh, Gail and Sara Louise are going at it hammer and tongs and Sara Louise is telling the old trout to basically butt out of her business, roysh, and warning her that if she doesn't, she's never going to see her granddaughter again, we're talking Bethany.

And I swear to God, roysh, I get this sudden flash of, like, inspiration, if you'll pardon the big words. I ring Orse Wipe on his mobile. He's out for dinner with the old dear, we're talking Roly's. He goes, 'Ross, what a wonderful surprise. I was just telling your mother the latest about Prisoner C080973, a.k.a my former inverted-commas friend. He's requested day release so he can go and watch the Schools Cup final. There's confidence – thinks Clongowes are going to make it that far. I said to a couple of the chaps out in Portmarnock, that alone should entitle him to compassionate leave.'

I'm there, 'Shut the fock up, you complete tool,' and he's like, 'Right away. What's on your mind?' I'm there, 'My five-and-a-half-grand hotel bill. The fockers won't restock the minibor until I pay up and my cord's maxed out,' and you're not going to believe this, roysh, but he *actually* storts humming and hawing, like he's thinking of not actually paying it, the tightorse that he is. He goes, 'Five-and-a-half grandingtons? It's a bit, er, steep, isn't it, Ross?' and I'm there, 'It's not *my* fault that I have to live in a hotel. I didn't ask for you two as parents,' and he's like, 'Fair enough, I suppose.'

I give him the old Sarah Lou manoeuvre then, roysh, except the opposite. I go, 'Here's the deal, roysh. If you don't settle that bill within the next hour, I'll make sure that you *see* your grandson,' and there's, like, silence on the other end of the line. I'm there, 'You wouldn't like that, would you? Skeletons coming out of the closet? What would the *chaps* say if they found out that your son had a working-class saucepan?' He goes, 'We're in the area. I'll swing by and settle up as soon as we finish dinner,' and I'm there, 'Very wise. And don't focking ask for me at reception. Just pay the bill and scram.'

I'll give him an hour, then I'll phone down, get Keira Knightley to bring me up a packet of Bourbons. I'm actually Hank Marvin.

*

26

Fionn looks at me as if *I'm* the one with the problem. He's like, 'Sorcha is as much a friend to me as you are, Ross,' and I go, 'Correction. *I'm* not your friend, dude,' and he's there, 'Well, I shall just have to reach an accommodation with myself over that,' and he thinks he's basically it with all his big words, the tosser.

I go, 'Same again?' pointing to his empty glass and he's like, 'Same again,' and I order two pints of Ken and I go, 'So, how was France?' and he's there, 'Great. I think I might be able to shed some new light on why Rimbaud gave up writing poetry at the age of nineteen. And not only that, but also his state of mind *before* Paul Verlaine shot him,' and he sort of, like, pushes his glasses up on his nose, roysh, and I give him this look, roysh, as if to say, *What* a focking waste of time.

I'm there, 'So you didn't see Sorcha over there, then?' and he's like, 'No,' and I go, 'Both of you in France at the same time and I'm supposed to believe that you didn't, like, bump into each other?' and he just, like, shakes his head, like I'm a child and he's trying to be, like, patient with me. He's going to have to have those focking specs surgically removed if he keeps that shit up. He's like, 'France covers an area of 547,000 square kilometres, Ross,' and I nod and I go, 'Big, in other words,' and he's there, 'Well, it's not exactly Termonfeckin. Sorcha was in Paris. At a fashion show. I was in Charleville, working on my PhD. Okay with you, Ross? You know, you *really* need to get over yourself.'

And I end up totally losing it then, roysh, and we're talking *totally* here. I'm there, '*Don't* focking yank my chain, dude. You're trying to get in there. You've always had a thing for her. I've seen the way you look at her,' and he goes, '*You* focked up what you two had, Ross. Stop looking around you for people to blame,' and I'm like, 'So you don't deny it, then? That you have feelings for the girl?'

And he goes – get this, roysh – '*Oh Venus, oh Goddess, I long for the days of antique youth, of lascivious satyrs, and animal fauns, Gods who bit, mad with love, the bark of the boughs, and among water-lilies kissed the Nymph with fair hair . . .*' and naturally, roysh, I'm looking over my shoulder to make sure no one else in the bor is listening. I'm like, 'What *is* that shit you're saying?' and he goes, 'It's actually a poem that Sorcha and I both like,' and I go, 'Doesn't even rhyme – how can it be a focking poem?' which he basically has no answer to, roysh, so he ends up going, 'Thank you, Edgar Allan Poe,' and I pick up my pint and knock back a mouthful, as if to say, basically, game, set and match.

So the two of us are just sitting there at the bor, roysh – we're actually in Gleason's in Booterstown – and all of a sudden I turn around and go, 'What do you mean, it's a poem that you and Sorcha both like? You mean you've been calling around to her focking gaff reading her poetry?' and he's there, 'She needed somebody,' and I'm like, 'That's total BS and you know it. You're trying to bail in,' and he thinks about this for a few seconds, roysh, and then he goes, 'I'm in love with her, Ross.'

He's lucky I've still got half a pint in front of me, roysh, otherwise I'd be, like, SO out of there. I end up just, like, looking away, roysh, and shaking my head. He goes, 'So now you know. I've always loved her. From the day I met her. For what it's worth, I don't think she feels the same way about me,' and I'm like, 'How could she? Look at you, with your, I don't know, glasses and your big focking words and all that useless shit you have in your head . . .'

He's like, 'Ross, I can understand you being upset, but I can't help the way I feel,' and I'm there, 'Answer me this one question – have you actually *been* there, or even tried to be?' and he just, like, throws his eyes up to Heaven and goes, 'Do you *have* to be such a Neanderthal? No, Ross, I haven't. That's sex, Ross. I'm talking about feelings,' and I'm like, 'And you're talking about my *wife*. Stay away from her or you can consider yourself decked.'

He goes, 'You know, I've watched the way you've treated her over the years. The number of times you broke her heart, humiliated her, left her in tears. I mean, the reception was a microcosm of your entire relationship . . . she can do better than you, Ross,' and I'm like, 'Meaning *you*, basically?' and he's there, 'When you look at her, I'm not sure you see what I see. If you did, you wouldn't hurt her like you do.'

I can't listen to this shit anymore. I'm there, 'You've had your warning, Fionn. Stay away from her,' and I get up to go. He's like, 'Well, I won't be making any promises I can't keep. She's cooking for me tonight,' and then, roysh, to hammer the point home, he goes, 'Wild boar casserole . . . with herb dumplings,' which she's obviously told him is my favourite.

So I end up totally losing it. I knock back the rest of my pint and I go, 'I'm going to get you for this. I'm going to get you in a *major* way,' and he laughs and goes, 'Not another war, Ross. You always end up losing,' and quick as a flash, roysh, I go, 'I might lose the war, but I'll win the battle,' which I have to say, roysh, I'm pretty pleased with. And then I just go, 'You're totalled. And we're talking totally totalled here.'

*

The old Wolfe rings, roysh, and I answer it and all I hear is this music in the background and it's, like, *'Deutschland, Deutschland über alles, Über alles in der Welt . . .'* and I'm thinking, that can be only one man.

Eventually, he's like, *'Von der Maas bis an die Memel,'* and I automatically go, *'Von der Etsch bis an den Belt,'* as in, straight back at you, dude. He goes, 'Hello, my child,' and I'm there, 'Hey, Father Fehily, how's it going?'

He turns off the record – he's got one of those old, like, gramophone things – and he goes, 'Like the fight put up by the l'Armée de Paris, Ross. I'm going to be brief,' and I'm there, 'Sure. What's up?'

He goes, 'You heard about our defeat last week?' and I'm like, 'Pres. Bray, yeah, that's pretty embarrassing,' and he's there, *'Embarrassing?* It's a humiliation, Ross. I'm going to level with you. In the six years since you left Castlerock College, this once-proud institute of learning has become the laughing-stock of Leinster schools rugby,' and I can hear him in the background, roysh, slamming his fist down on his desk. Then he goes, 'It's time the laughter stopped!'

I'm trying to, like, work out what he wants from me. I'm there, 'Are you asking me to come back and, like, repeat again?' but he cracks up laughing, roysh, and he goes, 'Lord, no. According to our records, you're twenty-three years old. Birth certificates can be doctored, of course. We've one or two past pupils working in the Births Registry, you know. Problem is, everyone remembers you from the great team of 1999. I mean, you were its heartbeat,' and I go, 'I suppose I *did* pretty much rock. So what can I do for you now?'

He goes, 'I want you to come back to coach the S this year,' which leaves me, like, totally speechless and we *are* talking totally here. He goes, 'Time is not our friend, child.

Our first match is a mere two weeks away. It's de La Salle, Churchtown. We'll pay you €2,000 a week, Ross, for every week that Castlerock stays in the competition,' and what can I say, roysh, but, 'I'll do it,' and he goes, 'Excellent,' and then he's like, 'I have to go to Rome for a few days – ecumenical business. Come to the school next week. Monday's good. Meet the players. Don't expect too much,' and I'm there, 'I'll see you then. Hey, thanks for the job,' and he goes, 'It's more than a job, Ross. I'm offering you . . . immortality.'

It's, like, six o'clock on a Thursday night in the Berkeley Court, roysh, and I'm bored out of my tree – I swear to God, roysh, if I watch that *Paula Abdul's Cardio Workout* DVD one more time I'll go focking blind – so I'm just, like, having a nosey around the hotel, just to, like, kill time I suppose and for whatever reason, roysh, I end up heading around to the Grafton Suite, where we had our reception, roysh, where it all went wrong, and through the doors, roysh, I can hear a band playing, 'Nothing's Gonna Change My Love For You'.

'I'd recognize that pretty little ass anywhere.' That's what I hear this goy's voice go, roysh. It's like, '*Ooh*, I'd recognize that pretty little ass *any*where,' and it's a real, like, gay voice, roysh, and I'm seriously getting ready to deck whoever said it. But when I turn around, roysh, it's, like, Trevor, as in the choreographer that me and Sorcha went to when we were, like, learning the steps for our first dance. He *is* actually gay, roysh, but he's still sound. His old dear sent him to ballet lessons when he was, like, five, so he can't help what he is, I suppose.

I'm like, 'Hey, how the fock are you, Trevor?' and I'm sort of, like, subconsciously – if that's the word – making my voice deeper, just so he doesn't get any ideas. He goes, 'Oh, you know this old queen – I'm never happy. I *do* have a fabulous new boyfriend, though,' and he sort of, like, leans close to me and goes, 'It's like a baby's arm holding an apple, in case you're wondering. It's *his* sister's wedding I'm at. Are you coming in?' and before I get a chance to answer, roysh, he goes, '*Ooh*, Glenn Medeiros! Quick, we're missing the first dance,' and he sort of, like, grabs me by the hand, roysh, and before I know it he's dragging me into the reception and there's all these, like, amazing-looking birds staring at me, giving me loads, and of course I don't want them thinking that I'm, shall we say, not their type – a steamer, in other words – so I'm sort of, like, mouthing the word, 'Friends,' as Trevor drags me up to the bor.

We sit on two high-stools and watch the couple do their last few, I suppose, rotations, then Trevor sort of, like, claps his hands together – like a girl, it has to be said – and shouts, '*Bravo . . . Bravo*,' then turns to me and goes, 'They had a good coach, of course.' I go, 'Do you want a pint?' and Trevor's there, 'What's up with your voice, Ross. Is it deeper or something?' and I'm there, 'Not that I've noticed. Pint?' and he's like, 'Heavens, no, Dorothy,' and he turns to the borman and goes, 'I'll have a Slow Screw Against The Wall, please. Make that two,' and a couple of minutes later these two Angel Delight glasses arrive with straws and umbrellas and focking fireworks sticking out of whatever piss it is we're about to drink.

So Trevor claps his hands together again and goes, 'I want to know *everything*, Ross. How's the delightful Sorcha?

Ooh, that *girl* – she's just like a young Judy Garland.' and I'm there, 'Oh, em . . . we broke up. But it's Kool and the Gang. I'm getting on with my life. I'm actually going back to rugby, in a coaching capacity,' and his jaw just, like, drops. He goes, 'Broke *up*? *No!* So there was *no* wedding?' and I'm there, 'No, no, we actually got married. It just didn't work out, I suppose,' and he's like, '*Didn't work out?* Ross, you got married *three* weeks ago. When exactly did you discover that you were growing apart?' and I'm there, 'Oh, about two-and-a-half hours after the ceremony, I'd pretty much have to say,' and he turns to the borman and goes, 'You'd better fix us a couple more of those.'

I don't know what it is, roysh, but I just find it so easy to talk to Trevor and I end up spilling my guts out to him about everything, roysh, we're talking the night I broke my duck with Tina, my old pair buying her off when they found out she was up the Ballyjames and the whole thing coming out at the reception. Trevor goes, 'Your father sounds like *quite* a man,' and I go, 'No, he's actually a total penis,' and it's only after I say it that I realize he's being, like, ironic, if that's the roysh word.

He goes, 'Well, you know what you've got to do, don't you?' and I'm there, 'Well, I've already phoned her a couple of times and tried to explain. I suppose I could send her flowers, if push comes to shove,' and he goes, 'I'm not talking about Sorcha. Ross, you've got to go and see your boy,' and it's probably the way he says it, roysh. *Your boy.* Not my kid, or my saucepan, or – as JP calls him – the fruit of my overactive loins. He's my boy. *My* boy. I have a boy. A son, I suppose you could call him.

So suddenly, roysh, I stort getting all, like, emotional and out of nowhere, roysh, I'm suddenly bawling my basic eyes out. So Trevor – he's funny, you have to give it to him – he leans over and, like, stirs my drink with the straw and goes, '*Ooh,* don't, Ross. People'll start talking,' and I sort of, like, laugh and go, 'I should go and see him, I suppose,' and he's there, 'Believe me, this isn't a time for sadness. Your parents, probably your friends as well, have been telling you that this is something to be ashamed of, when it's not. It's life. *Life,* Ross. Wonderful life.'

And I realize, roysh, that Trevor's roysh, he's totally roysh, and now the only questions going through my head all of a sudden are: What does he look like and is he good in school and is he into rugby and do all the girls in his class love him and . . . Trevor goes, 'Sorcha will come round, Ross,' and I'm there, 'What if she doesn't, though? What if she can't handle the idea of me having a kid with another bird?' and he's like, 'That's not the Sorcha I know. I dare say it's not the one you know either. She'll come round. Soon as she sees you facing up to your responsibilities. You know what you've to do, don't you?' and I'm there, 'Go and see Ronan?' and he's like, 'More than that. Be a man, Ross. It's time,' and I just, like, nod my head.

He goes, 'But before we say goodbye . . . a dance,' and he jumps down off the stool, roysh, and gets everyone to clear the dance-floor, then he says something to the band and all of a sudden they strike up the first notes of the song me and Sorcha had for our first dance, that pile of shite from *Dawson's Creek,* 'Kiss Me', or whatever. Trevor stands opposite me, roysh, with a big smile on his face and he goes, 'It's been three weeks, Ross. Let's see how much of this you remember,' and I go, 'Prepare to be amazed.'

*

I whip out the old Wolfe and bell Sorcha and she gives me the what-do-*you*-want? treatment when she answers. I'm like, 'How are things, Babes?' and she's there, 'Fine,' and it's real, like, frosty. I'm there, 'Hey, did you hear I'm actually coaching. Castlerock have asked me to go back and—' and she just goes, '*What*ever!' and then there's this, like, silence until I try to get the conversation going again. I'm like, 'Hey, I met Trevor last night,' and that gets a response. She goes, 'OH MY GOD, how *is* he?' and I'm there, 'He's drinking the Kool-Aid, Babes. Was asking for you . . . so . . . is Fionn there with you?'

And she totally flies off the handle when I say that, roysh. She goes, 'OH! MY! GOD! I've seen him, like, *once*, Ross, since he got back from France. I cooked him dinner. Oh my God, *what* is your problem?' and straight away I'm there, 'I actually don't like him,' and she's like, 'He's your *friend*, Ross,' and I go, 'Well, I don't trust him then. He has a thing for you. As in, the big-time hots,' and she's there, 'HELLO? He's a friend, Ross, that's all,' and I'm like, '*He* doesn't see it like that,' and she goes, 'Why am I even – *oh my God!* – discussing this with you? We've *nothing* to do with each other anymore. I can spend time with whoever I like.'

Just as I'm about to remind her, roysh, that she's still my wife, she goes, 'You still haven't been to see your son, have you?' and I'm there, 'Well, I'm actually going to. I'm actually thinking of going today, if you must know,' and she goes, 'If you spent a bit less time worrying about Fionn and a bit more time looking after your responsibilities, you might just succeed in winning back some of the respect I lost for you,' and she hangs up, roysh, leaving me there thinking how unbelievably spot-on Trevor was.

So what do I do, roysh, only bell Tina, then take my life – not to mention my new CD system – into my hands and hit the old Fleck Republic to see this kid, my kid, I suppose you'd have to call him. I have to say, roysh, I'm pretty nervous driving out there and it's not just because it's basically Dodge City. Being a father is something you usually get time to prepare for, roysh, but I've got this, like, instant seven-year-old son, but at the same time, roysh, I'm excited about finding out what sort of kid he is and all that shit.

So I'm driving through this estate – I mean, who the *fock* came up with that name to describe places like this? – and I'm looking for the gaff because it's, like, eight years since I was here. It's still like the focking Wild West, roysh, there's more horses in the gardens than cors and so many ugly birds in tracksuits that I'm wondering if the women's mini-marathon has taken a detour this year.

After, like, ten minutes of driving around, roysh, I finally pull up outside the gaff and it's all beginning to look familiar to me now, exactly the way I remember it, except eight years dirtier. I get out of the cor and lash the old alorm on. There's this little Ken Acker doing graffiti on the wall across the road, roysh, so I go over to him and I go, 'Want to earn ten lids?' and he just looks at me like I'm speaking a foreign language. I go, 'If that jammer's still got a full set of alloys and hasn't been keyed by the time I come back, there's ten sheets in it for you,' and as I'm walking away, roysh, I hear him go, 'Wanker,' but I let it go. The kid didn't ask to be born a peasant.

Then I go and knock on the door. Not being a snob or anything, but the place could do with a blast or six of Glade. Tina answers, roysh, and I decide it's important that she knows where she stands straight away, roysh, so I go, 'Don't get any notions about us playing happy families,' and she calls me . . . well, she calls me a few names and she tells me she already has a boyfriend – no, 'a fellah' – and then she makes a couple of not-too-favourable comments about my, like, performance that night. Sixty thousand birds would, like, testify that I've improved a bit since then, though after that little outburst, she'll never find out.

I decide to cut straight to the chase. I go, 'I'm here to see the little goy,' and I have to say, roysh, I'm suddenly kacking it, the old hort doing ninety to the dozen there on the doorstep. Tina goes, 'Did you not see him out there?' and this, like, horrible feeling hits me that it's the little skobe who just called me a wanker. Tina's like, 'There he is over there, at the wall,' and I turn around slowly, roysh, thinking that if I pegged it now, I could still ring Sorcha and tell her I *saw* the kid and I wouldn't be lying.

I turn around, roysh, but now there's, like, two kids standing next to the wall, the one who called me an oil tanker and then another kid, who's, like, two inches smaller than him, but who's, like, giving out yords to him. He's, like, pointing his finger in his face, roysh, and the bigger kid just has his head down and he's taking whatever the other kid's saying to him, then he hands over the spray can and this new kid pulls a wad of bills out of his Davy Crocket, peels off a couple and hands them to him, and the bigger kid beats it. The other kid crosses the road and comes into the gorden. He holds up the can and goes, 'Honest to Jaysus, Ma, have these kids nuthin' better to be doin' at all?'

Tina goes, 'Ronan, dis is Ross. 'Member I told ya abour im?' and he looks at her, roysh, then he looks me up and down, then he looks back at her and the two of them break their shites laughing. He goes, 'Sorry, Rosser, I thought you were that social worker back again. Nice to meet ye,' and he offers me his hand.

Doing the whole fatherly bit, roysh, I go, 'Hey, I've got something for you, young . . . goy,' and I go out and lash open the boot of the old GTI and give him a Leinster jersey, as in the new one, eighty focking sheets it cost me as well. He goes, 'Rugby, is it?' and I'm there, 'Yeah. You know, the man here was the best outhalf in the country in his day?' and he goes, 'Game ball,' and out of the corner of my eye, roysh, I catch him winking at Tina and I hear her go, 'I'll change it in Marathon durin' de week.'

I'm brought inside. I'm, like, bracing myself for the worst, roysh, but they've obviously come into a few bob since I was here last, roysh, because it's actually unbeliev-able inside. I'd say they shelled out a lot more for their furniture than my old pair, roysh, but none of it *goes* in a council Lego house. It's all, like, *chez longues* and big, fock-off ornamental rugs squeezed into these tiny little rooms. It's like Buckingham Palace, except shrunk in the wash, with giant plasma-screen television everywhere.

Tina goes off to the kitchen to make tea and Ronan and me sit there, chatting away, bonding, I suppose you'd have to call it. I tell him I'm married, though I don't mention the break-up, and that I'm one of the élite few people in the world who's a proud possessor of a Leinster Schools Senior Cup winner's medal. I'm there, 'Even Brian O'Driscoll would envy me this,' and I whip it out of my pocket and show it to him.

He tells me he plays 'ball', which is, like, Working Class for soccer, and that he's pretty good in school, except he hates it. I ask him what he wants to be when he grows up and instead of going, 'An astronaut,' or, like, 'A train-driver,' he turns around and goes, 'A solicitor specialising in personal injuries claims,' and I'm thinking, There's clearly a morket for that kind of shit around here. Smort kid.

I'm there, 'Are you sure you should be smoking?' He's just taken out a pouch of Old Holborn, which is full of, like, roll-ups and lit one up. I'm looking over my shoulder, expecting Tina to walk in any minute. He goes, 'Ah, relax, Rosser. She knows. I'm trying to get off them, but you know how it is.'

Tina comes in, puts the tray down on the coffee table, looks at Ronan and goes, 'I don't know *how* you can smoke dem tings,' and she focks off again and Ronan gives me a wink. I go, 'Whatever happened to Anto?' and he's there, 'Me Uncle Anto?' and I'm like, 'Yeah, my old pair really liked him. They'd love to know whatever happened to him,' though they're actually more interested in knowing what happened to the Jack B. Yeats original that went missing from the old man's study. Ronan goes, 'He's *insoyid*' and I'm thinking, No surprise there, and he's like, 'He got tree year. Ram-raided the offy in a robbed Peugeot, the fooken tulip.' I'm there, 'And you, Ronan? *You* stay out of trouble, I hope?' suddenly feeling all, like, I don't know, fatherly, I suppose. He goes, 'Acting the mickey in school, that's about the worst of it,' and I'm there, 'Kool and the Gang.'

After an hour or so, I get up to go, roysh, and I tell him I'll take a spin out to see him soon and we might, I don't know, hit town or something, or maybe go and see the Lions play in Donnybrook. He gives me his mobile number and he goes, 'Game ball, Rosser.' As I'm leaving the gaff I look across the road, roysh, and the kid who called me a wanker is back and he's got, like, a tin of white paint and he's painting over the graffiti he did earlier. He looks over his shoulder, roysh, and Ronan gives him the thumbs-up.

I get into the cor and stort her up. The kid shouts something at me, but I don't hear it. I turn off the Snoopster and wind down the window. He goes, 'No one touched your car, Mister,' suddenly all full of, like, respect for me. I'm there, 'Ten bills, isn't that what I said?' and he looks over at the gaff, then back at me and goes, 'No, er, Ronan already paid me.'

2. Caught in the Net

I pork the GTI out on the road, roysh, because I actually want to experience the basic sensation of, like, walking through the gates again. Above the orchway, it's like, CASTLEROCK COLLEGE in these big, like, wrought-iron letters and I swear to God, roysh, a shiver goes up my actual spine. It's, like, ten-to-one, we're talking lunchtime, and everyone's outside, roysh, throwing rugby balls around the place or, like, sitting around, basically eating their lunch.

Pretty much everybody stops what they're doing when they see me, roysh, and there's this, like, I suppose you'd have to say murmur in the air. Everyone's like, 'OH MY GOD! He's *actually* here!' and, 'Ross O'Carroll-Kelly – the legend returns!' which I have to say, roysh, is pretty flattering.

Someone throws a rugby ball to me and – six years out of the game, roysh – the reflexes are as good as ever because I catch it, look up, see the posts of the back pitch maybe fifty yards away in the distance and I drop-kick that baby straight over the bor. This, like, round of applause breaks out, roysh, then this big loud cheer and everyone's like, 'OH MY GOD! Did you *focking* see that?' and I look around at everyone and I go, 'Goys, your pride's just walked back through the door.'

I hit the staffroom. Fehily hordly ever goes in there, but I want to see the faces on the teachers when they find out that the man is back. I just barge straight in there, roysh, and McGahy, as in Geography, and old Lamb Chop Lambkin, as in Biology, are having some really interesting discussion – I *don't* think – about Iran, or Iraq, or wherever the Septics bombed the shit out of.

I don't say anything, roysh, just sit down, put the old feet up on the table and this bird – she's actually a new teacher, roysh, but not much to look at – she's just, like, staring at my Dubes, roysh, in total disgust, then she pulls her sandwiches away and sort of, like, tuts to herself. I'm like, 'Is there any coffee in that?' pointing to the machine in the corner and she's about to answer, roysh, when all of a sudden McGahy turns around to me and goes, 'I don't know where you *think* you are . . .'

I whip off my baseball cap, look around me and I go, 'I'm in the staffroom at Castlerock College. Hey, and you thought Geography wasn't my strong point,' and I crack my hole laughing. He's like, 'This room is reserved for members of—' and before he gets the chance to finish I just go, 'I *am* a member of staff. I'm coaching the S, as it happens. Fehily asked me to come back and bail out your sorry orses,' and of course being teachers, roysh, they're dying to, like, give me lines or detention or some shit, but all they can actually do is, like, throw their eyes up to heaven because they know I'm basically untouchable.

I'm sitting back with my hands behind my head, basically

loving it. I look at my shoes and I go, 'Think I need a new pair of Dubes. Of course, I can well afford it, what with my coach's salary of two grand a week,' and I see the new one turn around and look at McGahy with her mouth wide open and I know this is going to be, like, item number one on the agenda at the next teachers' union meeting. I'm there, 'You wouldn't be pulling in anything close to that kind of bread, would you, McGahy?' and he's looking at me, roysh – big focking bald head on him – and he goes, 'What I earn is none of your business,' and of course straight away, roysh, I'm like, 'Yeah, *what*ever!' and then I just go, 'Can't sit around chatting all day. Got a meeting with the Principal,' and on the way out the door, roysh, I turn around and I'm just like, 'Later . . . *Losers!*'

Fehily's cracking his hole laughing when I go into his office. He's like, 'Couldn't resist popping into the staff-room, eh?' and I'm there, 'Yeah. Wankers,' and he goes, 'Wankers is right. Always looking for *more* money. You know, I think some of them are under the impression that what they teach in class actually matters,' and I go, 'Unbelievable,' sort of, like, shaking my head. He goes, 'And on that self-same subject, there are one or two players on the senior team who are, shall we say, a little too interested in their studies. Got it into their heads somehow that the Leaving Cert. is important. Read what *that* says, my child,' and he points to this, like, plaque on the wall behind his desk.

I'm there, '*A violently active, intrepid, brutal youth – that is what I am after . . . I will have no intellectual training. Knowledge is ruin for my young men,*' and Fehily goes, '*Ruin*, that's right. It's from *Mein Kampf*. And you'd be wise to remember it. Don't be afraid to make changes, do you hear me?' and

I'm like, 'I watched the video you sent me – the Pres. match,' and he stands up and goes, 'Come and meet the players. Tell them the shame you felt watching your *alma mater* humbled by a school from a town of half-breeds.'

He brings me down to the gym, roysh, and all the goys are down there waiting for me, totally kacking it, roysh, and understandably so because the axe is about to fall in a major way. They all stand up when we walk in – they actually stand to attention – and Fehily goes, 'I take it this man ... needs no introduction,' then he's just like, 'I'll leave you to it, Ross,' and off he goes.

I look around the room at all the goys, roysh, shake my head and go, 'Sit down!' which they do. I'm like, '*Bray!* I mean, Bray, of all places! Someone says Bray to you, what do you think of? Slot-machines, pound shops, men with scaldy faces. You do NOT think rugby. Okay, they have a pretty tasty team this year, but they still shouldn't be in *our* league. Come on, what were you goys thinking? I watched the game and let me just say, I was ashamed of you,' and then I go, '*Ashamed*,' looking straight at Mouse Kelly, our so-called outside-centre who dropped the focking ball twice and handed them two tries. I'm just like, 'Be gone,' and when he finally cops what I'm talking about, roysh, he gets his shit together and focks off.

Next on the list, roysh, is Vaughan Anders, which I have to say is a seriously brave move by me, as it means breaking with the hundred-year-old tradition that the fattest goy in sixth year is automatically guaranteed a place in the pack. I know Fehily's probably going to get it in the ear from Brother Augustus and the other traditionalists on the board of management, but I know he'll back me 100 per cent, maybe even more, if there's actually such a thing.

I sort of, like, cup my hands around my mouth, roysh, and go, 'Come in, Vaughan Anders, your time is up!' which is probably a bit, I don't know, insensitive of me, roysh, but I want the rest of the goys to know that they're going to have to be, like, seriously fit if they want to play for Castlerock in future. I go, 'No man is bigger than the team,' and then I point at Vaughan's big flabby Ned and I'm like, 'although in his case, it's a pretty close call,' and everyone, like, cracks their holes laughing. He actually shoots me a filthy, roysh, as he's packing his bag and then, as he passes me on the way out the door he goes, 'Focking orsehole,' under his breath, but I'm actually big enough to ignore it. I'll tell Fehily I want him expelled this afternoon.

I'm there, 'Dead wood. Got to be swept out,' and Dessie Voyles – the tighthead prop – basically knows what's coming next because he's already, like, rolling his rugby gear into a ball and stuffing it into his bag. He's repeated his Leaving so many times, roysh, he's practically older than some of the teachers. I'm there, 'You understand, don't you? I've got to build for the future, dude,' and he sort of, like, stares into the distance, roysh, and goes, 'It's a short career alroysh. Washed up at twenty-seven . . .'

So there I am, roysh, walking around, looking them all up and down and, like, they're all scared to look me in the eye in case they're next. I go, 'You all know me and you know my reputation. You're going to find me a tough coach, but a fair one. I'll stand for a lot of things. I'll stand for players not being good enough. I'll stand for players being too hung-over to train. What I *won't* stand for is lack of pride in the Castlerock colours. And I can guarantee you one thing – by the time we go out to play de La Salle Churchtown next week, none of you will be too scared to look me in the eye.'

Then I'm like, 'Now, come on, cheer up. It's not all doom and gloom,' which it isn't, roysh. There's basically the nucleus of a decent team there – certainly good enough to beat de La focking Salle Churchtown. Francis Stadiem, our prop-forward, is good enough to make the Leinster schools team this year, according to Wardy, who also said in the *Indo* that Aodán Hannafy, our second row, is the best lineout jumper for his age in Ireland BAR NONE!

We've also got Andrew Pike – as in Pikey – and I don't need Wardy to tell me he is pound-for-pound the best all-round player in schools rugby at the moment, and reminds me a bit of myself actually, even if he is a bit, I don't know, full of himself. Then there's Lorcan, who's a focking unbelievable scrumhalf, but who I'm actually tempted to drop on account of the fact that he's, like, Fionn's brother and it would really piss off Eddie the Eagle. In the end, though, I don't, even though it's Lorcan that Fehily was talking about when he mentioned too many players being into, like, books and shit? I actually leave him in the team. He's good. And besides, I've decided he could have his uses.

It's, like, Saturday afternoon, roysh, and I bell Sorcha and ask her what she's up to. She goes, 'I'm in the Merrion Shopping Centre, if you *must* know,' and I'm like, 'In your mum's shop?' and she's there, 'We're doing a stocktake, Ross, not that it's any of *your* business,' and I'm like, 'So who's looking after *your* shop,' but she just ignores me, roysh, so I go, 'Doesn't matter. Just wondered did you fancy going for a coffee?' and she's there, 'And *why* would I want to go for a coffee with *you*, of all people?' and I'm like, 'No reason. It's just me and Ronan were, like, cruising around in the cor and we thought . . .' and she goes, 'What?' sounding all, like, interested all of a sudden.

She's there, '*Oh! My! God!* He's with you now?' and I'm like, 'Yeah. We're not a million miles away from you either. I was just showing him where the old Rossmeister General here went to school,' and Sorcha's going, 'Well, em, I suppose I'm *actually* due a break. I mean, I could squeeze in a skinny *latté*,' and I'm there, 'No, no, you've got, I don't know, frocks to count, shoes to put into pairs . . .' and she's like, 'Please, Ross. I want to meet him. I'd *love* to meet him. Please,' and I'm there, 'Okay, we'll see you in the coffee shop in there in, like, ten minutes?' and as I'm hanging up, roysh, I can hear her going, '*Oh my God, oh my God, oh my GOD!*' obviously pretty nervous about meeting him.

I'm actually nervous about meeting *her*. I haven't basically seen her since the day of the wedding. Ronan hasn't a care in the world. He's reading the *Racing Post* – 'studying the form', I believe is the expression. He's like, '*Harm's Way* in the 3.30 at Plumpton. I don't know – he's a fooken donkey, Rosser, but Barry Geraghty's on him. Suppose he's got to be worth a monkey each way,' and he whips out his Wolfe, roysh, presumably to ring his bookie.

I'm there, 'Now, Ronan, you'll be on your best be-haviour, won't you?' and he sort of, like, stops mid-dial and gives me this look, roysh, like I've just seriously offended him. Then he slips it back into his Davy Crocket, roysh, and goes, 'Okay, what's the story with you two again. Yiz are married but . . .' and I'm there, 'But we're having a bit of a break at the moment. Having a few problems, blah blah blah,' and he goes, 'I'll watch what I say then. Sorted,' and I'm like, 'And put that tin away, Ronan. You're not smoking in my cor,' and he just, like, smiles at me and goes, 'Game ball,' and it'd actually be hord, roysh, not to really like him.

Sorcha can't take her eyes off him. And he can't take his eyes off her. He's going, 'I know you said she was byooriful, Rosser, but I didn't think you meant *byooooriful*,' and he's actually spot-on, she *is* looking pretty tremendous, it has to be said, in her pink, sleeveless, cashmere poloneck and, I think, the grey Reiss trousers I bought her for her birthday last year. She's just, like, looking back at him, smiling basically. He goes, 'Sorry, Sorcha, I'm a bit quiet today. Always get that way in the presence of beauty,' and she laughs and goes, 'Well, you are *such* a handsome boy,' and the two of them look at me, roysh, as if to say, I don't know, where the fock did he get his looks from then, and the two of them crack their holes laughing.

Didn't take them long to break down the whole language barrier. It was actually a little bit awkward when they first met, roysh. She was there going, 'Ronan, it's *lovely* to meet you,' and he was like, 'The pleasure's all mine, Doll,' and he sort of, like, flicked his thumb in my direction and went, 'How'd you get mixed up with this sham anyway?' and of course Sorcha looked at me and I had to go, 'He's asking how we ever ended up being together,' and she was there, 'I don't know. It's like, OH! MY! GOD!' and of course Ronan was like, 'What's she saying, Rosser?' and I was like, 'She says she sometimes asks herself the same question,' and he went, 'Word from the wise, Doll, drop him like a hot snot,' and I turn to Sorcha and I'm there, 'He said you should . . . never mind.'

But they're getting on like a house on fire. Out of the corner of my eye, roysh, I cop one of the security gords having a look in – someone's obviously seen the Celtic jersey and reported it – but Sorcha just, like, mouths the words, 'It's fine, he's with me,' and the goy says something into his walkie-talkie and focks off.

My back teeth are focking floating, roysh, so I leave the two of them alone and head downstairs for a hit-and-miss and when I come back, roysh, Sorcha's going, 'They *have* actually force-fed her, but it's only, like, a short-term fix,' and I presume she's telling him about Aoife, who's, like, still in hospital. He goes, 'Is there any hope for her, is there?' and she goes, 'Actually, yeah. The doctor who's, like, attending her now, he's really gained her confidence, which is, like, SO important,' and Ronan just, like, nods and goes, 'You're obviously a good friend to her,' and Sorcha just gives him this, like, really warm smile, then turns to me and goes, 'I better get back. Mum'll have a search porty out looking for me,' and she gives Ronan a hug, then thanks me for the *latté* and the carrot cake, says it was nice to see me and then gives me this, like, peck on the cheek.

I drop Ronan home. We're, like, crossing the East Link and Ronan whips out the old Wolfe again, hits a number on speed-dial and asks whoever's on the other end how *Harm's Way* got on at Plumpton. Then he hangs up and goes, 'Fell. That's a few bob saved,' and then I get a text message, roysh, from Sorcha as it turns out and it's like, **Ross, hes gorgeos I luv him & it realy was nic2 cu** and I put the old Wolfe back in my tennis racket and I think, Today really was a good day.

When he's getting out of the cor, Ronan goes, 'Sort it, Rosser,' and I'm like, 'Sort it?' and he's there, 'She's an unbelievable boord. Sort it,' and I tell him I'll see him next week and then I go, 'And don't forget to look out for our result in the paper. Remember, it's Castlerock,' and he just, like, waves his hand at me as he disappears up the path and into his gaff.

I'm, like, pulling into the cor pork of the Berkeley Court, roysh, when my phone rings and caller ID says it's, like, Sorcha. I'm there thinking, Easier than I expected, but when I answer, roysh, she's bawling her eyes out and she goes, 'Have you seen *VIP*?' and if it's not the most stupid question I've ever been asked, roysh, it's pretty focking close. I'm there, 'What's wrong? You sound upset,' and she goes, 'Erika sent them one of our wedding photos, just to be a bitch. They printed it. The caption's like, *Ross O'Carroll-Kelly and Sorcha Lalor on their happy day,*' and I sort of, like, groan and I go, 'I'll have a word with her,' and she's like, 'Actually, Ross, I think you've done enough. It's just brought it all back to me again,' and she just, like, hangs up on me.

We did beat de La Salle Churchtown, roysh, but by nothing close to the margin we expected. Thank fock for Pikey is all I can say, roysh, because he kicked all fifteen of our points and our defence performed basically heroics to keep them to two tries, which they failed to convert because their kicker basically couldn't hit a focking rhino's orse with a tennis racket. It was actually a cracker of a match, roysh – '*the best advertisement for the game of rugby that you are likely to see in this hemisphere all year,*' in the words of the great man, but we should really have beaten them out the gate. The goys are pretty down about it and they need serious picking-up, what with our second match, we're talking St Paul's here, coming, like, five days later.

Lorcan played totally focking kack and I swear to God,

roysh, if I had another scrumhalf with two hands and even partial vision, the goy would be dropped quicker than a focking Ag. Science student's knickers at the UCD Valentine's Ball. The thing is, roysh, he's one of the best scrumhalves I've ever seen, but it's, like, the same problem that a lot of coaches are finding – what with all the pressure to get, like, points in the Leaving, blah blah blah – goys are becoming more and more, I suppose, reluctant to, like, skip classes. And that's Lorcan's problem. He's more interested in becoming a clone of his focking geeky brother than in, like, realizing his potential as a rugby player. It's all, like, books and notes and education.

I basically realized it was becoming a problem, roysh, a couple of days before the match, when I copped him and Aodán, our second-row, filling out their CAO forms in the library. We're talking during lunchtime here, when they should have been out training, or at least thinking about their game. It was, like, pretty clear watching the de La Salle match that neither of them was properly concentrating on their rugby.

So the day after the game, roysh, I bell Lorcan on his mobile. It's, like, eight o'clock at night, roysh, and I am not bullshitting here, the goy is actually *still* studying. I'm there, 'Why aren't you watching "Jackass"?' and, calm as you like, roysh, he goes, 'I'm doing some extra grinds. I need to get an A1 in chemistry.' Surprise, sur-focking-prise, of course, I can hear Fionn's voice in the background, roysh, going, 'Who is it?' and it's obviously him who has Lorcan like this, not giving a fock whether his brother leaves schools with a Leinster Schools Senior Cup medal or not. I just lose it, roysh. I go, 'Lorcan, I need to talk to you. Couple of rugby matters. I'll be out there in ten.'

So I hop into the old GTI, roysh, and I arrive out to the gaff in Monkstown, which is a pretty impressive pile of bricks, it has to be said. Fionn's old dear opens the door and I push past her, ignoring her offer of a slice of date-and-goat's-cheese quiche, and head straight for the study, roysh, where Lorcan and Fionn are both sitting with this, like, massive chart spread out in front of them, with all these, like, stickers and initials and all sorts of, like, big words on it, basically gobstoppers, and it looks seriously focking complicated.

There's, like, big-time tension between me and Fionn. I go, 'What the fock is *that*?' and Fionn goes, 'It's what Leinster need to do to reach the quarter-finals of the European Cup.' I'm thinking, at least it's, like, rugby-*related*. I go, 'I didn't actually realize there were so many teams in it,' but then Lorcan laughs, roysh, and he goes, 'Actually, Ross, it's the, em, Periodic Table of Elements,' and I wonder will the little focker sound so smug when he finds out that I'm actually thinking about dropping his sorry orse. Fionn looks at me and goes, 'Just a little joke, Ross. It's the arrangement of chemical elements according to their atomic numbers to illustrate periodic law. Formulated by the Russian chemist, Dmitri Mendeleev. You didn't need me to tell you that, of course.'

I go, 'I need to talk to Lorcan. In private. It's about rugby. You remember that game? You were shit at it,' which isn't actually true, roysh, he was a pretty decent back, but I'd never focking tell him that. He looks at me, roysh, then at Lorcan and then he goes, 'I'm just going to surf the 'net, Lorcan. Don't be too long. I want to go over that stuff again about Mendeleev's role in predicting the existence and properties of scandium, gallium and germanium,' which is said for my benefit, of course. When he focks off, I turn around to Lorcan and go, 'Your brother needs to get out more. And so do you.' He's there, 'It's January, Ross. The Leaving's only five months away. There'll be plenty of time for going out once the summer's here. What did you want to talk about?' the cocky focker that he is.

I walk over to the window and look out. Caitlin, their next-door neighbour, who I ended up being with two years ago at the Loreto Foxrock debs, is getting out of her cor. She's still hot. I go, 'Lorcan, I'm hearing rumours,' and he shoves his glasses up on his nose, roysh, just like his focking brother. He's like, 'Rumours?' and I'm there, 'Yeah, rumours.' I let that sink in for a couple of minutes, roysh, then I'm like, 'I hear you're thinking of entering the Young Scientist of the Year competition,' and he relaxes all of a sudden, like it's not a big deal, and he goes, 'Oh, *that*. I'm not *thinking* about entering it, Ross. I *am* entering. It's a project on the effects of additives like beta-carotene on skin pigmentation. What I'm doing is –' and I'm there, 'Whoa! Lorcan, you don't know how little inter-est I have in what you're about to say. All I'm here for is to tell you that I'm worried. I'm worried that all this … education, I suppose you'd have to call it … is affecting your rugby.'

He goes to say something, roysh, but I'm like, 'I'm open to contradiction,' throwing in a big word, just to remind him that I'm not exactly thick myself, 'but I don't think you can combine the two. So you think on,' and I turn around and head for the door, roysh, before he has a chance to say anything. Fionn's standing outside, obviously been listening to every word. I give him daggers, roysh, and I go, 'If Lorcan ends up like you – a focking geek who can't get his Swiss in a brothel with a fistful of fifties – he's going to end up hating you forever,' and then I hit the road.

And that should have been that, roysh, except that deep down, I knew there was trouble coming. It turns out, roysh, that this project he was doing on the effects of . . . well, whatever . . . basically involved him drinking six litres of Sunny D a day while, like, noting changes in his basic skin colour. I actually thought he looked a bit orange when I saw him in the dressing-room before the de La Salle match, but he had spent New Year in Colorado with his old pair skiing, roysh, and I just presumed he had a Peter Pan.

The night before our second-round match against Paul's, roysh, he sends me a text, telling me he can't play because he's in, like, hospital. Of course, straight away, roysh, I peg it up to the Blackrock Clinic to see what the Jackanory is and there he is, roysh, sitting up in the bed like a focking Oompa Loompa, as in bright focking orange. Fionn is actually taking photographs of him.

Lorcan goes, 'Hey, Ross, thanks for coming. I overdosed on beta-carotene. Isn't it exciting?' I'm there, 'I've no focking scrumhalf for tomorrow. How is that exciting?' Fionn's checking his last shot on the camera, one of those digital jobs, which I'm about to insert up his focking orse, and he's like, 'Lorcan's been asked to present his findings at an international dermatological conference in Boston in August.' I just flip the lid then, and who can blame me? I turn around to Lorcan and I go, 'If you want to fock-up the most important year of your life, go ahead. Here, I brought you these,' and I fock this bag of fruit at him. Of course, it's only when I'm in the cor pork, roysh, that I remember they were oranges. They're probably up there pissing themselves over that, like the tools that they are.

I'm actually pretty focked off, it has to be said, with Erika over what she did. Sorcha's actually stopped replying to my texts, roysh, so Tuesday morning, the actual day of the Paul's match, I ring her up, roysh, and I'm ready to give her a serious earful, but she ends up, like, totally throwing me by answering the phone like she's actually pleased to hear from me. She's like, 'Hey, Ross, long time, no speak,' and I end up going, 'Er, hey, Erika. How are you?' and it's true, roysh, I am *such* a sucker for a pretty face and Erika *is* a ringer for Denise Richards.

She goes, 'I'm great, Ross. I've an *amazing* new boy-friend,' and I'm there, 'So the stockbroker goy . . .' and she goes, '*Oh my God*, Ross, he's, like, SO last month. I'm with Stephen now. He's a lawyer. Going places. They're saying he's going to be the youngest Attorney-General in Ireland. *Ever*,' and I'm there, 'Cool.' She's like, 'I'm in Fitzpatrick's, Ross, trying on shoes. Was there something?' and I'm there, 'Oh, em, look, I just want to ask you a question, don't have a knicker-fit, probably wasn't you anyway, but I have to ask – you didn't send that picture of me and Sorcha in to *VIP*, did you?' and straight away she's like, 'Yes,' and I'm there, 'Oh, roysh, well . . . em . . . I presumed you were going to say no. Why? As in, why did you do it?' and she's like, 'Because I'm a bitch, Ross. Does that come as a surprise to you?'

I actually don't know what to say next. She goes, 'I'm only disappointed they didn't print the other one I sent, when that *wan* showed up – you know, the mother of your child? I suggested they use it as a before-and-after thing. Dublin's *Jerry Springer* wedding. *Oh my God*, is it, like, *possible* anymore to buy shoes *without* a pointy toe?' I'm there, 'You've actually upset Sorcha,' trying to sound tough basically, but Erika goes, 'Ross, I'm going to be finished in town in about an hour. Would you like me to swing by the hotel on my way home and you can have sex with me?' and I'm like, 'Em, well . . . okay then,' suddenly finding it in myself to forgive her. But then she just, like, laughs at me, roysh, and goes, 'Yeah, you're really worried about Sorcha being upset, aren't you?' and then she just, like, hangs up. And presumably she's no intention of swinging by the hotel either.

My head is hopping, roysh, but when the phone beside the bed rings, I make the mistake of, like, answering it. It's Knob Head. His first line is, 'Watch out, a certain E. O'Sullivan of Moylough, County Galway, your job's under threat,' and I'm there, 'What the *fock* do you want?' He goes, 'Just wanted to extend my congratulations. I was at the Paul's match. You didn't just beat them, Ross, you rubbed their noses in the dirt, which is what they deserved.'

I'm there, 'Finished?' which he ignores, roysh, and just goes, 'Everything's going goodo right now. Fionnuala's got those frightful Funderland people on the run – they'll soon be folding up their tents for where they belong, Tallaght, or Darndale, or one of those wretched places – my son is proving himself to be the best young coach Ireland has produced since, dare I say it, the Dagger himself, my short game is the best it's been since the early 1990s, and

Hennessy is looking down the barrel of a ten-stretch, quote-quote, thank you very much indeed.'

I go, 'Oh, and don't forget to mention how you focked up my marriage,' and he's there, 'That'll blow over, Coach. Don't you worry your head about that,' and in the background, roysh, I hear the old dear going, 'Charles, your dinner's going cold. It's roasted salmon fillets with Pecorino and pesto topping,' and then he goes, 'Sorry, Ross, under orders to wrap it up this end. Well done, though. I mean, 30–12, that's not a victory, that's a massacre, with a capital M,' and I manage to go, 'You're the world's biggest penis,' before he hangs up.

It was actually 31–9, roysh, not that I'd expect *him* to remember. It was a miracle we won by so much, roysh, what with Conall Gillen, our stand-in scrumhalf, having the mare that he did. We need Lorcan back, roysh, doesn't matter whether the focker's orange or purple with yellow spots. Our next match is against Clongowes, who might be tossers, but they're no mugs, and they'll totally destroy us if we're as slow getting the ball out of the scrum again.

Pikey was out of this world. Didn't miss a single kick and capped a Man of the Match performance with our fourth try, though if I'm being honest, roysh, I'd have to say that I have my concerns about him. Saw him after the game, roysh, surrounded by birds, we're talking a lot of Mounties, giving him, 'Congrats,' and '*Oh my God*, you were, like, SO amazing,' and 'You played SUCH a good game,' and it's not, like, jealousy or anything, I just worry about where the goy's head is at.

So there I am, roysh, lying in bed, trying to work up the energy to lash on the *Atomic Kitten* DVD and have an Allied Irish, when all of a sudden my mobile rings and it's, like,

JP. He's there, 'Dude, you've been offline for a few days. Everything okay?' and I go, 'Just busy – saw Ronan and then it's, like, the team and shit?' and he's there, 'A big ten-four on that one, Ross. I'm hearing you loud and clear. Hey, you fairly went to town on Paul's, didn't you?' and I'm like, 'Might do them a favour in the long run. Northside schools shouldn't be playing rugby anyway,' and he's like, 'Agreed – motion carried.' Then he goes, 'I saw Sorcha in Blackrock Shopping Centre this morning,' and I'm there, 'Really?' probably sounding a bit too eager. I'm there, 'Did she mention anything about seeing the result of the match?' and he's like, 'Negative, dude. She was with Fionn, Ross,' and I'm there, 'What do you mean, with him? As in *with him* with him?' and he goes, 'No, they were just coming out of L'Occitane. I think it's, like, Amie with an ie's birthday this weekend. Watch him like a hawk, Ross, that's all I'm saying,' and I'm there, 'Hey, I've actually come up with a plan to fix him big-time,' and I tell JP I'll bell him back, roysh, because I've another call coming through.

Of course who is it, roysh, only Lorcan, and I can tell straight away from the tone of his voice that he, like, wants something. He's like, 'Hey, I'm out of hospital, Ross . . . I mean, Coach,' and I'm there, 'Why are you calling me Coach? What am I coaching you?' and he goes, 'Well, rugby,' and I'm just there, 'You obviously know something I don't,' and there's, like, silence on the other end of the line.

It's pretty obvious, roysh, that he's been looking around at the other goys, seeing the kind of scenario they're pulling and he wants a bit of that himself. I actually need the little focker – beating Paul's is one thing but it's, like, Clongowes in the quarter-final and you don't beat Clongowes unless your scrumhalf is shit-hot – but I am SO going to make the little focker grovel.

I go, 'You're cut from the team. I have to say, we seem to be doing pretty well without you,' and he goes, 'Oh. It's just that, er, well, I heard you gave Conall a serious bollocking. Said he couldn't pass off his left hand,' and I'm like, 'Well, he's not Peter Stringer, but he has *some* good qualities,' and I swear to God, roysh, the little focker sounds like he's about to burst into tears. I'm there, 'Must be hord for you?' and he's there, 'What?' and I'm like, 'Watching from the sidelines while your old team-mates enjoy the spoils. They're a pretty popular bunch with the ladies. And they're only two games away from a Schools Cup final. Must be hord knowing you were port of that and, like, threw it away,' and that tips him over the edge, roysh, and on come the focking waterworks. He goes, '*Stop it!* It's been difficult enough hearing that from the goys in the Rotary Club,' and I'm thinking, The focking *Rotary Club?* This goy has NERD written above his head in big focking neon letters.

He's like, 'Ross, please, I'm begging you, give me another chance,' and I go, 'I have doubts about you, kid, there's no getting away from that. I have doubts about your … loyalty,' and he's there, 'I *am* loyal, Ross,' and I go, 'Are you loyal to the team, Lorcan. Or are you loyal to your brother?' and he's like, 'The *team*, of course,' and I'm there, 'If only I could think up of some kind of way of *testing* that? Some kind of, I don't know, trial. To prove your loyalty to me over that … four-eyed freakshow,' and he's there, 'Anything.'

I'm there, 'Okay, get this. Your brother keeps a diary. It's a big green ledger. I've seen it. He records all his, like, intimate thoughts in it, which I'm sure is really riveting stuff. I want you to get it for me,' and he's like, 'Steal my brother's diary? Ross, I couldn't . . .' and I'm there, 'Enjoy your life with the Rotary geeks. I hear the Youth Leadership Awards are going to be a focking howl this year,' and I leave him there hanging on the line for, like, ten seconds, roysh, then eventually he goes, 'Okay, I'll do it,' and I'm there, 'I'm picking the team for Clongowes at lunchtime on Wednesday. If I have that diary in my hand, you'll be in the team.'

Fionn is one sick focking puppy. Get this, roysh:

Monday, 10 February 2003
Called to see S. She was upset about something Ross said to her and needed a friend. I brought her a present – *Closing Time* by Tom Waits. It was actually for Valentine's Day but I didn't want to give it to her 'on the day' in case it embarrassed her. I love that album for the same reasons that I love her – its sincere sentimentality. I told her to listen to 'I Hope That I Don't Fall In Love With You' – for obvious reasons! – and also 'Grapefruit Moon', which is my song for her, though she doesn't know it.

Then it's like:

Friday, 4 April 2003
I've been trying to keep busy, but it's still hard. S has only been in Indonesia for two weeks now, so why does it feel like two years? The truth is that the endangered species of the Sumatra region are almost certainly beyond saving, but I admire her spirit so much. And yet I miss her so much it hurts. I'm trying to be

60

strong, but I can't bear the thought of her being there with that
. . . uncultured oaf.

And underneath it, roysh, he's written this, like, poem, called 'Sorcha' and it's like:

> *A rage that can't be quieted,*
> *A love unrequited.*

What a wanker. You'd need a focking dictionary to understand half of this shit anyway. I'll give him uncultured oaf when I see him. I turn around to the borman and I go, 'Rack 'em up again, will you? Make it another double,' and he's like, 'Certainly, Sir. Shall I charge it to your room?' and I'm there, 'You got it.'

Thursday, 21 December 2003
The wedding is just days away now. I phoned S tonight with the intention of saying, 'Don't do it. Don't marry *him*. Marry me instead,' but, like the Danish prince, in the eye of the moment, my nerve failed me and, 'Good luck on the big day,' was all I could force through my lips. The only way I know of soothing this torrent within me is to put my feelings into verse.

> *Unending devotion,*
> *Overwhelming emotion,*
> *While life goes by*
> *In slow motion*

He really is a steamer. His focking glasses are SO getting broken when I see him.

Tuesday, 6 January 2004

Spent the night sitting with S, nursing her broken heart. I am balm to her wounds, as she is to mine. When I held her tonight, I knew something of how Rimbaud felt when he wrote:

Je ris au wasserfall blond qui s'échevela à travers les sapins:
à la cime argentée je reconnus la déesse.
I laughed at the blond waterfall that tousled through the
pines: on silver summer I recognized the goddess.

I'm in, like, Cocoon, roysh, in Trap One, as it happens, dropping a load, and I can hear these two goys outside, roysh, standing at the trough, going, 'Did you see Pikey against Paul's?' and the other goy's like, 'He was un-*focking*-believable, wasn't he?' and the goy's going, 'They'd be SO focked without him this year,' and the other goy's like, 'He da man,' and then the two of them stort going, *'He da man! He da man!'*

I'm in Kiely's with the goys, roysh, we're talking Christian, we're talking JP, we're talking Oisinn, who reckons that he's actually only, like, weeks away from putting the finishing touches to *Eau d'Affluence*, which he then reckons Hugo Boss is going to give him a million squids for.

He's going, 'Today was a *big* day, goys. See, for months I couldn't understand what it was that was drowning out the citrus notes. But I figured it out – it was the amber accords,' and we're all nodding, roysh, like we know what he's talking about. It's actually pretty funny, roysh, to call around to his gaff and see him there in his, like, long, white lab coat, with all these bottles with, like, funny-coloured liquids in them, bubbling away over all these, like, Bunsen burners, which he, shall we say, borrowed from the science lab in Castlerock. He's been doing it for, like, the guts of a year now and I suppose you have to admire him for, like, sticking with it.

Christian gets his round in – always does, fair focks to him. I go, 'Haven't seen you in a while – how's the job going?' and he's like, 'Good, but . . . see, the problem is, I never manage to get my wages, like, *out* of the shop? Spent four hundred bills today on a five-foot model of IG-88,' and he can tell from my expression that I haven't a focking bog what he's talking about because then he goes, 'The droid assassin turned bounty-hunter?' and I'm like, 'Oh, *that* goy.'

He turns around to me then and he goes, 'Is it true you've been to see him, as in Ronan?' and I'm like, 'Twice now,' and he's like, '*Whoa!* What's he like?' and I'm there, 'Well, old,' and he's like, 'You mean for his age?' and I'm there, 'Scarily so,' and he goes, 'You'd want to get his midi-chlorian count checked out,' and I end up going, 'That's a good point,' because it's actually easier than getting into it with him.

Fionn – the focking snake – arrives in, roysh, with these four birds, one of whom I think is called Julie-Ann, nice enough rack, but she's got a brace on her Taylor Keith, and what does she do, roysh, before I've had the chance to, like, check her out properly, only shoots me a filthy, a total filthy, basically, and goes, 'Sorry, *you're* Ross O'Carroll-Kelly?' and I'm like, 'The one and only,' still playing it like Steve Silvermint in the face of unbelievable hostility, if that's the word. It's nice to be nice. She goes, 'You might remember my sister, as in Carragh?' and I'm there, 'It's not ringing bells for me, Babes,' and she goes, 'Oh, think horder. She brought you to her debs. You puked all over her dress, then scored her best friend,' and I'm like, 'Doesn't exactly narrow down the field. What school are we talking?' and she's like, 'Muckross,' and it's actually coming back to me now. It's like, *There may be trouble aheeeaaad* . . . I go, 'Yeah, she was, like, head girl,' and she goes, 'Deputy. You are SUCH a wanker,' and – tired of playing Mr Nice Goy – I end up going, 'Hey, that was, like, two years ago. Tell your sister to get herself laid, then get herself over it.'

So off they go, roysh, in a total strop, and Fionn turns around to me and goes, 'That was a tad harsh, Ross,' and I'm like, 'Why, is she *la noyau de mon monde?*' and I watch his face go totally red, because it's actually straight out of his diary, roysh, as in:

Monday, 13 October 2003
I'm sitting on the DART, watching the graffitied walls zip by, and I'm beginning to feel that Rimbaud is shadowing my life:

> *In the wheelhouse there are lewd*
> *Graffiti, ithyphallic, crude.*
> *O let my heart be cleaned, renewed*
> *By wondrous waves immersing it!*
> *Oh, S, you are la noyau de mon monde.*

Of course, he'll peg it home tonight and check if his diary is still there, which it will be. I gave it back to Lorcan yesterday after getting the Keira Knightley bird at reception to, like, photocopy the entire thing for me; she's actually developing a bit of a thing for me. Anyway, it shuts Fionn the fock up. So there I am, roysh, just sort of, like, idly looking across the far side of the battle-cruiser, and who do I see, only Pikey, as in Andrew Pike, surrounded by scenario – total lashers most of them, and we're talking totally here – and he's making out like his shit doesn't smell just because Eddie O'Sullivan tipped him as, like, a stor of the future on television the other night.

JP goes, 'Hey, Ross, that Pikey's some man for one man, isn't he? Reminds me of you in your day,' and I'm *majorly* pissed off now. He's giving it the whole ladies' man act, all these birds hanging on his every word, and I decide the goy needs to learn that he doesn't know everything yet, so I walk over to him, roysh, and I can tell from his face that he hadn't been expecting to see me. He's like, '*Ross!*' and I'm there, 'This could probably have waited until training on Monday, but I might as well tell you now – you're dropped from the team,' and I wish I'd had a camera phone with me, roysh, just to get a shot of him being brought crashing to Earth. All the birds are going, '*Oh my God!*' and '*Oh! My! God!*' and '*Oh my God?*' flapping around, all confused, like when you scatter pigeons with a BB gun.

Pikey's like, '*Dropped?* But I'm the *captain*. And . . . you named the team on Wednesday. I was in it,' and I go, 'And now I'm changing it,' and he's there, 'But . . . *why?*' and I'm like, 'Your lifestyle, frankly,' and he holds up his glass and goes, 'But Ross, this is, like, Diet Coke I'm drinking,' and I'm like, 'Hanging out in pubs, playing Jack the Lad . . .' and he's there, 'It's Saturday night.'

I can tell from his boat race, roysh, that he wants to have a serious go at me, but he can't, roysh, because that'd be him totally focked. He's a smort boy. He goes, 'You can't beat Clongowes without–' and I'm like, 'Without *you?*

You think you're Bertie Big Bollocks, don't you?' and he goes, 'But you said yourself after the de La Salle match that I was *the man*,' and quick as a flash, I go, 'Well, now you're the dropped man,' and I head back over to the goys and I can hear all the birds going, '*Oh! My! God!*' with the odd, 'That's, like, SO unfair,' thrown in for good measure.

Of course, I've no intention of dropping him, cocky as he is. Clongowes would wipe the floor with us without him, but it'll stop him getting too up himself. I head back to the goys, with a big shit-eating grin on my boat. JP goes, 'Ross, you look like a focking gynaecologist who's just seen Cameron Diaz walk through the door,' and I'm there, 'Maybe I am, dude. Maybe I am.'

I don't know what it is, roysh, but I can't stop thinking about Ronan. It's probably the whole father–son thing, blah blah blah, but I wake up in some bird's house in Booterstown this particular Sunday morning, roysh, and I bell Tina and ask her if it'd be okay to, like, call out to the gaff. She goes, 'Jaysus, you're not scared of out-staying your welcome, you, are ye?' and I'm there, 'Oh, but I just thought . . .' and she's like, 'I'm only messin' wi' ye, Ross. Ronan tinks de wurdled of ye. Come on out for yisser breakfast.'

So all of a sudden there I am, roysh, eleven o'clock in the morning, sitting in a kitchen in darkest Knackeragua, roysh, watching Tina's old man make fried bread, or some other peasant food, listening to him crapping on about 'de yoot of today, jaysus sakes', while Ronan's chatting away on his Wolfe, making all these, like, references to 'supplies' and 'storage' and 'profit margins', and every so often he

66

looks at me and, like, mouths the words, 'Little bit of business,' and, 'World of commerce never sleeps,' and I'm sitting there just, like, staring at him, unable to believe that this kid is actually mine.

Tina's nipped around to one of the neighbours to get her hair done, leaving orders that we're not to go out until she arrives back and, of course, I'm beginning to feel like I'm trapped in the 'Fair City' omnibus. Her old man's going, 'Problem wi' de kids today is deev no respect, knowhorramean? You'd be too young to remember oul' Lugs Brannigan. Now dare was a copper. Bate the fooken shite out of ya as quick as he'd look at ye, would oul' Lugs, but you respected him all de sayim. If he cot yiz walkin' down de roa-id tree- or four-abreast, he'd grab ye by the ear, trun ye down on de ground an' pump six bullets into de back of yisser head. An' if you went home cryin' to yisser mudder or fadder, deed say ye musta deserved it so ye must, den *deyd* pump six bullets into yisser head as well. But he had de respect of de comyooo-nity, knowhorra-mean? Matter o' fact, not tellin' ye a word of a loy, he killt all moy family, me mudder an' fadder, me brudders an' sisters, shot ever last one of dem, but sure they were royt bowsies so dee were, an' I respected um for dat. Not sayin' he was an angel, or athin like it, but in dem days we knew de law was dare to protect ye. Sure nowadays the kids is runnin' woyild.'

He puts a plate down in front of me with, like, two pieces of batch bread, deep-fried in grease. He goes, 'Spose ye heard about young Anto, did ye? Tree year done ourruv his life. For wha'? A few oul' bottles of cider.'

Ronan gets off the phone. He's like, 'There you are, Rosser. Get some saturated fat into your arteries, no better start to the day,' and I laugh and go, 'How's it going, Ronan?' and he's there, 'I'm game ball, man. Let's hit town, will we?' and then he nods down at my plate and, like, winks at me, as if to tell me to eat it all up, so as not to hurt his granddad's feelings. There's, like, cigarette ash on it, roysh, but I eat it all, gagging after pretty much every mouthful.

Tina arrives in. A frizzy perm – there's a shock. She gives me a bit of a lecture – don't let him wander off on his own, make sure he doesn't hot-wire any cors, blahdy, blahdy, blah – then I throw on the old Henri Lloyd while Ronan bums a cigarette off his granddad, who goes, 'Told ye befower, you shouldn't be smokin' till yer at least torteen. In anyway, didn't I give ye tree dis mornin'?' and Ronan's like, 'Go on ourra that, I'm fooken gaspin', so I am,' and he ends up giving him three more out of his box.

We go outside and there's, like, three kids washing my cor, as in *washing* it, not keying it, and they're all, like, thirteen or maybe fourteen, and when they cop us, they go, 'Howiya, Ronan?' and Ronan goes, 'How's it goin', boys?' and he storts, like, inspecting the cor and then he goes, 'A good shine.'

I point the old GTI in the direction of the city. The big dilemma, of course, is which side of town do we hit. I'd sooner be boiled in my own spit than go anywhere near the O'Connell Street and Henry Street end of things, roysh, and I'm sure Ronan feels the same way about Grafton Street. It's like he can read my mind. He goes, 'What's it gonna be, your soyid or mine?' and before I say anything, roysh, he goes, 'Let's check out your soyid. Wouldn't be safe for you north of the Liffey, not dressed like that. Any of my contacts see us together, you're a social worker and I'm out on TR, *capisce?*' and I just, like, crack my hole laughing.

So we pull up at the lights next to Heuston Station, roysh, and totally out of the blue, Ronan says something that basically knocks me sideways. He's there, 'Who was that bird you were with in Annabel's last night, then?' and I'm thinking how well him and Sorcha are getting on – they're actually *texting* each other now – so I think, Tell him nothing, he's just fishing. I go, 'What bird would this be then?' and he's like, 'Small, red hair, nice set of jugs, pink top, denim skirt . . .' and I end up nearly driving into the focking wall of the actual Guinness brewery.

I'm there, 'How the *fock* . . .' and he goes, 'Rosser, I've eyes and ears all over this town. You were with a bird in Lillie's last Saturday as well. What are you playing at, Rosser?' and I'm like, 'Look, it's complicated, Ronan.' I look at him and he shrugs his shoulders and goes, 'It's complicated because you're married and you're roidin udder boords. You eeder love her or you don't,' and I crack up laughing and go, 'What would you know about love? You're, like, seven?' He's there, 'Hey, I've one or two emotional scars meself, you know,' and I crack my hole again.

He goes quiet for a bit, roysh, then he's like, 'Was it over me, was it?' and I'm there, 'What? The break-up?' and he just, like, nods. I look at him. He only *acts* like he's hord as nails. I don't think it would take much to hurt him, so I go, 'Not *you*, as such, Ronan. It's just that, well, she didn't know anything about you until the day of the wedding. *I* didn't know anything about you.'

He goes, 'Doesn't sound like a very good reason for you to be roidin udder boords. Has she got anyone else?' I'm like, 'No. I mean, she's not the type to go . . . well, she's not like me, I suppose. There is one goy sniffing around.' Ronan goes, 'Do you want me to sort it. I know a few heads,' and I'm there, 'I'm sure you do. No, I've got it in hand,' and he nods and doesn't say anything for ages and then he goes, 'Fix it, but.'

We hit BT2. I'm a bit worried about whether the security gords will let him in, but you could have, like, knocked me down with a feather, roysh, when the dude on the door with the walkie-talkie turns around and goes, 'How's it goin', Ronan?' as we're going in. I turn around and I'm about to say something, but Ronan just goes, 'Like I said, eyes and ears all over this town.'

We stort looking at threads. I try to interest the kid in a few things, roysh, but anything I show him he just goes, 'Bent . . . bent . . . bent . . .' I'm buying a pair of chocolate-coloured Sonetti chinos and new rhythms – we're talking Hugo loafers here – and there I am, roysh, standing in the queue, when all of a sudden I notice the bird behind the counter basically giving me the mince pies on a grand scale. She's a total honey, roysh – her and Beth Ostrosky must have been, like, separated at birth – and when I get to the desk, before I even have a chance to use any of my killer lines, she goes, 'You're Ross O'Carroll-Kelly, aren't you?' and bear in mind, roysh, she hasn't even seen my credit cord at this stage. I'm there, 'No prizes for guessing which paper you've been reading,' thinking she probably saw John O'Sullivan's profile of me in *The Irish Times*.

She goes, 'Sorry, *paper?*' and I hand her my credit cord and I'm there, 'Hey, don't be embarrassed about making the first move,' playing it cooler than Huggy Bear's frigid sister. She's there, 'No, you don't understand,' and I nearly fell over when she turned around and went, 'I'm Jessica. Andrew's girlfriend. As in Andrew Pike?'

He does well, I'll give the focker that. Quick as a flash, roysh, I'm like, 'His girlfriend? How many other girls are saying that at the moment?' and she ignores this, roysh, but rips the receipt out of the little credit cord machine like she's imagining tearing off my dick. She goes, 'So why was he dropped?' and I'm like, 'That's strictly team business,' and she's there, 'He's the best player you have. What about the two tries he scored against Blackrock last year? *And* he was only in, like, fifth year then.'

As I'm signing the receipt, I'm going, 'If you must know, I dropped him because I didn't like the way he was living,' and she gives me this look, roysh, and I'm there, 'Out practically every night of the week, playing Jack the Lad,' and she's goes, '*Oh my God!* That is SO not the case. He trains, like, SO hord. He only goes out, like, one night a week. HELLO? He *lives* for rugby, Ross,' and I go, 'Hey, passions are running a little high here. Why don't I treat you to a cappuccino? What time do you get your break?' and she looks me up and down and goes, 'You *must* be joking,' but there's an attraction there, roysh, and there's no doubt she feels it as much as I do. I pick up my bag and go, 'Later,' and she gives me this, like, scowl, I suppose you'd have to call it.

Ronan's waiting for me at the bottom of the escalator. He goes, 'Jaysus, I'd have to be dug ourra that boord,' and I'm laughing, basically thinking, like father, like son.

My phone rings and I check the time and it's, like, ten o'clock in the morning, roysh, and I'm going, 'What kind of a focking lunatic . . .' and I answer it, roysh, and this voice goes, 'This is Thaddeus Pike,' and even though I'm still half-asleep, roysh, I know what's coming next, so I just go, 'And?' and he's like, '*Justice* Thaddeus Pike,' and I'm there, 'I know who you are. What do you want?'

He's a pompous tosser, this goy. He's like, 'I would like an explanation, please, as to why you've dropped my son from the school team,' and I go, 'Because I *decided* to drop him. Look, I don't come down to your courtroom and tell you who to throw in the slammer, so you don't tell me how to run my team.'

He's there, 'You really enjoy this, don't you? Playing God with people's lives?' and I'm there, 'I'm not *playing* God. As far as Pikey's rugby career is concerned, I *am* God,' and I hang up on him.

The bird I was with in Annabel's on Saturday night, the bird Ronan was talking about, is actually called Leilani, roysh, and it was the usual crack, chatted her up, back to her gaff in Dalkey, do the business, casual sex and whatever you're having yourself but – unusually for me, roysh – I actually hung around for an hour the next morning, didn't try to moonwalk out of there without giving her my mobile number.

I've got, like, no *real* interest in her – she's got red hair and I've never really been into kippers – but the one thing she does have going for her, roysh, is her knowledge of computers, she's doing, like, computer science in Trinity, and that was the whole idea of putting in the extra couple of hours on Sunday morning, roysh, basically to keep her sweet. As I was focking off out the door to go to pick up

Ronan, I told her I'd like to see her again, though she wouldn't have thought I meant eleven o'clock on Monday morning.

I grabbed a Jo into town, roysh, rang her and arranged to meet her in The Buttery. Not being bigheaded or anything, but the girl can't believe her luck. She's going, 'OH MY GOD! I can't *actually* believe you called to see me. That's like, *Aaarrggghhh!*' and I'm there, 'That's my number one problem, Babes. When I, like, really like someone, I have to let it show,' and she's just lapping it up, the sap.

Then she goes, 'What have you got there?' and she nods at this, like, stack of paper under my orm. I'm there, 'Oh, this? It's just stuff. To be honest with you, I've been running around town all morning looking for someone to set up a website. I suppose there is Gail, who's in UCD, but she has it pretty bad for me and I don't want to lead her on,' and straight away, roysh, Leilani goes, 'I'll do it for you,' and I'm there, 'No! You *wouldn't,* would you?' and she's there, 'It's actually very easy, Ross. What kind of a website is it?'

We join the queue and we order two coffees, which Leilani insists on paying for, the total focking walkover that she is. I'm there, 'I want to put a diary *online,* if that's the word,' and she goes, '*Whoa!* You don't mind the world's four billion people having access to your secrets?' and I'm like, 'Not *my* diary. Someone else's,' and she's there, 'Whose?' and I go, 'It's a friend of mine.' We sit down and she looks at me all confused. She goes, 'Why would you want to put your friend's diary online?' and I'm there, 'Because he's a focking tosser,' and she sort of, like, pulls away from me, like she's weighing the whole thing up, and I know she's going to turn around, roysh, and say it'd be unethical – like that doctor's receptionist I scored when I tried to persuade her to let me see Fionn's medical file.

I can tell she has a problem with it, roysh, so I go, 'I was thinking of asking you out for dinner. I see Peploe's has a new menu,' and eventually she goes, 'Okay, I'll do it. I do NOT want this traced back to me, though,' and I'm there, 'Hey, it'll be Kool plus Friends, I promise.'

She storts, like, flicking through the pages of the diary and she stops and reads the entry that's like:

Tuesday, 2 December 2003
Only S understands the precocity of the boy poet in me.

> HE – *Your breast on my breast,*
> *Eh? We could go,*
> *With our nostrils full of air,*
> *Into the cool light*
> *Of the good morning that bathes you*
> *In the wine of daylight?*
> *When the whole shivering wood bleeds,*
> *Dumb with love*

I'm there, 'Bent, isn't it?' and she goes, 'Oh my God, *no!* I love Rimbaud. I studied French literature in Paris,' and I'm thinking that these two – as in Fionn and Leilani – focking belong to each other. She goes, 'He must really love this girl, S?' and I'm there, 'Yeah, *what*ever! Can you put these on the website as well?' and I give her these pictures, roysh, of Fionn the time we all went to Playa del Ingles and he looks like a weedy little focker in his glasses and his Speedos.

She goes, 'Sure. And his name's Fionn?' and I'm there,

'Yeah,' and she's like, 'I could call it Fionn's Blog,' and I go, 'I don't care what you call it. Just get it out there on the World Wild Whatever the fock you call it,' and I get up to leave. She goes, 'Em, what night were you thinking for, you know, Peploe's?' I'm there, 'Maybe the weekend. Just get that done, then call me,' and she goes, 'It should only take me a couple of days,' and I'm there, 'Whatever. Quick as you can,' and then I fock off.

'Enjoy it while it lasts, Ross.' I'd know my old man's big focking foghorn voice anywhere. He's like, 'Enjoy it while it lasts, Ross.' He's coming out of Avoca with the old dear in tow, the stupid focking weapon, and I was unlucky enough to be walking past on my way to The Bailey. I'm there, 'Enjoy *what* while I can?' and he goes, 'Your last few weeks of being able to walk around this city unmolested. Because when Castlerock win that Leinster Senior Cup, Year of Our Lord 2004, there'll be no one in the country who hasn't heard of the great Ross O'Carroll-Kelly, if that situation doesn't already pertain,' and I just go, 'You are the world's biggest penis, do you know that?'

The old dear holds up this bag and goes, 'I got some of that champagne shallot mustard you like, Ross. Why don't you come out for your dinner next weekend? I might do a marinade,' and the old man's all smiles and I'm just there, 'Didn't I tell you after the wedding that I actually never wanted to focking see you two again. What port of "I never want to focking see you two again" do you not understand?'

The old man goes, 'Everything's working out wonderfully well. Ross here is on his way to becoming the best coach Ireland has had since our friend the schoolteacher from the West. And next week, Hennessy goes on trial. Ten years is Eduard's bet. The courts have got to send out a strong message, you see – no more Ray Burkes and what have you.'

Then the old dear, roysh, turns around and goes, 'Charles, you haven't told Ross *my* news,' and the old man's like, 'Oh, yes. Big news, with a capital B,' and the old dear goes, 'Ross, you remember your friend Simon?' and it's, like, Simon as in Simon who captained the S the first year we got to the final. I'm there, 'What about him?' and she goes, 'Well, you remember his mother, Sally?' and I'm like, 'Oh yeah, we *all* remember Sally,' because in fairness, roysh, she was a total MILF, as in Mother I'd Like to Fock.

The old dear goes, 'Well, she's arranging this yummy-mummy calendar,' and I swear to God, roysh, suddenly I'm feeling weak and I can, like, hear the blood in my ears. I'm just, like, staring at her. She goes, 'It's *for* charity, Ross,' and I'm there, 'Let me get this straight – you're *actually* proposing to take your *actual* clothes off and *actually* be photographed for a calendar?' and she goes, 'It's for breast cancer awareness. Christian's mum's doing it, too,' and I'm like, 'Yeah but she's *actually* worth looking at,' which of course I'm in a position to know.

She goes, 'It'll all be very tastefully done, Ross. These things are all the rage in the States,' and I'm like, '*No!* It's not focking happening. Take a look at yourself, woman – you're *hordly* yummy-mummy material,' and she looks at the old man, roysh, for, like, reassurance and he goes, 'Don't listen to him, Fionnuala. You could give that Liz Hurley a run for her money and anyone who likes can quote me on that.'

I'm there, 'He's focking lying. You are bet-down. And

you are SO not making a holy show of me,' and she goes, 'I've given Sally my word now,' and I'm there, 'Well you can basically ungive it,' and she goes, 'And I have final approval of what shot they use,' and I'm like, 'Are you focking deaf as well as ugly?'

I am in no mood to talk to Leilani when she rings. I just, like, answer the phone going, 'What?' and she's there 'Oh. Ross, it's . . . it's Leilani,' and I'm like, 'I *know* who it is. I've got caller ID,' and she goes, 'Oh, em . . . I just wondered had you seen it yet? As in the website? It's, like, fionnsblog.ie,' and I'm like, 'You've finished it, then?' and she's there, '*Oh my God*, it was just like studying for exams. I stayed up, like, *all* Monday night and most of Tuesday night to type it in,' and I'm there, 'You're a bigger focking fool than I thought then,' and she obviously thinks she's misheard me, roysh, because she just ignores it and goes, 'So what are you doing tonight?' as in, like, Thursday night. I'm there, 'I'm taking a beautiful lady out to dinner,' and she's like, 'Oh?' and I can hear the excitement in her voice. I go, 'You know Peploe's, don't you?' and she's like, 'Yeah, the *foie gras* is supposed to be like, *Oh my God!*'

She goes, 'What time will I meet you there?' and I'm there, '*Meet me?*' and she's like, 'Yeah, as in *for dinner?*' and I go, 'What a focking hilarious misunderstanding. I said I was bringing a beautiful lady out to dinner and you thought that meant *you,*' and she goes, 'No, seriously, Ross,' thinking I'm ripping the basic piss, but I go, 'Look, I was only using you to get that work done. Get over it. I'm not into kippers. Never was, never will be,' and I hang up, roysh, and tip straight down to the old business centre.

I get online I suppose you'd have to call it, lash in the old www dot, then fionnsblog and then the old dot ie and after a couple of seconds, roysh – focking hilarious – up comes that picture I took of Fionn in the Parrot Park in Playa del Ingles a couple of years ago, looking like the dude out of the focking Mister Muscle ad, with his focking weedy little body and his glasses and a basic focking cockatoo on his shoulder. I look down in the corner, we're talking bottom left, roysh, and the site's already had, like, 2,767 hits in like – what? – one day.

I love the homepage, if that's the actual word for it. I basically wrote it myself, roysh, and it's like, 'I'm a poet – and you didn't know it,' which I have to say I'm pretty proud of – well at least it, like, rhymes. Then it's like, 'Hey there, fellow geeks! My name is Fionn and the things I'm into are basically reading, knowing loads of shit . . . and poetry. I have the big-time hots for a girl called Sorcha, but she's totally in love with this really, really, really good-looking, kick-orse rugby player, which means that all I have are my fantasies. Why not click on the little pair of glasses below and read about some of the sick shit that goes on in my head in my online diary . . .'

I click and Leilani, fair focks to her, she has it all laid out, roysh, month-by-month, year-by-year, and she's added a few little touches of her own, roysh, like pictures of this Rimbaud steamer he seems to be into and, like, Tom Waits with his big stupid focking head. She's done herself proud here.

I whip out the old Wolfe and bell Sorcha. I'm there, 'Don't hang up on me, Babes. I was just, like, surfing away on the internet there, checking out a few websites on endangered animals, basically seeing how they're all doing, when all of a sudden I came across—' and she goes, 'I already know. Claire rang me,' and I'm there, 'Well, it gives me no pleasure whatsoever to know that one of my friends is a focking psychopath. I'm not trying to, like, put the shits up you or anything, but I think he's actually capable of killing,' preparing the ground before I offer to come over and keep her company.

She goes, 'Fionn wouldn't hurt a fly, Ross,' and I'm like, 'Let's not take that chance,' but then totally out of the blue, roysh, she goes, 'I actually think it's quite sweet.' I'm there, '*Sweet?* After all the things he was writing about you? He's a focking sicko, Sorcha. *Listen* to this shit,' and I read the entry for Friday, 1 August 2003, and it's like:

> *Could it really be that I have lost*
> *You to some undeserving fool*
> *Who sees none of the beauty in you?*
> *If so I will bear my loss like a man.*
> *But in my dreams*
> *We'll walk through bullion fields*
> *And on a bed of wheat,*
> *Skin on skin,*
> *We'll consummate*
> *That which we are afraid to feel*

I'm like, 'What fields? What wheat?' and she goes, 'Look, Ross, I know in some ways it's like, OH MY GOD! But it's actually quite, I don't know, flattering,' and I'm there, '*Flattering?* You know, the day he wrote that was the day we announced our engagement. He was like, "I'm SO pleased for both of you," to our faces, then he goes home and writes this shit? I'm telling you, Babes, a goy who writes so-called poems like that is well capable of going over there and killing you. I know things aren't great between us at the moment, but I have to say I'd be pretty upset if the Feds ended up finding your body rolled up in a corpet and, like, dumped in a lay-by somewhere.'

She goes, '*Oh! My! God!* You're the one who's *actually* freaking me out, Ross. Okay, I have to say, I was surprised by what I read – I was like, OH! MY! GOD! – but I blame myself. I should have seen that he liked me. I, like, SO should have. Now I feel like I led him on.' I go, 'Just make sure your bedroom window is locked tonight,' and she's like, 'Well, at least I can say that there's someone out there who cares enough about me to write *actual* poems for me,' and I go, 'Cool, we'll read a couple of them out at the funeral.'

She gives me the silent treatment for ages, roysh, then eventually she goes, 'You know, Ross, you haven't got, like, a romantic bone in your body. I can't remember the last time you did something to *actually* impress me.'

3. 'Twixt Love and Duty

Stitching up the Boy Poet puts me in cracking form for the day. I head back to the hotel, order a club sandwich to my room, watch a porno, kip for a few hours, then ring Christian, who's in work but who, as it happens, is meeting Oisinn for a pint in the M1 later.

So I go to meet the goys, roysh, and I have to say they're in, like, top form as well. Christian is telling me about the time that all the Hutts were evicted from the Komonor system by the ruling warlord and Jabba the Hutt hired Dyyz Nataz to hunt him down and kill him and I'm there going, 'Cool,' while Oisinn is saying he can definitely smell *212* by Carolina Herrera and he keeps asking me am I absolutely positive that Hazel, as in third year Orts UCD, wasn't in, and I just tell him to shut the fock up and get the Britneys in, which he does.

When he's at the bor, roysh, he turns around to me and goes, 'Have you heard from Fionn?' and I'm like, 'I presume he's too scared to show his face,' and he's there, 'You've seen it then? Pretty heavy stuff, wasn't it? Whatever

81

about thinking that shit, you don't put it on a focking website. You seem cool about it,' and I'm like, 'He's obviously a sicko, he's more to be pitied than anything,' and then Oisinn turns around and hands me and Christian our pints and goes, 'The old *212,* huh. Pure focking alchemy. Modern, innovative and radically feminine,' and I'm like, 'That certainly sounds like Hazel,' and I'm, like, grinning from ear to ear, roysh, because I've been there loads of times.

So then, all of a sudden, roysh, I feel this, like, tap on my shoulder and I turn around and who's standing behind me, only Jessica, as in Andrew Pike's piece. I'm playing it cool as an Eskimo's piss, of course, going, 'Hey, Babes. Pull up a stool,' and she's like, 'I'm not staying. I just want to make, I suppose, an eleventh-hour appeal for clemency,' and I haven't a focking bog what she's on about, though I suspect she's asking me to put Pikey back on the team. The thing is, roysh, he was never actually dropped in the first place, though I'm enjoying her squirming too much to tell her that.

I'm there, 'I don't think he's the man for us,' and then I, like, put my hand on her orm and I go, 'I don't think he's the man for you either,' and she goes totally ballistic then, giving it, 'How *dare* you! You don't know *anything* about me, *or* him,' and I'm there, 'I know his type,' and she goes, 'HELLO? I think I know him better than you, seeing as we've been together, like, two years?' and I just, like, turn back to the goys and throw my eyes up to Heaven as if to say, you know, she must have a starring role in a period costume drama, roysh, but Jessica just, like, grabs me by the shoulder and spins me around and goes, 'You think you're SO cool, don't you? Playing

God with people's lives,' which are the exact same words that Andrew's old man used, so I think it's pretty fair to say there's been some kind of family conference about me.

I just, like, shrug, take a whack out of my pint and go, 'Answer me this: has he ever done the dirt on you?' and she doesn't answer. I'm there, 'I'll take that as a yes,' and she's like, 'That was Becky's fault. She came on to him when he was drunk. And she SO did it to piss me off,' and I nod really slowly, roysh, cracking on that I understand where she's coming from, but it's, like, mission accomplished, roysh, because I've planted that seed of doubt in her mind. I go, 'Where is he tonight?' and she's there, 'Having an early night. He's getting up early tomorrow to practise his kicking. *See?* He's still practising, Ross, even though you cut him from the team.'

I'm there, 'That's what he told *you*,' and she goes, 'No, that'd be the *truth,* Ross. We trust each other,' but I can tell from her boat, roysh, that she's not exactly convinced. She storms off then, roysh, but I know she'll be back.

Oisinn turns around to me and goes, 'You've two hopes there, Ross,' and I'm like, 'Meaning?' and he's there, 'Meaning Bob and No. I know a goy who's in her class in UCD. Every goy in Commerce has chanced his orm with her and ended up crashing and burning. She's been going out with that Pikey goy for years,' and I'm like, 'I love a challenge, Oisinn, you know that,' and Oisinn goes, 'She actually looks a bit like that Beth Ostrosky.'

Half-an-hour later, roysh she's back – surprise, sur-focking-prise – her *Volume Effet Faut Cils* all over her boat from where she's been crying. She goes, 'His mobile's switched off. And the home phone's been engaged for, like, thirty minutes.' The poor focker's probably on the internet or some shit. I'm there, 'He's strayed before, Jessica. What's to say he wouldn't do it again?' and I just, like, slip my orm around her waist and when she lets me leave it there I know she's, like, putty in the hand.

I give her an hour of you-deserve-so-much-better horseshit and a bit of the old you-need-a-man-not-a-boy, and an hour later, roysh, she's kicking off her Dubes back in Room 404 of the Berkeley Court and I'm pleasuring her like she's never been pleasured before. She knows a few tricks herself, if the truth be told, and I'd actually give her a good eight out of ten.

Of course, while we're doing the bould thing, I'm thinking, You're not so shit-hot now, are you Pikey? Stor of the school team you might be . . . and then I accidentally go – out loud – '. . . but they all still want The Master,' and Jessica stops and goes, 'What did you say?' and I'm there, 'Oh, I . . . em . . . asked you did you want me to go faster,' and she buys it.

Of course, then the inevitable happens. Four o'clock in the morning, she gets the kind of attack of conscience that a man of my vast experience has come to expect. She actually wakes me up with her *Ohmygod! Ohmygod! Ohmy-God!*s. She's like, 'I cannot *believe* I did that,' and I'm lying there going, 'Do you mind? I'm actually trying to sleep here. Do your focking soul-searching somewhere else,' and she gets out of the Margaret and storts throwing her threads back on and, like, sobbing to herself about how she promised Andrew that the pre-debs was a one-off and it wouldn't, like, happen again, but now it has, which makes her a – OH! MY! GOD! – *total* slapper.

As she's leaving, roysh, I turn around and go, 'And put

the Do Not Disturb sign on the door,' and she actually does it, the sap.

Pikey's like a dog with two mickeys when he hears the news. I'm there, 'You're back on the team,' and for a minute, roysh, I actually think he's going to hug me. He's like, 'And I'm still captain?' and I go, 'Yeah, but I want to see maximum commitment from you. No more nights out. No more distractions, of a romantic or otherwise nature,' and – get this, roysh – he goes, 'I'm actually going to talk to Jessica tonight, tell her I want to cool it for a while, at least until after March seventeenth.' I'm there, 'March seventeenth? You're thinking in terms of the final – I like that,' and he goes, 'Why not? We're better than anything else in the competition,' and I'm like, 'For now, let's just concentrate on beating Clongowes tomorrow,' and he goes, 'You are not going to regret this, Mr O'Carroll-Kelly,' and he focks off, roysh, feeling like I'm doing him a favour rather than the other way around.

My phone rings and I can see from my caller ID that it's, like, Ronan and it's weird, roysh, but I get this, like, feeling of excitement in my stomach, butterflies, I suppose you'd have to say. I answer and he goes, 'Alreeet, Rosser?' and I'm there, 'Hey, Ronan. What's the *scéal?*' and he's like, 'You know yourself, don't want to say anything to incriminate myself,' and I laugh. He goes, 'You've got that match tomorrow, right?' and I'm there, 'Clongowes, yeah. It's in Donnybrook. Why don't you come along? I can talk to your mother,' and he goes, 'Don't take this up the wrong way, Rosser, but rugby's a faggot's game. If that's what you're into, it's what you're into. But don't forget,

I've a rep in this town,' and I'm there, cracking up again, going, 'Sorry, I forgot about your *rep*,' and he's there, 'If some of me contacts found out I was into that kind of thing, well, you know ... but I just wanted to say good luck.'

Two days after we beat Clongowes, I'm still buzzing off what Wardy wrote, and I know it basically off by hort at this stage. It was like, With former star flyhalf Ross O'Carroll-Kelly at the helm, MAKE NO MISTAKE, Castlerock College have gone from being rank outsiders in the Leinster Schools Senior Cup to THE team to beat after yesterday's seismic events in Donnybrook.

We ended up lashing Clongowes out of it, we're talking 57–13, and we're talking seven tries as well, four of them from Pikey, who had the game of his life. He kicked focking everything. He was unbelievable, roysh, and so was Lorcan, who got a try himself, and as we're running circles around them, I'm looking over at Gerry Thornley, who actually tipped this shower to win it this year, and I'm, like, wondering what he's thinking now.

The next day I find out. His report is like, Not only were Clongowes beaten yesterday, they were anni-hilated. It rained tries at Donnybrook. But that was only part of the story. Castlerock lit up a miserable afternoon with their fast-running game that put this writer in mind of – dare I say it – their young coach Ross O'Carroll-Kelly in his prime, and I'm just reading it, going, 'Yes, you dare say it. All is forgiven, Gerry.'

Then he's like, Andrew Pike was outstanding —
but then, isn't he always? It would be selling him
short to describe his performance as mesmeris-
ing and, though only a couple of thousand souls
braved the elements to watch yesterday's match,
many thousands more will, in years to come, claim
to have been there to watch his five-star performance yesterday.

Then it's like, Yet the most impressive aspect of
the performance, from this observer's point of
view, was Castlerock's dominance up front, with
young hooker Francis Stadiem proving himself the
immovable object of popular cliché, while in the
lineout Aodán Hannafy jumped like his legs were
spring-loaded.

I'm actually glad he, like, singled other goys out, roysh,
because I didn't want to take all the credit for the result,
although I have to say, my pre-match talk was pretty amazing, we're talking real, like, stirring stuff, if that's the word.
All the goys were there in the dressing-room with their
heads down and their game-faces on, basically psyching
themselves up, and I was just, like, pacing back and forth
in front of them going, 'Look at me! LOOK AT ME!'
and they all, like, looked up and I went, 'What do those
jerseys mean to you? Because they mean EVERYTHING
to me. *EVERYTHING!* Let me tell you something, I
don't actually care if we lose out there today. Clongowes,
okay, they're wankers, but they're a bloody good team. It
won't bother me if they beat us — just as long as every one
of you can still look me in the eye when you walk off that
pitch in a little under two hours' time,' and at that point,
roysh, Francis Stadiem jumped up, pointed at me and went,

'I WILL FOCKING *DIE* FOR THIS MAN!' and out they went. Clongowes didn't know what hit them.

I pulled Pikey to one side and I was like, 'Where's your head at?' and he was there, 'In a good place. Had the chat with Jessica,' and I'm there, 'That's good. How'd she take it?' and he goes, 'Not well, but I can't afford to dwell on that. This is my only focus roysh now. And if you'll excuse me, I have business to take care of,' and he turns around and I just go, 'YOUDA MAN, PIKEY!' and under my breath – I'm a dickhead, I know – I go, 'But *I* was the man on Monday night.'

JP rings me and before I have a chance to ask him, roysh, how those new gaffs in Edgeworthstown are selling, he goes, 'I take it that it was you? Who put Fionn's diary on the internet?' and I'm there, 'What makes you think that?' and he's like, '*Hey there, fellow geeks . . . really, really, really good-looking, kick-orse rugby player?*' and I crack up laughing and I go, 'Couldn't resist that bit. Focking hilarious, isn't it?' and JP's like, 'Not from my POV. I actually think you're like Grant Mitchell's phone – *bang* out of awder. Sorry, dude.'

I'm there, 'Hey, when I told you I was going to fix him you thought it was great,' and JP's like, 'I thought you were going to, like, do an Ivana in one of his Dubes or, like, use his Ralph as a jizz rag – the usual shit we do. I think you crossed the line, dude. I met Fionn today and he is NOT a happy camper,' and I'm there, 'You *told* him it was me?' and he goes, 'Ross, the goy's studying for a PhD. He's got an IQ higher than mine, yours, Oisinn's and Christian's put together – you think he needed to be told? Ross, you need to sort your shit out,' and I'm there, 'What's that supposed to mean?' and he goes, 'Just that – sort your shit out,' and he hangs up on me, my *so-called* friend.

I'm flaked out on the bed, roysh, stretched out, watching a DVD of our next opponents – as in the boggers of Newbridge College – beating Mary's in the quarter-finals and I'm, like, basically analysing their strengths, weaknesses, blah blah blah. The next thing, roysh, there's a knock on the door and who is it only the focking Boy Poet himself, and I can tell straight away that he's bulling.

He comes in, but he doesn't say anything, just plonks himself down in the ormchair in the corner, so I go back to watching Newbridge. After a few minutes I go, 'I think I've spotted a weakness in their back row,' and Fionn goes, 'I know it was you, Ross,' and I just stare at him, as if to say, basically, prove it, and he's there, 'She rang me. Your friend, Leilani. She felt bad about what she did,' and I look at him as if to say, *Whatever!*

I think we're actually going to murder this team in the lineout. He goes, 'I went to see Sorcha tonight,' and I'm there, 'What did you do – shout poems up at her focking window?' and he's like, 'I came here to apologize, Ross,' and I pause the match, thinking, Grovelling, this is more like it. He goes, 'My feelings for Sorcha are real. It's just I should have told you years ago.' What a tool. I go, 'Apology accepted.'

He goes, 'But what *you* did, Ross, was an unforgivable violation of my privacy,' and I'm there, 'I was actually trying to get you off Sorcha's case. I wanted her to see what kind of a focking wacko you really are. Poems that don't rhyme? What were you focking thinking of?'

He sits down on the side of the bed, takes off his glasses and rubs his face. The focker looks tired, like he hasn't slept in a week, which he probably hasn't. He puts his glasses back on and goes, 'I was surprised, you know. At how well Sorcha took it. She actually said she thought it was sweet. Well, not that it ended up on the internet obviously, but the fact that I had all these feelings for her and was able to subjugate them for so long.'

I don't believe it, roysh, the focker's actually got me feeling sorry for him. I grab a couple of Britneys from the minibor, crack them open and hand him one. I go, 'Did you tell her it was me who put it on the internet and shit?' and he's there, 'No. I told her it was me,' and I end up dribbling a mouthful of beer down the front of my new Ralph. I'm like, 'Why would you do that?' and he goes, 'She *loves* you, Ross. I know how much it would devastate her to think you'd be capable of doing something like that,' and I'm there, 'So you took the hit?' and he goes, 'Not for *you*, Ross. I did it for Sorcha.'

He knocks back a couple of mouthfuls of beer, then he goes, 'I haven't said anything to Lorcan. I know he gave you my journal, but I can understand *why* he did it. You manipulate people, Ross. It's all about getting what *you* want,' and I just, like, shrug my shoulders, as if to say, basically, that's the nature of the beast.

He finishes his beer and gets up to go. I put out my hand and I go, 'No hord feelings,' but he just, like, refuses to shake it. He goes, 'Don't misunderstand anything I've said here tonight, Ross. I *will* get you back for this. And that's a promise.'

*

90

JP texts me this joke, roysh, and it's like, **Why did God invent orgasms?** and the answer, roysh, is, **So northsiders would know when to stop riding.**

Lauren's in bits, roysh, and it's pretty understandable, I suppose, what with her old man looking at a ten-stretch. We're standing outside the Four Courts and she's got her head buried in Christian's chest and she's going, 'This is, like, SO unfair. He's being hounded, like some common criminal,' and Christian's reminding her that Han Solo's friends didn't give up on him, even after he was frozen in carbonite and hung like some decoration on the wall of Jabba's Palace, but it doesn't seem to cheer her up at all.

She's going, 'But he's *innocent*, Christian,' and of course I have to bite my tongue to stop myself pointing out that he's *actually* pleaded guilty. I'm not about to go joining any escape committee to get Hennessy out of the slammer. The goy can rot in there for all I care – the old man gave him a hundred and fifty thousand sheets to stick in an offshore account, basically as a deposit on a gaff for me one day, roysh, but the last time Toss Features went to visit him in the Joy, the dude refused to see him, his *so-called* best friend, so it's pretty obvious the sponds are history.

I'm not one to hold a grudge – I'll get the bread out of the old man anyway – and though I couldn't give a fock if Hennessy ends up spending the rest of his days sewing mailsacks and shitting in a bucket in a six-by-four cell, Christian and Lauren are my friends and I want to, like, be there for them, just like they've been there for me. See, some of us have what we call sensitivity, though where I

inherited it from I don't know. I see Knob Head coming from a focking mile away and it's obvious, roysh, that he's only come here to gloat, not giving a fock about Lauren, who's supposed to be, like, his goddaughter. He breezes along the road towards the court, roysh, a big stack of, like, papers under his orm, just to make him look important, and just as he's passing Charlie Bird, roysh, he looks into the TV camera and he goes, 'Let's cut the cancer of corruption out of our society once and for all,' then he turns around and asks the cameraman if he got that on tape, or if he'd like him to do it again. Charlie Bird – who obviously hasn't got a bog who the old man is – just, like, butts in and goes, 'We're waiting for Hennessy Coghlan-O'Hara to arrive,' and the old man's like, 'Just thought you might value the view of one of your licence-payers.'

The old nosebag in the Joy mustn't agree with Hennessy, roysh, because when he arrives he looks about five stone underweight – must be down to about sixteen now – and as these two heavy-looking Feds are leading him from the back of the prison van into the court, Lauren's giving it, 'I love you, Daddy,' and he's going, 'I love *you,* Lauren,' and they're both bawling and I have to say, roysh, you'd have to be pretty hord-hearted not to be moved by . . .

My Wolfe rings. The screen's like, **Private Number**, but I answer it and it's, like, One F from *The Stor.* He goes, 'Seems your success with Castlerock has made you a wanted man. The grapevine is, shall we say, abuzz with rumours that we're soon going to be seeing you plying your coaching wares at a certain club out Stradbrook way in the not-too-distant. I'm thinking in terms of World Exclusive here. I'm thinking, eighty-four-point banner headline. Care to comment?' I go, 'Are you serious?' and he's like, 'I'm as serious as the Tet Offensive,' and I'm there, 'Sorry, One F, you'll have to talk to my agent,' only remembering after I hang up that my agent – the goy who got me my boot deal with Elverys – is up there in the dock in Court Two.

Me, Christian and Lauren sit at the back of the public gallery and the rest of the goys arrive together, we're talking Oisinn, we're talking JP and we're talking Fionn, who carries on like nothing ever happened between us. The old man stands up for the entire hearing, leaning over the rail, making hangman gestures to Hennessy, like he's in *The Godfather* or some shit. The actual case itself, roysh, is pretty boring – it's all blah-blah-this and blahdy-blah-that – and I end up spending most of the morning getting an eyeful of these two lawyer birds, wondering how many shekels it'd cost to keep something like that interested.

Bang! Seven years, with the last two suspended, which is a result basically. He'll be out in, like, three. Hennessy's got this big, like, shit-eating grin on his face, but Lauren's howling like a focking banshee, roysh, and Christian has to take her outside. Wank Features leans over the railing and goes, 'JUSTICE WAS NOT SERVED HERE TODAY!' and the judge tells him that unless he's careful, he'll cite him for, like, contempt and the old man turns to some total stranger beside him and storts muttering about the disgrace of tax evasion and, like, hospital ward closures.

The stupid tosser catches my eye then and he goes, 'Justice was most certainly served at Donnybrook last week. I was at the game, Ross. Wonderful rugby,' and before I get the chance to call him a tool and tell him to drop dead, some old dude in a suit just, like, sidles up to him and goes, 'Charles O'Carroll-Kelly?' and the old man goes, 'No interviews, I'm afraid. I'm keeping my powder dry in case "Questions and Answers" want me on,' and the goy goes, 'No, I'm not a, em . . . look, Adam Bagshaw is my name. From Baggot and Leggit Solicitors. We instructed counsel for Mr Coghlan-O'Hara in this case. Our client asked that I give you this,' and he hands the old man a piece of paper. The old man's like, 'What is it, a recipe for a cake with a file in it?' and the dude looks over his shoulder, roysh, and goes, 'It's the number for a bank account in Liechtenstein. Hennessy moved your money there when he found out the Revenue were on his case. He didn't want to see you in Mountjoy that day because he was afraid he was being *listened to,* if you know what I'm saying.'

Knob Head's just left standing there in, like, total shock. I just walk off. Christian's managed to calm Lauren down, though he's got half her face on his new Henri Lloyd. He's saying he's not going back to work and she's going, 'You have to, Christian. You've got that consignment of Clone Wars animated figures arriving. I know how much that means to you,' but he goes, 'I think this is, like, *slightly* more important,' and it's true, roysh, the goy *is* a focking rock.

Ten minutes later the old man suddenly, like, emerges and breezes down the steps of the court. TV3 are interviewing people outside, asking them if they thought that justice had been basically served. The old man nearly breaks his focking Gregory trying to get on. He goes, 'There'll *be* an appeal, you can bet your last dime on that. This is not justice. It's mass hysteria generated by bloody Commie journalists who wouldn't know *how* to do a hard day's work, never mind fan the flames of the economy like that good man, who we've just seen hauled off to prison in handcuffs, like someone from one of these frightful local authority housing estates. What I want to say to your viewers tonight is: Judge not lest you be judged yourself, with a capital J.'

Birds are, like, total focking headwreckers. I get, like, two calls in the space of, like, five minutes, roysh, and the first one is from Jessica and she's going, 'Andrew's finished with me, you are SUCH a wanker,' and I'm there, 'Hey, the goy wants to concentrate on his rugby. They're saying he's going to captain the Irish schools team Down Under, as in basically Australia,' but it does fock-all to win her around. She storts, like, bawling her eyes out, giving it, '*Oh my God,* I SO want him back,' and I'm there, 'Just give him his space, just until Paddy's Day,' thinking I don't want her wrecking *his* head like she's actually wrecking mine.

She goes, 'It's, like, SO hord, though. I miss him SO much,' and I swear to God, roysh, I am SO tempted to tell her to ring the Samaritans, or at least someone who actually *gives* a shit, except that I need her to be cool roysh now. I don't want her getting all hysterical and telling Pikey in a moment of honesty that I boned her. I'd totally lose the dressing-room, and we are seriously talking totally here.

Wouldn't say we *beat* Newbridge College in the semi-final as much as totally rubbed their noses in the dirt, which is where they belong, being boggers and everything.

Fehily called me into his study the day before the game and he goes, 'Intellectually, I'm no five-eighths of a man, Ross, I know this team of yours are no world-beaters. We have – what? – four, maybe five good players. The rest of them are a joke and not even a good one. And yet what you

97

have achieved, with the limited resources at your disposal, is a miracle on a scale not witnessed since Jesus wept bitter tears over the tyranny of death, the last enemy, and Lazarus got out of the bed and walked,' and I'm there, 'That's pretty high praise,' but he just, like, raises his hand and goes, 'But, my child . . . it will all have been for nothing if we lose to this shower of shite tomorrow.'

I'm like, 'I know. Why do they have to let schools like that into the competition in the first place?' and he's there, 'It's all in the name of social ecumenism,' and I go, 'Totally,' cracking on to know what he's talking about.

He goes, 'I don't think it's any secret, Ross, that I've got something of a . . . *regard* for our friend – the painter from Brauna am Inn. As you know, he considered the theory that all men are created equal to be the most deceitful lie. These people are from, dare I say it, the *country*, Ross. How many of our Taoisigh went to school there? How many of our great men of industry? Of commerce?' and I'm like, 'None?' and he's there, 'Your answer is both correct and wise, my child. We cannot afford to lose this match.'

I'm like, 'We won't. I've studied them. I know their weaknesses. They've no pace on the wings, they've no decent lineout jumpers, their number thirteen doesn't like being tackled and their back row is focking shite, if you'll pardon the French,' and he goes, 'That's not French, Ross. That's vulgarity, and I like it. It demonstrates anger. Reveals passion. Channel it and a place in the Leinster Schools Cup final is ours for the taking.' I'm just there, 'And we're talking *totally*,' and I get up to leave, roysh, and as I'm going out the door, he goes, 'Either the world will be ruled according to the ideas of our modern democracy, or the world will be dominated according to the natural law of force; in the latter case the people of brute force . . . will be victorious,' all of which basically translates as, KICK ORSE!

My big fear was, like, Jessica. I had a feeling she'd end up showing her face. So she turns up in Donnybrook, roysh, with a whole focking gaggle of her UCD mates – one was a honey, the other three were total ditch-pigs – and I'm straight over to her and I'm like, 'What's your focking game?'

It has to be said, roysh, she's looking pretty well. She's dressed to kill and she reeks of *Dazzling Gold* by Estée Lauder. She's just like, 'It's a free country,' and I go, 'Do you think it'll be good for Andrew's head to know you're in the crowd?' and she's there, 'HELLO? There's, like, two thousand people here. I don't *think* he's going to see me,' and I'm like, 'He focking dumped your orse. Learn to live with it. It'll make it easier in the long run,' and then I head for the dugout.

There were actually more than two thousand people there. The ground was like Howl at the Moon on Mickey Tuesday – basically rammers – and the atmos was, like, electric. It was one of those times when the goys didn't need a pre-match talk. They were, like, so psyched up they wouldn't have heard it anyway. I just went, 'You don't need me to tell you what's at stake here today. Let's *do* them.'

Pikey scored two tries – one at the end of a sixty-yord run – and Lorcan got over for another after taking a sly little tap penalty. Pikey converted all three and kicked, like, five penalities without reply and at half-time, roysh, I told the goys not to be afraid to showboat a bit in the second half. I'm like, 'Don't be worried about humiliating this crowd. Bogball is their game. They need to learn that, even if it is the hord way,' and the second half was just, like, champagne rugby, the goys passing it to each other through their legs and everything.

I don't usually buy *The Stor*, what with it being a news-paper for poor people, but One F was like, Hold the front page – Castlerock are back! The pre-viously misfiring southsiders hit Newbridge College like a Tonkin gunboat yesterday to clinch a place in the Leinster Schools Cup final for the first time since they lifted the cup in 1999. What-ever was said in the wake of the school's rather patchy performance in their winter friendlies has certainly worked. And perhaps that should come as no surprise, for the man pulling Castle-rock's strings now is none other than Ross O'Carroll-Kelly, once a legend as a player, now a legend as a coach. They still have a few more clicks to travel, yet it's hard to believe that this boy general, who plotted his team's passage all the way to Lansdowne Road, is still only twenty-three . . .

I'm thinking, he could have added, 'And available'.

Sorcha rings me – no mention of me steering possibly the worst Castlerock team in probably twenty years into the final of the Leinster Schools Senior Cup – and instead, roysh, she storts giving it the whole Pretending To Be Getting On With The Rest Of My Life vibe. She says the new shop, as in the one in the Powerscourt Town-house Centre, is doing SO well at the moment and – *Oh my God!* – she's *actually* storted seeing someone, some total tosspot by the sound of it, who goes to Trinity and who's taking her to see the Suleyman Erguner Ensemble and the Whirling Dervishes perform the Sema at the National Concert Hall.

No, how are you Ross. No, good luck for the final against Blackrock. And what the fock *is* a Whirling Dervish anyway?

A word of warning, roysh – do NOT go to see *The Passion*. Two hours I sat through it and despite the title, there's fock-all riding in it. This was basically the joke I cracked in JP's cor the other night, roysh, but Emily and Medb – these two birds we took to the flicks – didn't find it funny. Emily is just like, 'HELLO? *The Passion* is *actually* the suffering of Jesus Christ from the Last Supper to the point of his crucifixion,' me totally forgetting that Emily's in the folk group in Foxrock church, and JP turns around to me and goes, 'Know your audience, Ross,' and gives me a wink.

Two God-botherers, just our luck. Probably no chance of bailing in now either, and they're both pretty babelicious, which makes it worse. Emily is JP's one. She's doing, like, a TEFL course in Mountjoy Square, roysh, and he chatted her up in The Bailey a couple of Saturday afternoons ago. They storted talking about, of all things, Jesus and God and all that basic stuff. JP owns a CD of Elvis Presley gospel songs – that's where his knowledge of this shit storts and ends. So this Emily bird mentions that she is SO going to go to see the new Mel Gibson movie when it comes out, and JP says he's dying to see it as well and suddenly, roysh, before they know it, they've talked themselves into a date.

So Thursday night, roysh, we're talking two hours before they've arranged to meet, Emily springs the news on JP that one of her friends is tagging along, as in Medb, who's her best friend and who's also in the folk group. Of course, the last thing JP wants is some Klingon putting the dampeners on the night, so he asks me to tag along – give it the whole *double*-date vibe? – and, because he's a mate, roysh, I agree to take a bullet for him. Anyway, it's not a bullet at all, roysh, because Medb turns out to be a lasher, basically a dead ringer for Tara Reid – as in Tara Reid from, like, 'Scrubs' – and suddenly it's, like, 'Late Late' country: there's something for everyone in the audience.

Fifteen minutes into the film, of course, my hand goes for a bit of a wander, up the old kilt basically, but it's only gotten as far as her knee when Medb grabs it, roysh, and bends three of my fingers back to the point where I practically scream and I know straight away, roysh, that tonight's a dead loss, that you'd have to basically marry this bird before she'd let you even feed the toothless gibbon. JP's not getting on much better either, because I can hear Emily giving him an earful, roysh, and though I can't hear what she's saying, once or twice I catch the word, 'Respect'.

So two hours later, roysh, we're on the way home and it's, like, roasting in the cor and there's a very good reason for that. Emily, according to JP anyway, has the best rack this side of Lola Ferrari, but she's wearing a jacket that looks like she stole it from a hot-water tank – we're talking a bubble jacket that's, like, five sizes too big for her – and she hasn't taken it off all night, roysh, which is why JP is, like, turning up the heat, bit by bit, to try to get her to, like, unzip it at least, so I can cop an eyeful in the rear-view.

Yes, it's childish, but then so is taking a bird to the flicks and ending up going home with all your bullets still in the chamber.

So there's me and JP up the front, roysh, and the two birds are in the back and it's like a focking sauna in there and Emily's giving it, 'Is it just me, or is it, like, hot in here?' and JP's there, 'Don't feel it myself. What about you, Ross?' and I'm like, 'No, I'm just perfect,' and JP goes, 'I'll lash on the old AC,' which is, like, Estate Agent for Air Conditioning, but instead of turning on the cold air, he turns the heat up another notch or two.

I'm still making the effort with the two birds, of course, but I'm pissing into the wind basically. I ask them what they think of this, like, smoking ban that's coming in and Medb's like, 'I'm in favour of it,' and I'm there, 'They're saying The George is going to be the most popular pub in Dublin next weekend,' and it's basically a joke about the smoking ban. Medb goes, 'The George, as in the gay bor?' and I'm there, 'Yeah, it's the only pub in Ireland where you can still have a pint and a fag,' but neither of the birds even smiles. I lean forward and flick the temperature up another ten degrees.

Out of nowhere, roysh – and I'm not making this up – JP turns around and goes, 'Is it true that Mel Gibson took all the goriest bits out of the four Gospels and put them in the film?' and Emily goes, 'Well, I know that only one of the books of the New Testament mentions Jesus being scourged,' and Medb's like, 'But then only Luke tells us about the robber repenting on the cross beside him. Matthew, John and Mark make no mention of it and yet it's taken as, pardon the pun, gospel,' and JP goes, 'I must sit down one day and actually *read* the thing from cover to cover,' and I'm looking at him, roysh, unable to decide whether he's actually serious or he's trying to get in at them from another angle.

Emily goes, 'I'm sorry, it is *ab-so-lute-ly* roasting in here. Can you even, like, open a window?' and JP goes, 'I can't. It'd mess up the, er . . . the refraction,' and even though JP did, like, physics for the Leaving Cert, roysh, I happen to know he made that word up. I know what Emily's talking about, though. I'm sweating like Dot Cotton after a twelve-hour shift in the laundrette, but me and JP are cracking on not to notice, roysh, and we're sitting there, copping sly looks at Emily, wondering basically how much longer she can hold out. I could *suggest* she takes off her coat, but I don't want her to think I'm a perv.

JP turns around to me and goes, 'So, two days to go to the big game. How's the team looking?' and I'm there, 'Weak in some areas, strong in others. I don't think Blackrock are all they're cracked up to be, though,' and JP nods and the two birds must have no interest in rugby, roysh, because neither of them asks, like, a single question.

JP turns the heat up again. It must be, like, a hundred degrees in the jammer at this stage and I'm going to have a focking Peter Pan when I get out. Emily's, like, fanning herself with her hand and blowing her face. Medb's got her head back and her mouth open, trying to find some air to breathe in, but she looks like she's losing the will to live. JP goes, 'Hey, how's that kid of yours doing?' and I'm there, 'Pretty good, actually. He's making his, like, Communion in a few weeks,' and all of a sudden, roysh, Medb sits forward in her seat and goes, '*Excuse me?* You've got, like, a child?' and I'm there, 'Yeah?' as in, *so focking what?*

She goes, 'So, you're married?' and I'm there, 'Yeah,' and

she's like, 'I went on a date with you and you didn't mention that you were, like, *married,* with a child?' and I go, 'No, I'm not married. Well, I *am* technically, but not to Ronan's mother. I just had a kid with her, but I'm actually married to another bird, though we're supposed to be getting a divorce or, I don't know, an annulment or some shit . . .' and she goes, 'STOP! STOP JP! Let me out of this car. NOW!'

I end up just losing the rag, roysh. I go, 'I'd *hordly* call it a date, anyway. I got fock-all out of it. Maybe I should have told you I had a wife and a kid. But you should have told me you were a frigid Holy Mary,' and while we're arguing, roysh, JP's given us another ten degrees and I'm turned around, roysh, looking at Medb, but my vision's getting all, like, blurred and my speech is all, like, slurred and my eyelids suddenly feel like heavy weights.

The next thing I remember is waking up, roysh, lying across the bonnet of the cor with JP standing over me, cracking his hole laughing. I'm going, 'What the fock happened?' and he's going, 'You fainted, dude. Must have been the heat. You've been out for, like, twenty minutes,' and I'm there, 'Where's the birds?' and he's like, 'Home, I presume. They flagged down a Jo,' and then he storts, like, cracking his hole laughing. He goes, 'Got to tell you something, though, and this registers, like, a ten on the Comedy Richter Scale. When we got you out of the cor, Medb said that the first rule in first aid was to keep the patient warm. So Emily took off her coat and put it over you. She took off her coat, dude! And you were out for it all!'

*

I can't believe that focking Orse Breath would ring me at a time like this. I answer it. I *actually* answer it. Sometimes I'm, like, too nice for my own good. I'm there, 'What the fock do you want?' and he goes, 'Ringing to tell you the big news, Ross. Don't want you reading it in your *Irish Times* first,' and I'm like, 'What are you crapping on about?' and he goes, 'I've decided to stand in the local elections. Yes indeed, you heard me right. Oh, yes, Mister. I'm doing it for Hennessy and Beverly and all the others who've had their names dragged through the mire by certain so-called journalists whose names I won't give them the pleasure of mentioning,' and I don't bother my orse even answering him, roysh, I just flip the old Wolfe shut and turn it off.

I'm actually at assembly in Castlerock, roysh, well actually I'm sort of, like, backstage, waiting for Fehily to introduce me because we've got, like, the final tomorrow and he wants me to say a few words, but first he wants to read them something from, like, the Bible basically. He's there going, 'A reading from the Book of Exodus. Now Moses was tending the flock of his father-in-law, Jethro, the priest of Midian, and he led the flock to the far side of the desert and came to Horeb, the Mountain of God. There the angel of the Lord appeared to him in flames of fire from within a bush. Moses saw that though the bush was on fire, it did not burn up. So Moses thought, "I will go over and see this strange sight – why the bush does not burn up."

'When the LORD saw that he had gone over to look, God called to him from within the bush, "Moses! Moses!" And Moses said, "Here I am." "Do not come any closer," God said, "take off your sandals, for the place where you are standing is holy ground." Then he said, "I am the God of your father, the God of Abraham, the God of Isaac and the God of Jacob." At this, Moses hid his face, because he was afraid to look at God.

'The LORD said, "I have indeed seen the misery of my people in Egypt. I have heard them crying out because of their slave-drivers, and I am concerned about their suffering. So I have come down to rescue them from the hand of the Egyptians and to bring them up out of that land into a good and spacious land, a land flowing with milk and honey – the home of the Canaanites, Hittites, Amorites, Perizzites, Hivites and Jebusites. And now the cry of the Israelites has reached me, and I have seen the way the Egyptians are oppressing them. So now, go. I am sending you to Pharaoh to bring my people, the Israelites, out of Egypt." This the word of the Lord,' and everyone's like, 'Thanks be to God.'

Fehily goes, 'Boys and girls, the story I've just told happened about twelve hundred years before the Coming of Christ. More than a thousand years before he sent his son, the Lord sent Moses to lead the Israelites out of captivity in Egypt into Sinai. More than three thousand years later, He sent *us* a saviour to lead us from the wilderness of schools rugby . . . into the Promised Land of the Leinster Senior Cup final,' and everyone storts cheering and clapping and basically giving it loads.

He goes, 'Castlerock is justly proud of traditions – as an institute of learning and a nurturer of athletic excellence, particularly in the sacred game that is rugby union. We have come to see success as our right, much like the Israelites considered the land promised to Abraham in Genesis 15. In January, I made a covenant with a man who I believe was sent to us by the Lord. And now here we are, camped on the Planes of Moab, east of the River Jordan, about to enter the Promised Land of Lansdowne Road. Ladies and gentlemen, I give you . . . Ross O'Carroll-Kelly,' and the whole place goes totally ballistic, roysh, everyone giving it, 'ROSS! ROSS! ROSS! ROSS!' and, 'LE-GEND! LE-GEND! LE-GEND! LE-GEND!'

When the noise dies down, roysh, I'm just like, 'I never believed that five years ago, when I stood here before you as a player, I'd be back again quite so soon. But, as you heard Father Fehily say, back at the stort of the year, he came to me and he went, "Will you coach Castlerock this year?" and I'm not going to basically lie to you, I had my doubts. I doubted whether the bunch of goys I was going to inherit had the same hunger to win that we had in 1999. Fitness was a major problem. Then a few too many of them were way too interested in passing their Leaving Cert,' and I give Lorcan in the front row a big wink and he, like, waves his fist at me, roysh, as if to say, You rock! Thank you for changing my life. I go, 'But I was wrong. There was a hunger there. There was a desire. All it needed was someone to, like, bring it out of them.'

Believe it or not, roysh, I haven't got an actual note in front of me. This stuff is coming straight from the hort. I'm there, 'Where once there was laziness, suddenly there was whatever is the opposite of laziness. I think these goys – who I'm about to ask to join me here on the stage in a moment – have learned a lot about themselves in these past eleven weeks. They've learned that within each of them there *is* talent. Within each of them, there *is*, like the song says, a hero. Like I said, they've learned a lot about themselves, but they've learned a lot about each other, too. They've learned about teamwork, about friendship, about loyalty, about trust. And that's what Blackrock will be facing tomorrow. And God help them!'

And the whole audience just, like, explodes, roysh, that's the only word for it. Everyone's giving it, 'WE ARE ROCK, WE ARE ROCK, WE ARE ROCK . . .' and I'm telling the goys in the front row – the team basically – to come up on the stage and they do, roysh, and they're hugging me and high-fiving me and clapping me on the back and telling me that I'm a legend and thanking me, basically, for helping them unlock their potential, while in the background Fehily's going, 'Let it be known that in triumph lies also defeat, and in defeat lies also triumph. I had to go through both to see where the end lies . . . the end that is not an end, death that is not death, human life that is not all of life . . .'

I hit the sack early – as in eleven – what with tomorrow being one of the biggest days of my basic life. I've been asleep for, like, an hour when the old Theobald goes. It's, like, Jessica and she's basically bawling her eyes out, roysh, shouting something down the line about a yearbook. I've just gone, 'I can't hear what you're saying. Ring me back when you're less focking hysterical,' but she calms down, roysh, and she's like, 'Don't tell me you haven't seen it yet,' and I'm there, 'Seen *what?*' and she goes, 'There's an interview with Andrew in the Castlerock yearbook. It must have been done before we, like, broke up. They asked him who was his biggest inspiration and he said . . . he said, "My girlfriend, Jessica". '

Then she's like, 'I can't live with the guilt of having been with you anymore. I'm sorry, Ross, but Andrew and I have always told each other the truth,' and she just, like, hangs up and I'm left there going, '*Oh fock!*'

Pikey bells me at, like, nine o'clock on Paddy's Day morning, roysh, and I tell him I hope he got a good night's kip, fully rested for the final, blah blah blah, and he tells me I'm a wanker and a snake and also a dickhead and he's basically going to deck me, roysh, and I can tell from the tone of his voice that he's not a happy camper and it's pretty obvious he knows that I gave Jessica an old rattle.

I'm actually having a bit of brekky in Café Java in Blackrock with the goys when he rings, their way basically of saying well done to the Coach of the Century for steering a team of losers to the Leinster Schools Cup final.

I actually didn't think Jessica would spill the beans, but the news that he actually knows hits me like a focking Johnny Hayes tackle. JP goes, 'What's wrong, Ross? You look like someone's just splashed your Dubes at the trough,' and I'm there, 'He *knows*. Pikey knows,' and Fionn and Christian are going, 'Knows what?'

Only JP and Oisinn know that I boned Jessica, but it doesn't take long for the other two to catch up on the story so far. Fionn goes, 'You never learn, do you?' full of sympathy as usual. Oisinn goes, 'I told you he was going to find out,' and I'm there, 'Well, I *knew* he would. Birds can't hold their piss. I just thought we might have at least been able to keep it on the QT until after the match.'

Christian shakes his head and goes, 'You were just hours away,' and JP goes, 'So what's the SP, Major? He's not going to play for you surely?' and I'm there, 'He said he wants to meet me. Twelve o'clock at Lansdowne Road

Dorsh station,' and straight away, roysh, Fionn – who's loving this – goes, 'You're like Gary Cooper in *High Noon*. Waiting for the noonday train to get your orse kicked,' and I give him the finger, roysh, but then he storts giving it, '*Do not forsake me, oh my darlin*,' and the rest of the goys – even Christian – break their holes laughing.

I'm there, 'Will anyone come with me?' and JP just, like, shakes his head and goes, 'One-on-one. Sounds like a fair fight to me, dude,' and I look at the goys and it's pretty obvious they're not going to offer me any back-up. I go, 'You're *supposed* to be my friends,' and Fionn goes, 'You slept with his girlfriend, Ross. You need to learn that sometimes there's a price to pay for that kind of shit,' and it's obvious, roysh, that he's, like, poisoned their minds against me over that diary business, the steamer.

Christian looks like he's wavering, though, and he's about to say he'll come with me when Fionn sticks his big, bent oar in and goes, 'You don't discriminate, do you, Ross? You'll do it with anyone – other people's girlfriends, your best friend's mother?' and when he says this I can't even look Christian in the eye.

I finish my Americano and get up to go and face my, I suppose, fate, at Lansdowne Road Dorsh station. As I'm leaving, Fionn's drumming on the table, going, '*The noonday Dorsh will bring young Pikey, if I'm a man I must be brave, and I must face that deadly outhalf, or lie a coward, a craven coward, or lie a coward in my grave . . .*' and just as I'm pulling open the door, Oisinn goes, 'Don't forget your stor, Kane,' in this, like, cowboy voice, the fat focker.

When we played rugby together, we had this rule, which was, like, one in, all in, but that's obviously totally forgotten now, and we are talking totally. I pork the cor on Baggot

Street and it's only when I go to stick a couple of squids in the meter that I realize my hands are, like, trembling. I head towards the Dorsh station. It storts to piss out of the heavens. I'm about, like, twenty minutes early, roysh, and I use the time to try to think of something that will basically save me a beating, roysh, and still get him to play against Blackrock, who'll piss all over us if he's not playing.

I'm standing at the crossing, roysh, and suddenly the barrier storts coming down and there's a train pulling in, and all of a sudden, roysh, I come up with what I have to admit is a pretty decent line. I'm sort of, like, craning my neck, roysh, trying to see if Pikey's getting off and all of a sudden I see the dude stomping his way down the ramp towards me and opening up his blue Henri Lloyd sailing jacket, like he's getting ready to deck someone – basically me. Quick as a flash, just as he's getting near me, roysh, I turn around and go, 'If it's any consolation, *she* was the one who came on to *me*. She was basically gagging for it,' but the goy's in no mood to listen to reason and all of a sudden – BANG! BANG! BANG! – three punches and the next thing I know I'm lying in, like, a puddle and he's leaning over me, roysh, and he has me by the scruff of the neck and my head's focking spinning and there's a taste of, like, blood in my mouth.

I'm waiting for the kicks to stort coming in, but then I hear this voice go, 'That's enough,' and I look up and there's, like, three blokes there and, even though my vision is blurry, I sort of, like, vaguely recognize two of them as bouncers from, like, Reynord's. Pikey goes, 'He slept with my girlfriend,' and one of the goys goes, 'And now *you've* had your fun with him. But that's enough. You're not hitting him again.'

Pikey looks down at me, roysh, then at him, then back at me again, then he lets go of me – my black DKNY shirt is basically focked – and he goes, 'Don't bother showing your face at the match this afternoon. I've spoken to the rest of the goys and they've all agreed: if you're coaching us, no one's playing,' and off he goes.

One of the bouncer dudes – he actually focked me out of Cocoon once before and Reynord's twice – he hands me a mobile and goes, 'There's a telephone call for you,' and I hold it up to my ear, roysh, which feels pretty badly bruised from where Pikey caught me when I was on the way down, and I'm just there, 'Hello?' and I hear this voice and it's just like, 'You're some fooken tulip.'

It's Ronan.

My head's too sore to even *stort* working this out. I'm there, 'How did you . . .' and he goes, 'I told you, Rosser. I've eyes and ears all over this town. The boys there are good friends of mine. I told them you were in a spot of bother. How were they, alreet?' and I'm like, 'They could have got here a bit quicker,' and he's there, 'They've been there for an hour. I told them to let him get a few digs in on you. He was *entitled*, Rosser. And it might knock some bleedin' sense into you.'

Doesn't matter what side I lie on, roysh, my face still hurts. Haven't, like, checked my boat out yet, but I'd say I've got at least one black eye, the left one, and my ear on the other side feels pretty bruised and I've got this, like, ringing noise in my head. The clock on the Savalas says it's, like, half-five in the afternoon. I go to the window and I can see the last few stragglers making their way past the Berkeley

Court and back towards town. There's, like, six or seven Castlerock goys taking the total piss out of these two Blackrock heads, which gives me a fair idea of the result.

I wander back to the bed and think about sticking on an old grown-ups' movie to try to, like, cheer myself up, but I've seen them all at least three times at this stage. I check my mobile. I've, like, one missed call. I dial 171 and it's, like, Fehily, talking in this, like, whisper. He's there, 'I'm sorry, my child, you cannot be with us on our day of glory. A sin of the flesh, I am told. We have all fallen, my child.'

Then he goes, 'You have no doubt pondered on the fact that, with you absent today, Scripture has been fulfilled. Moses worked hard to lead his people to the Holy Land, but he never made it there himself. His crime was to doubt the Lord when his flock was dying of thirst in the Desert of Zin. Yours was something quite different, I know, but let me read to you from the Book of Deuteronomy. I hope it will bring you succour in this lonely hour.'

He goes, 'On that same day the Lord told Moses, "Go up into the Abarim Range to Mount Nebo in Moab, across from Jericho, and view Canaan, the land I am giving the Israelites as their own possession. There on the mountain that you have climbed you will die and be gathered to your people, just as your brother Aaron died on Mount Hor and was gathered to his people. This is because both of you broke faith with me in the presence of the Israelites at the waters of Meribah Kadesh in the Desert of Zin and because you did not uphold my holiness among the Israelites. Therefore, you will see the land only from a distance; you will not enter the land I am giving to the people of Israel.'

He goes, 'But at least, my child, like Moses you got to enjoy the view from Mount Nebo. And for that you were blessed ... *Ein volk, ein Reich, ein Rock! Ein volk, ein Reich, ein Rock!*'

4. God's Gift

Having a hangover is bad enough without having to listen to the biggest knob in the universe crapping on while I'm trying to watch 'Ricki Lake'. I don't actually know why he rings with all the shit I throw at him. Must be, like, a glutton for punishment. He's going, 'I still don't understand why you weren't there, Ross. For your team's big moment of glory,' and I'm like, 'I told you already, I was Moby. Get that into your thick skull,' but he just won't let it go.

He's there, 'Wardy, for one, can't make head nor tale of it. Mysterious non-appearance, quote-unquote. Gerry's the same. I mean, that chap who lifted the cup, that young Justice Thaddeus Pike's boy, he never mentioned you. Not so much as a thank-you-very-much-indeed in his speech. Said the players were all grateful to Father Fehily for stepping in at such short notice to coach them on the day.'

He's like, 'I take the afternoon off from helping put together my good friend Hennessy Coghlan-O'Hara's appeal to watch my son lead Castlerock to glorious victory, only to find he's been written out of the script. That's ingratitude with a capital I, Ross. I said it to Hooky in the Berkeley Court afterwards. I said, "Put me on that show of yours and I'll tell the world",' and I can't listen to any more of this, roysh, so I end up going, 'IF YOU MUST KNOW, I KNOBBED PIKEY'S BIRD!' and there's, like, total silence on the other end of the line and after, like, twenty seconds of that, I just hang up.

I'm lying there, thinking of lashing on *Hot in the Caribbean* for the tenth time this month when Keira Knightley rings and tells me that JP's at reception. I'd ask him up here except I'm pretty much going stir-crazy in my room at this stage, so I hop in the elevator and go down to meet him in the lobby. The dude goes to high-five me, roysh, but before I can respond he turns around and goes, *'Fock!'*, obviously copping my eye and the general state of my boat. He's there, 'Was that, like . . .' and I'm there, 'Pikey? Yeah, it was. He did this to me after my *so-called* friends deserted me,' and he's, like, suddenly on the defensive, going, 'Hey, it was one-on-one, dude. Sounds like a strategic fit to me,' and I just, like, shrug my shoulders and go, 'There has to be a price to pay, I suppose, for being so desirable to the opposite sex, not to mention a red-hot lover,' and I can see Keira Knightley giving me the big-time mince pies, roysh, her interest in me having gone through the roof since she saw the shiner. Birds love a bad goy.

JP goes, 'Dude, there's a reason I'm here. I have an idea. I want to run it up the flagpole and see if you salute,' and I'm just there, 'Shoot,' and he's like, 'Well, as you may or may not know, my grandmother is going into hospital on Good Friday to have that botox operation she had reversed,' and I'm just, like, looking at the goy in, I suppose you'd have to say, disbelief. I'm there, 'Are you *sure* this is the conversation you came here to have with me?' He's there, 'Listen up for a second. My old pair were supposed to be taking my grandparents to the Holy Land for Easter Week. This has put the kibosh on it, and we're talking big-time. What I'm basically saying is that I've got a holiday for four – free, *gratis* and for nothing – and I just wondered did you want a piece?'

I'm just hoping Keira Knightley hasn't heard a word of this conversation, roysh, otherwise my street cred is out the focking window. I'm there, *'The Holy Land?* As in . . .' and he goes, 'Israel,' and I'm like, 'We're talking a pilgrimage? You're *actually* suggesting that I go with you on a pilgrimage? As in, Holy Mary and how's your father?' and he's there, 'It won't *be* like that, Ross. Come on, think outside the square for once. Take a look at this,' and he puts this, like, brochure in front of me and it's got this, like, picture of a beach, roysh, and it's, like, wall-to-wall Blankers Koen, we're talking stunners as well, with unbelievable top tens.

I'm there, *'This* is more like it. Where's this – Spain?' and he goes, 'It's Tel Aviv, Ross. That's where we're staying. We're in the Crowne Plaza, roysh on the beach.' I'm like, 'You had to actually *ask* me was I interested? What's the line-up?' and he goes, 'Christian can't get the time off work. And he wants to be around for Lauren,' and I'm there, 'Understandable. Oisinn?' and he's like, 'Yeah, he's already given me a big ten-four,' and I go, 'Cool. Which leaves one more place. Who can we ask?'

JP goes, 'Come on, Ross, you *know* who,' and I'm there, 'No focking way, JP. You *know* him – he'll ruin the whole atmos with his guidebook and his focking glasses,' and he goes, 'Ross, he's our friend. We can't *not* ask him. Anyway, it's about time you two buried the hatchet.'

I'm in Dún Laoghaire, roysh, using the old drink-link next to Café Mao, when who do I see coming out of, like, Meadows and Byrne only Erika and it has to be said, roysh, she's looking shit-hot. She goes, 'Hey, Ross. What happened to your eye?' and I'm like, 'Casualty of war, Babes,' and she's there, 'It makes you look very handsome, I have to say. I'm having some of the girls around on Good Friday, Ross, for a comedy night,' and I'm like, 'A comedy night?' and she's there, 'Yes, we're going to watch the video of the wedding,' and I can tell from her face, roysh, that she's actually not joking. She's like, 'I was going to text you, ask you to come along,' and instead of telling her to go and fock herself, roysh, I end up going, 'Em, no, I'm actually going to be in Israel,' and I end up hating myself for being so focking weedy. She goes, 'What a pity.'

I try to, like, change the subject. I'm there, 'How are things going with that goy, as in, like, the lawyer dude?' and she just goes, 'Gone,' with this really, like, cruel, I suppose you'd have to call it, look on her boat. I'm there, 'I'm sorry,' and she's like, 'So is he. Wants me back, of course. It's quite fun watching him embarrass himself. He couldn't satisfy me, Ross. *His* problem, not mine,' and I'm there, 'Oh well,' and she goes, 'I have to say though, I *do* enjoy watching men cry. No, I've got a wonderful new boyfriend. He's an orchestra conductor. His parents are loaded.'

*

Freya Farrell is this bird I met in, like, Café en Seine about six months ago, roysh, and who's been on my *To Do* list ever since. Well, I've been pretty busy, roysh – what with, like, getting married and shit? – which is the reason she hasn't heard a dickie-bird from me since I nipped her in the laneway beside the Shelbourne Hotel cor pork and asked for her phone number. Of course, she's probably thinking her chance has passed her by, roysh, but little does she know that I'm about step back into her life and make all her dreams come true. The thing is, roysh, Ronan has me totally paranoid at this stage, we're talking *actually* scared to even look at another bird when I'm out on the lash with the goys. I'll get a text, roysh, and it'll be like, **Blondie bird, denim skirt, black boots. Heads up Rosser - yur being watched**, and I'm, like, looking around me, roysh, wondering how the fock he knows this shit.

So what's happened is, roysh, I'm actually having to fall back on my old contacts to get my Nat King Cole and, it has to be said, roysh, that Freya is a total cracker, brown hair, amazing eyes, huge baps, has that whole Eva Longoria thing going on. She's actually a vet, of all things, roysh, and she shares a practice with her old man in, like, Wicklow town, of all places, so this particular Wednesday lunchtime, roysh, I decide to drive down there and have a sniff around.

She's actually surprised to see me, roysh, though shocked is probably more the word. I'm there, 'Sorry I haven't been in touch. I've been up to my eyes,' though it's probably best I don't go into specifics. She's like, 'Ross? *Wow*, it must be, like, a year?' and I'm there, 'No, must be, like, six months,' and she goes, 'No, it's a year. It was before I sat my finals,' and I'm not going to argue with her, roysh, because she doesn't seem that pissed off with me.

She's got one of those long, white doctor's coats on her and it's really doing it for me, and we're talking in a big-time way. She goes, 'Look, Ross, I'm, em . . . well, working at the moment. You should have phoned before you . . .' and I'm like, 'What are working on?' cracking on to be really interested, which is basically a trick I have with birds. She looks over her shoulder and goes, 'Oh, I just have a pup back there, in the recovery room,' and I'm like, 'Hey, I focking loves dogs,' giving it the whole Dr Dolittle bit, and I burst straight into the room. It actually turns out not to be a dog at all, roysh, but a baby seal, which also happens to be called a pup, and he's laid out on this, like, operating table. He smells like focking Moore Street at eight o'clock on a Friday morning. Freya goes, 'Isn't he beautiful? He was found washed up on Wicklow beach,' sort of, like, petting his head and I'm there, 'Hell of a hum off him, isn't there?' and she laughs and goes, 'That'd be the sea, Ross. It's funny how you get used to it.'

He is actually a cute little thing, roysh, you'd have to say, lying there with his eyes closed, totally out of the focking game. I'm there, 'What is he, nearly dead or something?' and Freya goes, 'I hope not. No, he's under a general anaesthetic,' and I'm there, 'So what's basically wrong with him?' and she's like, 'Periodontal disease,' and I'm like, 'I take it that's a bad thing?' and she goes, 'Well, it's not life or death. It's only gum disease, but the swelling in his mouth was so bad it was starting to affect his vision. It's lucky Dad's a qualified ophthalmologist,' and I'm like, 'It *really* is,' obviously not having a focking clue what she's talking about.

She goes, 'We administered an anti-inflammatory to his left eye, cleaned out two empty tooth sockets, which seems to have been where the infection started from, then sutured them closed,' and I'm not sure, roysh, whether it's all the talk about, I don't know, disease and empty tooth sockets and scabby eyes, but I've actually gone off the idea of trying to score Freya, the other reason being that, mad as it sounds and everything, it's pretty obvious that she's absolutely no interest in me. She's being quite friendly, roysh, but I'm picking up on the vibe that what happened a year ago happened a year ago and that's basically that, which is her loss.

So now I'm wondering how I get out the door without being rude. I'm like, 'Do you want me to wake him up?' and Freya sort of, like, raises her eyebrows at me and goes, 'And how do you propose to do that?' and I'm like, 'I don't know, sort of, like, slap him across the face a few times. Lightly, of course. Maybe throw a cup of water over him,' and Freya laughs and goes, 'If only it were that easy. Anaesthetizing seals is a very tricky business, you see. Have you ever heard of Marine Mammal Diving Reflex?' and I'm like, '*Duh!* Of course I have,' but she obviously sees straight through it, roysh, because she explains it to me anyway.

She goes, 'Marine mammals that are predisposed to diving have a very unusual physiology. At very low depths, seals can almost completely shut down their vascular systems, so that their blood oxygenates only the heart and the brain and not the other, lesser organs,' you can imagine me, roysh, I'm like one of them focking nodding dogs. She's like, 'A seal can slow his heart rate down from 140 beats per minute to as few as ten. Dogs, cats and birds breathe as normal under general anaesthesia. The problem with seals is that when you administer an anaesthetic, it triggers that same breath-holding response. Means you have to revive them slowly and carefully,' and I'm there, 'Well, thanks for clearing that up for me, Freya. So when are you expecting him up?'

She sort of, like, lifts the lids of his eyes, roysh, and goes, 'Pretty soon. I took him off the ventilator about twenty minutes ago. Pulse, temperature, oxygenation rate – everything's normal. He should be opening his eyes within the next hour,' and I'm like, 'Wish I could hang around and meet him, but I've got to split,' and she goes, 'Okay. Well, it was very . . . *unexpected* to see you,' and she goes to shake my hand, roysh, she *actually* shakes my hand, and I'm just there thinking, Yeah, well maybe *I'm* embarrassed about nipping *you* – has that crossed your mind?

I'm actually turning the key in the engine, roysh, when all of a sudden she comes running out of the . . . I suppose it's, like, a surgery? She's going, 'Ross, wait!' and I'm thinking, Too late for regrets, Baby, but it turns out it's not that at all.

She goes, 'Ross, I need your help,' and I'm there, 'What, did he sleep through his alorm call?' but she's in no mood for jokes, even mine. She goes, 'There's a circus on the way from Rosslare. They're in Gorey. They've a giraffe with an injured fetlock,' and I'm there, 'I actually wouldn't know what to do. To be honest with you, Freya, I was just cracking on to know what you were talking about in there,' and she goes, 'I'm not asking you to go and treat the giraffe, Ross. I'm asking you to look after the surgery for an hour. Dad's in town doing a necropsy,' and I'm like, 'No way. It's, like, totally out of the question. What if *he* wakes up in there?' and she goes, 'I'll probably be back by then. Even if he does, he's just a pup. He's very passive.'

And being basically too nice for my own good, roysh, I

eventually give in, which is how I end up sitting there with my feet up on Freya's desk, having a nosey through her drawers and watching this little baby seal basically spitting zeds. And of course after five minutes, roysh, you can guess what comes into my head. I'm there thinking, How cool would it be if Sorcha were here, roysh, what with her being into that whole Save the Animals vibe, and I'm thinking what a pity it is that she isn't going to get to see this, I don't know, caring side to me and then I end up getting this idea, roysh, which at the time, like most of my ideas, seems like the best idea that anyone's ever had in the world – *ever*.

The focking thing weighs a tonne, roysh, and it's a good job I've kept in shape since I quit playing rugby, otherwise I would never have got it out to the cor. I whip open the boot and sort of, like, slowly lower him into it, roysh, then I hit the road. A couple of times on the way I have to actually lower down the old Snoopster, roysh, because I keep imagining I can hear the thing, I don't know, borking or whatever the fock seals do. I know they clap actually. But I check on him when I pull into this, like, petrol station in Bray, of all places, and he's still out of the race.

I go up to the goy in the forecourt, who isn't the brightest, it must be said – they don't tend to recruit from the universities, these petrol stations – and I go, 'I'm looking for some oil,' and he goes, 'Do you want me to check your oil, Sir?' you know, in the way that people from Bray talk. I'm there, 'No, I want *used* oil,' and he sort of, like, scrunches his face up and goes, 'That's been bled from an engine, like?' and I'm there, 'Exactly,' and he's like, 'What would you be wanting that for?' and I go, 'Never focking mind. There's twenty focking sheets in it for you. All I'm looking for is a litre,' and he takes the moolah, disappears around the back of the garage and comes back five minutes later with a 7-Up bottle filled to the top with this, like, black gunk.

I pork opposite the Dorsh station in Killiney, lash open the boot and manage to hoist the focking animal over my shoulder, which makes it easier to carry down the steps, under the railway tracks and onto the actual beach. A couple of old biddies out walking their dogs stort staring at me, roysh, so I turn around and I go, 'MIND YOUR OWN FOCKING BUSINESS!' and they look away and I hear them muttering about 'language' and 'disrespect'.

I lie the seal down – actually I end up dropping him, but it's, like, an accident – then I whip open the bottle and pour the oil all over him, though making sure not to get any in his eyes because I *am* actually a nice goy underneath it all. Then I bell Sorcha on her mobile. She answers by going, 'Ross, I'm busy,' and I'm like, 'Drop whatever it is you're doing, grab a bottle of washing-up liquid and get your orse down to Killiney beach – we're talking NOW!' and she's like, 'I said, I'm busy,' and I'm there, 'There's a baby seal down here, Babes. Looks very much to me like he's been caught in some kind of oil slick. I'm trying to keep him alive here. Not sure I can do it on my own,' and then I shout, 'DAMN YOU OIL COMPANIES – PLACING PROFIT ABOVE ANIMALS!' but then I'm, like, worried all that I might have overdone it.

But I listen closely, roysh, and I can hear the *Oh my Gods* storting up and they get quicker and quicker, roysh, until she eventually goes, 'Mum, I have to go out. Will you tape the end of 'Family Affairs'?' and five minutes later, roysh, she's coming down the beach. Of course it's only then that

I remember the 7-Up bottle beside me, which I'm practically sitting on, and I end up burying it in the sand just as she arrives on the scene with a large bottle of Persil Citrus Burst, her old man's gorden hose and a face on her like a bucket of smashed crabs.

She goes, 'How is he?' and she storts, like, petting his face and I'm like, 'Pulse, temperature, oxygenation rate – everything's normal. Be careful handling him – looks very much to me like a case of Marine Mammal Diving Reflex and, I don't know, basically vascular systems and shit,' and I'm thinking, If only I could have remembered stuff like that at school maybe I wouldn't have got, like, *nul points* in the old Leaving. I can actually feel her looking at me, roysh, in total awe, and I actually *mean* total.

I whip open the washing-up liquid and I basically squirt it all over him, roysh, and Sorcha goes, 'I'll get water,' and of course I'm looking at the sea, wondering how she's hoping to persuade it to go up the hose. But she races over to the jacks, roysh, where there's an outside tap and she, like, unravels the hose, fixes it to the tap, then turns it on and by the time she makes it back over to me, roysh, there's water coming out of the top of it and she aims it at the seal, while I keep rubbing him down with a bit of cloth I found and lashing on more and more washing-up liquid.

Fifteen minutes later, roysh, the thing is, like, finally clean again and – un-focking-believable timing this – suddenly storting to wake up. Of course, Sorcha thinks this is a focking miracle. She's practically hugging the focking thing to death, going, 'We saved him, Ross!' and I am SO tempted to go, 'What's this *we*, Kemosabe?' but I don't. I end up going, 'I just hope and pray there aren't more out there,' and she stands up, squints her eyes and looks out to sea, like she's expecting to see a focing oil tanker or something.

She goes, 'I was on the Greenpeace Ireland website an hour ago and there was nothing about a spillage. I'll have to ring them,' and quick as a flash I go, 'Okay, you do *that*, while I bring this little chap off and release him,' thinking I've still got a chance to get him back down to Freya before she's finished doing whatever she's doing to that focking giraffe. But no, Sorcha has to throw a spanner in the works – she wants to come with me.

I'm like, 'I'm actually going to drive him pretty far. As in Wicklow. There's seals down there. I saw them in the paper. He looks to me like he's one of their crew,' and she goes, 'Ross, I *have* to be there. Please. I think this has really brought us closer together again,' and there's no answer to that of course except, 'Kool and the Gang.'

So I hop into the jammer, roysh, and Sorcha sits in the back, with the thing across her lap, petting and making, like, baby-talk to him and I'm doing ninety on the motorway all the way to Wicklow, thinking, How the fock am I going to get out of this? And of course the answer is, I'm not.

I don't know if it's that she's getting suspicious, roysh, but she's certainly asking me a lot of questions all of a sudden. She's like, 'What were you doing on Killiney beach anyway?' and I'm there, 'Walking and thinking. About all the stupid mistakes I've made,' and she goes, 'How come you knew so much about seals earlier?' and I'm there, 'This might come as a bit of a surprise to you, Sorcha, but I actually love animals,' and she's like, 'I didn't think you did. You told me I was a sap when I sent my birthday money to the World Wildlife Fund,' and I'm there, 'I'm trying to concentrate on the road, Babes.'

There's no getting out of this. I carry the seal over my shoulder down onto the beach. There's, like, six or seven other seals in the water and they suddenly stort borking in our direction. Sorcha goes, 'I think I'm going to call him Persil,' and I can see she's got, like, tears in her eyes as she's saying her goodbyes. She kisses him on the nose and, like, hugs him two or three times – she's going to end up smelling like the focking Borza if she keeps that up. She goes, 'I suppose we'd better put him back in the water,' and I look up and I go, 'Hey, wouldn't it be cool to fock him off one of those cliffs?' and she gives me this filthy, roysh, and I go, 'HELLO? It was, like, a *joke?*' which it most certainly was not.

I carry Persil down to the edge of the water and put him in and he swims straight over to his mates and suddenly, roysh, he's borking louder than the rest of them and I like to think what he's actually saying to them is, 'See that goy there in the Leinster – he's *some* man for one man.'

My phone rings and I make the mistake of answering it. It's Freya and she's having a total focking conniption fit. I have to get out of earshot of Sorcha, then I go, 'Calm down, will you. He woke up. I let him go. No big deal. Now, how's the giraffe?' and she's like, 'YOU LET HIM GO? WHERE? WHERE DID YOU LET HIM GO?' and I'm there, 'Wicklow focking Main Street! Where do you think I let him go? The beach!' and she's like, 'YOU HAD NO RIGHT . . .' and I just, like, blow into the phone a couple of times and go, 'Freya, you're breaking up,' then I hang up and, like, turn the phone off because you basically can't talk to birds when they're like that.

I wander back down towards Sorcha, who's staring out into the water with, like, tears streaming down her face. She doesn't say anything for ages. I'm like, 'I suppose we'd better get back,' and she goes, 'The way you handled that, Ross, it was like, OH! MY! GOD! Remember I said that you never do anything to actually impress me anymore?' and I'm there, 'No,' and she goes, 'It was when we were talking about that stuff Fionn wrote. I said you never did anything romantic. You never do anything to actually impress me anymore. Well, Ross, you just did. And it's like, OH MY GOD!'

My face is actually sore, roysh, trying *not* to crack up laughing in her face. I go, 'I just hate to think of animals suffering,' and I put my orm around her and, with the sound of crashing waves and happy seals borking away, we walk slowly back to the cor.

She seriously focking smells, though.

Me and the goys are having a few scoops in Finnegan's the night before we go away, roysh, and I'm making an extra-special effort with Fionn, asking how his PhD is going and blahdy blahdy blah. I actually think things are, like, Kool plus Significant Others between us now, and I seriously doubt that he's going to be looking for revenge.

The goys are in cracking form. Oisinn's been seeing this bird called Anna – used to be the best-looking bird in her year in Loreto on the Green – but he gave her the flick because the old PCS was wrecking his head, as in the Purring Cat Syndrome, as in she *seems* really relaxed and, like, chilled out, but as soon as you try to make a move she doesn't like, she digs her claws in. He's like, 'Didn't take too kindly to the idea of me going away with you goys, so she ended up getting the straight red,' and we're all there, 'You da man, Oisinn! You da man!'

Fionn goes, 'It's a pity Christian's not coming with us,' and JP's like, 'Lauren's not good, apparently. She's talking about not sitting her finals. Too upset about her old man,' and all this talk of, like, parents reminds me of something. I'm there, 'Goys, have any of you heard from Simon recently?' and JP looks at me like I've got, like, three heads. He's like, 'He went to the old US of A, didn't he? Got a rugby scholarship,' and I'm like, 'Yeah, I know, he got the place *I* turned down . . . em, has anyone heard about this, like, calendar that his old dear's doing?' and Oisinn's there, 'Oh yeah. MILF of the Month. I think it's for, like, charity.'

JP's like, 'Hey, why the big interest, dude?' and Oisinn goes, 'Christian's old dear's obviously agreed to pose nude, has she?' which she has actually, roysh, and the goys cracks their holes laughing, roysh, but I don't, and JP's the first one to cop it. He's like, 'Don't tell me your . . . Ross? *Your* old dear's going to be in it?' and I'm like, 'So she focking thinks. She won't survive the editing process,' and no one says anything.

I'm there, 'Goys, she's hordly yummy-mummy material,' but everyone's just, like, smiling to themselves and the only one who says anything is Oisinn, who goes, 'I don't know . . . speaking for myself . . .' and I'm like, 'She has a face like a focking blind cobbler's thumb. Goys, you SO can't be serious,' and they just carry on smiling and eventually Fionn goes, 'I think it's my round.'

The goys have stitched me up, roysh, and we're talking *totally* here. JP thinks I didn't hear him asking the bird at the check-in desk to put him, Oisinn and Fionn together in one row, roysh, with me in the next row behind them, basically so I'd be left talking to some Holy Joe, which is exactly what happened, roysh, except they weren't Holy Joes as much as Holy Josephines, we're talking two old biddies here, de salt o' dee ert Dooblin types.

'Have you a devotion to Our Lady?' That's what one of these old biddies *actually* asks me, when we're only in the air about ten minutes. She's like, 'Have you a devotion to Our Lady?' I've a devotion to *the* ladies, I'm tempted to tell her, but I want to get to Tel Aviv with as few words as possible passing between us, so I pretend to be asleep, though that doesn't, like, discourage her.

She goes, '*I've* a devotion to Our Lady. I've had a devotion to Our Lady me whole life,' and then, like, thirty seconds later, she goes, 'Haven't I, Mrs Mulligan?' and Mrs Mulligan – who's, like, sitting at the window and who's totally Mutt and Jett – goes, 'WHAT?' and the biddy beside me – Mrs Holt is her name; they're friends for fifty focking years and they're still not on first-name terms – she goes, 'I'M JUST TELLING THE YOUNG MAN HERE . . . THAT I'VE A DEVOTION . . . TO OUR LADY,' and Mrs Mulligan goes, 'Our Lady, yes,' and I swear to God, roysh, we're talking *literally* five minutes later, she turns around and goes, 'I WAS TELLING HIM . . . I'VE HAD A DEVOTION TO OUR LADY . . . ME WHOLE LIFE,' and Mrs Mulligan goes, 'Life, yes.'

Of course, the goys are loving this. Oisinn shouts back to me, 'Did you get any numbers yet, Ross?' and JP and Fionn think this is the funniest thing they've ever heard. We're barely out of Ireland and I'm already losing the will to live. I call one of the flying waitresses and I go, 'Does this plane have, like, parachutes?' and she's there, 'No, but if you were listening to the safety instructions earlier, you'll know that there's a lifejacket under your seat in the event—' and I'm like, 'Are we over water now?' She looks out the window and goes, 'Yes, we're over the English Channel,' and I go, 'Get that door open and tell the pilot to fly low. I'm going to take my chances,' and she laughs, roysh, thinking I'm not actually serious.

Half-an-hour into the flight, roysh, the trolley arrives, offering us basically a drink before our meal. I ask for, like, eight JD miniatures, roysh, deciding that the only way to cope with these two is to get totally focking mullered. Of course, Mrs Holt doesn't approve. She goes, 'I've a grand-son your age and he's a pioneer. I'M JUST SAYING, MRS MULLIGAN … I'VE A GRANDSON HIS AGE … ALICE'S SON … AND HE'S A PION-EER,' and of course back comes the response, 'A pioneer, yes,' and I knock back the first four bottles by the neck, roysh, not even bothering to pour them.

I conk out, roysh, and end up missing dinner. An hour later, not asleep but not really awake either, I can hear Fionn chatting to the goy across the aisle from him, going, 'I'm not a believer myself, but I'm going to enjoy seeing the holy sites from a purely historical perspective,' and I'm thinking, He's off again.

I open my eyes and sit forward, to see are the goys getting any of this, but they're, like, both asleep. Fionn's like, 'To me, Jesus was just a religious charismatic who was judicially put to death – an unremarkable enough event in Palestine under Roman occupation. And yet, in death, he became the most influential human who ever lived, shaping world history, even setting the template for a morality shared by believers and non-believers such as myself.' The

goy he's talking to – he's a septic – goes, 'The One Com-
mandment. *Love one another as I have loved you,*' and Fionn's
there, 'What a wonderful world that would be,' and I swear
to God, roysh, I'm practically reaching for the vom-bag.

'Mrs Mulligan needs the toilet.' I'm like, 'What?' She
goes, 'Mrs Mulligan needs the toilet,' which means I'm
going to have to get up out of my seat again to let her out.
I'm there, 'This is, like, the third time in an hour,' and
she goes, 'Oh, she's a martyr to her waterworks is Mrs
Mulligan,' and she turns around, roysh, and goes to say
something to her friend and I go, 'Do NOT repeat that,
I swear to God!'

She *brings* her to the toilet, as in actually goes into the
little cubicle with her and, no, I don't want to think about
it either. Ten minutes later, they're back, just as I'm knocking back the last of the JDs. I go, 'Would it maybe make
more sense if *I* sat at the window? That way, you can
get out more easily,' and she goes, 'Oh no, Mrs Mulligan
has to have her window seat,' and Mrs Mulligan goes,
'Seat, yes.'

Four-and-a-half hours later, roysh, the pilgrimage has
already witnessed its first miracle: we arrived in Tel Aviv
without me focking the two of them out the window. The
plane hits the tarmac and as we're, like, taxiing to the
terminal, Oisinn rubs his hands together and shouts, 'Jew-
ish Princesses, here we come!'

Look at that one. No, look at that one. No, no, look at the
one behind her. I swear to God, roysh, our first day on the
beach in Tel Aviv and I've, like, fallen in love probably
twenty times. You see some bird who's, like, the love of

your life, roysh, and your eyes follow her down the beach and then, all of a sudden, the girl of your dreams walks the other way. The local scenario is unbelievable and, just like the brochure said, it's basically Funbag City.

Obviously, roysh, we've brought the rugby ball down onto the beach and me, JP and Oisinn are, like, flinging it around, with our tops off, giving the locals a good eyeful of the talent that's just rolled into town, while Fionn sits there on the sun-lounger, with his glasses and his little weedy body, reading the focking guidebook, like the little swot that he is, and every now and then shouting out basically facts and figures like, 'Israel is actually smaller than Wales,' and 'Unlike the Christian religions, Judaism doesn't recognize priests as intermediaries between God and the faithful. Rabbis are simply teachers, revered for their knowledge of the *Torah* and the *Talmud*.'

I turn around to JP and I go, 'Imagine coming all this way to read a focking book,' but I say it quietly, roysh, because I'm not really sure if Fionn not giving me a dig-out with Pikey on Paddy's Day actually counts as him getting me back for the diary thing. JP goes, 'I don't know, I thought it was very interesting what he was saying earlier, about Hebrew being virtually extinct when it was adopted as the national language of the new state in 1948,' and I look at Oisinn, roysh, and he's nodding – he's *actually* nodding – and I'm there, 'Sorry, am I the *only* one who's actually looking for his Nat King Cole?' It's unbelievable that I have to actually remind them why we're here.

Those couple of months working with Castlerock have left me pretty fit, it has to be said. I'm pegging it around like the Dricmeister himself and the goys can't get a tackle in on me. Then Oisinn – probably out of frustration at being made to look the lardorse that he is – just, like, tackles me high, roysh, and I end up flat in the sand with all sixteen stone of him on top of me.

We're just, like, lying there, cracking our holes laughing when all of a sudden we look up and there's Fionn, roysh, being chatted up – not *chatting up*, actually *being* chatted up – by these two total honeys. We're talking *total* as well. Using the less challenging, geeky friend as a gateway to his good-looking mates is the oldest trick in the book, roysh, and it's one that birds the whole world over know only too well.

Of course there's, like, a stampede to get over there. Fionn – he looks so focking puny in those Speedos – he pushes his glasses up on his nose and goes, 'Goys, this is Debra and this is Shifra. Girls, this is Oisinn, JP and Ross,' and we're all like, 'Hey, girls.' Debra's a total honey, roysh – I'm not saying that Shifra's not – but Debra is a ringer for Candice Hildebrand and there's an instant attraction, which you would have to say is mutual from the way she's, like, checking my pecs.

Shifra's like, 'So what are you guys here for?' and I'm about to go, 'Sweet loving,' when Debra gives it, 'Shifra and I could drive you around to see some of the sites,' and I'm there, 'Big time. You took the words out of my mouth. I want to see them all.' Debra looks at me and goes, 'Well, you're not going to see them all in four days. Which ones in particular would you like to see?' and I'm looking at the goys to throw me a rope but, not for the first time in the last couple of weeks, they leave me to drown.

Debra goes, 'Well, what about the Via Dolorosa?' and I'm there, 'You actually read my mind. I think there's, like, a connection between us,' and Oisinn goes, 'What's the Via

Dolorosa?' and I look at Debra and she goes, 'It's the path Jesus took to his crucifixion. You know the Stations of the Cross?' and I'm remembering being dragged to it as a kid every Good Friday in Glenageary church.

Fionn – trust *him*, roysh – he goes, 'It literally means Way of the Cross. It storts with the Condemnation of Jesus by Pontius Pilate and follows the route of his suffering to his death and the placement of his body in the tomb, from where – according to Christian teaching – he was resurrected three days later.'

He *actually* thinks that kind of talk's going to impress them. I go, 'Is it, like, near here? Could we walk it?' and Shifra looks at me like I've got ten heads and goes, 'No, it's in Jerusalem. Maybe an hour's drive,' and Debra goes, 'We can come back for you in the morning,' and we're all like, 'Kool *and* the Gang.'

I thought I was onto a winner when I found out I was rooming with JP. Oisinn snores like a focking elephant and Fionn, well, Fionn is Fionn, a tool basically. But get this, roysh, seven o'clock that night, roysh, we're getting ready to go out on the total lash and I'm throwing on my new black Sonetti shirt when all of a sudden JP's standing beside me in the bathroom, roysh, leaning against the doorframe, going, 'Ross, what do you think of God?'

I look him up and down, like I'm wondering is he feeling well. I go, 'You *know* what I think of him. He's a legend. We've had our differences over the years, mostly involving birds, but I'd be the first one to say he should captain the Lions next year.'

JP's there, 'No, not *him*. I'm talking about God, as in

actual God,' and I'm like, 'Oh, *him*. I try not to think about him. Hey, what's all this about?' and he's there, 'I don't know. It was all that talk about the Crucifixion earlier. Made me realize how little I know about my actual religion,' and I go, 'The only religion we should be interested in tonight is the worship of beautiful young ladies,' but I'm not reaching him.

He goes, 'I'll be back in a minute,' and off he goes, roysh, hopefully next door to seek the wisdom of Fionn, who'll tell him that it's all focking fairy stories. I'm actually looking really well, it has to be said. The shirt is pretty tight and it actually shows off my abs pretty well, roysh, and the old quiff is the perfect length. Five minutes later, roysh, JP's back with a copy of the Bible, of all focking things, which he bought downstairs in the gift shop. He flops down on the bed, roysh, and storts reading it, we're talking *actually* reading the thing.

I'm there, 'What's the Jackanory, JP? Are you not having a shower?' and he goes – unbelievable, roysh – he goes, 'I'm going to chill tonight, Ross. Still pretty jetlagged. Wouldn't mind an early night.'

Oisinn can't believe it when I tell him. He goes, 'Has he been at the minibor?' and I'm there, 'He's sober as a judge,' and Oisinn's like, 'He *was* very quiet on the beach earlier.'

So me, Oisinn and Fionn end up going out by ourselves, roysh, and basically having the time of our lives. We were giving it loads and all the locals loved the Irish accents, though none of us pulled, roysh, and we all ended up in Hot Pants, a, shall we say, gentlemen's club that some taxi-driver took us to.

Five o'clock in the morning, roysh, we all arrive back at the Crowne Plaza and when I stick the cord in the door,

I'm shocked to find JP's still awake and *still* reading the Bible. Of course, I stort telling him some of the stories from the night – Fionn's glasses getting all steamed up when that bird had her funbags in his face – but he doesn't answer me, roysh, he basically blanks me and just, like, carries on reading. What with the birds calling for us at ten o'clock in the morning, I decide to get some kip.

The next morning, another miracle happens: all four of us are up in time for breakfast and it's pretty obvious, roysh, that it's all to play for today. We have the crack, roysh, mostly talking about the fun and games in Hot Pants and also slagging Fionn for eating the local fare, which is basically meat and olives and all sorts of shit. During all this, JP says nothing at all.

The birds arrive bang-on ten o'clock in Shifra's old man's people-carrier and all the goys dive in. Oisinn gets in the front, roysh, and it's pretty obvious he's settled for second prize. He tells her he loves *Tommy Girl*, roysh, and she asks how he knows it and he tells her it's the clash of the camellia petals and apple blossoms with the spearmint and mandarin orange and Shifra throws her head back laughing, roysh, thinking the dude's actually making it up as he goes along, and Oisinn goes, 'Not to mention that intoxicating bouquet of honeysuckle, desert jasmine and Dakota lily that gives it its unmistakable sensual vibrancy,' and then there's, like, silence in the cor, until Debra goes, 'So what did you guys get up to last night?'

Of course there's great amusement at that and eventually I go, 'We went to a museum,' barely able to keep a straight face. Shifra looks around and goes, 'What kind of museum did you find open at night?' and Oisinn goes, 'I don't know, but Ross seemed pretty taken by one particular relic,' and what can I do, roysh, but lean forward and, like, high-five the dude.

We arrive in Jerusalem. Shifra porks the cor and we go and find a tour guide called Bakir, who mentions in the first ten seconds that even though he's a Palestinian, roysh, he loves Christians and Jews as much as he loves Muslims because we are all brothers under the same God, and if anyone asks us to come into their shop during our tour of the Old City we should tell them No because they are thieves and criminals and he can take us instead to his brother's shop and he will offer 10 per cent discount to Irish customers.

The place is jammers, roysh, what with it being Good Friday, and there's millions of people milling about the place, we're talking monks, we're talking nuns, we're talking normal people, we're talking Muslim birds with their faces covered, we're talking all these dudes with long beards and hats and then kids with, like, skullcaps and ringlets, who Fionn says are called Ascetic Jews, which is all very fascinating . . . I *don't* think.

Bakir was spot-on, though. Everyone in the place is trying to port you from your shekels, *literally* shekels because that's what the currency's called over here – obviously someone's idea of a joke. People are selling, like, rugs and sandals and walking-sticks made of real Mother of Pearl, whatever the fock that is, and pipes and hand-crafted chess sets and all sorts of shite. It's all, 'Come in, I give special price.' Debra says she's embarrassed at how commercialized the Via Dolorosa has been allowed to become. In between the Sixth Station, where Veronica wiped Jesus' boat, and the Seventh, where the dude fell for the second time, I point out this little, like, coffee shop and I go, 'Look, that's where Jesus stopped for hummus and a cappuccino,' and she looked at me, roysh, like I was the devil, even though I was basically agreeing with her.

So suddenly, roysh, she ditches me and storts walking next to Fionn, who's spouting all sorts of BS about the Armenian Quarter and the Christian Quarter, roysh, and he's even telling the tour guide shit he didn't know, the nerd that he is. By the time we get to the Tenth Station – where Jesus was stripped of his, like, garments, thank you, Fionn – the two of them are having this really intense discussion about, like, the political situation in Israel and I've basically decided that Fionn's welcome to her.

It's too late for a tactical switch, though, because Shifra looks totally smitten with Oisinn. Meanwhile, JP is walking, like, twenty yords ahead of the rest of us, deep in conversation with Bakir about – of all things – religion. We go and see the spot where Jesus was crucified and this tomb, roysh, where he supposedly rose from the dead and it's like, 'What*ever?*' but me and Oisinn actually had to drag JP away from the tomb, roysh, because he was just stood there for, like, twenty minutes, staring at it like a total spacer.

So before he frog-marches us to his brother's shop to buy overpriced Susan's Ears of our visit to Jerusalem, Bakir brings us for coffee, which is very generous of him considering it's me who ends up paying for it. So there we are, roysh, sitting in this little place, JP just, like, sitting there – we're talking picture, no sound – Fionn telling the two birds how he would love to come back and work in a Kibbutz, and me and Oisinn listening to Bakir banging on about how people are the same, no matter where you go. He goes, 'I have met people from all over the world . . .'

and he reaches into his pocket and pulls out a stack of business cords, which he storts laying down on the table, one by one, going, '. . . from Russia. From England. From Brazil. From Iceland. From Japan. From Albania. Even from USA.'

I look at the USA cord. It's some dude called Paul Sperber who's, like, senior vice president of Casteneda, Sandys, Mewshaw and Partners, whoever the fock they are, in Boulder, Colorado. 'Whip it.' That's what I hear Oisinn whisper. I look at him and he goes, '*That* one. Go on, whip it,' and when Bakir turns around to tell the owner how much he loves the coffee, I whip the cord out and slip it into my Davy Crocket.

We buy a whole heap of tat from Bakir's brother, then head down for a gander at the Wailing Wall, which, according to Specs Express, was called the Wailing Wall because it was here that the Jews lamented the destruction of their temple by the Roman emperor Titus in AD70, though now it's more popularly known as the Western Wall. The birds have to wait outside while me and the goys walk towards it. Fionn gets involved in some really deep conversation with a couple of locals while me, Oisinn and JP put on the old skullcaps and write out, like, wishes, which you then stick in between the bricks in the wall, to be supposedly read by God.

In the cor on the way back to Tel Aviv, I ask Oisinn what he wished for and he went, 'That Giorgio, Yves or *somebody* recognizes me soon,' and he asks me what I wished for and I went, 'That I get loads of birds while I'm here,' but that was a lie, roysh, because what I really wished for was that Sorcha would take me back and that we'd live, like, happily ever after, roysh, but I didn't say that because it sounded too bent.

I asked JP what he wished for and he said it wasn't a wish, it was a prayer, and when I asked him what he prayed for he didn't answer and I'm beginning to wonder whether I'm the only normal person on this trip.

Oisinn opens the door. The first thing he says is like, 'Where's JP?' and it's obvious I'm not the only one worried about the dude. I go, 'Remember when we went to Australia for the World Cup? That CD he kept playing night and focking day in the Chick Wagon?' Oisinn's like, '*Elvis's Gospel Hits*,' and I'm there, 'Exactly. I think this has always been in him, Oisinn. We should ring Father Fehily. *He'll* know what to do,' and Oisinn goes, 'Let's just give it the weekend. It might pass,' and then this real, like, evil look passes across his face, roysh, and he goes, 'There *is* one phone call we should make, though. I'm there, 'Who to, dude?' and he tells me to get out the business cord that I whipped from Bakir.

He says I have to do the talking, roysh, because I do a pretty good American accent, but he says he'll tell me what to say. The phone rings three times and then a voice answers and it's like, 'Casteneda, Sandys, Mewshaw and Partners. Good morning, how may I direct your call?' and I'm thinking, Morning? – oh yeah, I forgot about, like, the time difference and shit – I'm there, 'I'd like to speak with Paul Sperber, if I may,' and she's like, 'Certainly, Sir,' and she puts me through.

He answers on the first ring. I'm like, 'Is that Paul Sperber?' and he goes, 'It most certainly *is*.' He's obviously one of those really big, jolly septics you see hanging around the lobby of the Westbury, the big fat ones in elasticated jeans; for years I thought the Westbury was a focking health farm. I'm there, 'This is Agent Ross O'Carroll-Kelly. I'm with the FBI,' and chirpy as you like, roysh, the goy goes, 'And how may I be of assistance?'

I'm like, 'Hey, I'll ask the questions if you don't mind,' which is actually a line of my own and Oisinn, roysh, who has his ear next to the receiver so he can hear the other side of the conversation, gives me a wink to say basically, nice touch.

There's, like, silence on the other end of the phone. Oisinn goes, 'Ask him did he recently travel to Israel?' and I'm there, 'Mr Sperber, did you at any time in the recent past basically travel to the country of Israel?' and he's like, 'Yes. In January. My wife has a sister in—' and I'm there, 'I'm . . . not . . . interested. During your time in Israel, did you meet with a man named Bakir?' and I can't think of a second name, roysh, and Oisinn shrugs his shoulders and goes, 'St Laurent,' and it sounds stupid when I say it, but the goy buys it. He goes, 'Bakir St Laurent? I don't *think* so.'

Oisinn gives me the next line. I'm there, 'Can you think of a reason why your business cord should be found in his aportment, Sir?' There's, like, silence for a few seconds, roysh, then he goes, 'Bakir? Yeah, we *did* meet a guy called Bakir,' and I go, 'Oh, your memory's improving. This is good,' and he goes, 'Yeah, he showed us around the Holy City,' and I'm like, 'He *did* work as a tour guide . . . among other things.'

He goes, 'But he told us his name was Bakir al-Omary,' and you can tell the goy knows he's in deep shit here, roysh, because all this, like, verbal diarrhoea storts spilling out of his mouth. I don't say anything, of course. I just let him stew in it. He goes, 'He seemed like a very nice man. He had as much love for Jews and Christians as he did . . . well, my wife remembers the exact quote. She remembered it verbatim. He was very nice, though . . . he knew a lot about the Holy City. I suppose he'd have to being a tour guide . . . er, how is he?'

I go, 'I don't know, Mr Sperber. By the time they found him, all that was left was his boots and cloud of smoke. You know what I'm saying?' and he's like, '*No!* He wouldn't have . . .' and I go, 'Oh, you feel you can vouch for this man?' and suddenly he's on the big-time retreat, giving it, 'No, I don't even know him! He was just our tour guide,' and I'm there, 'Do NOT raise your voice to me, Sir,' and he's like, 'Look, I'm sorry. I'm so sorry. I'm just trying to get you to see that this man, this Bakir St Laurent as you call him, he was just our guide. My wife wanted to walk the Via Dolorosa. He was a nice man and I gave him my card and said that if he happened to be in Boulder, Colorado . . .'

I'm like, 'You invited him to the United States, Sir?' He goes, 'No, I didn't *invite* him as such . . . I know how this probably looks to you,' and I'm there, 'Well, *this* is how it looks to me – you're in a whole bunch of trouble. Go and stand in front of your building. We're going to send a cor around for you,' and he goes, 'A car?' and I'm like, 'Unless you want a scene . . .' and he's like, 'I don't want a scene. Look, I've just made partner here,' and I'm there, 'Well, go and stand out front, then. And before you go . . .'

I nearly laugh out loud when Oisinn gives me the next line. I'm there, 'Are you concealing anything under that shirt?' and he's like, 'My shirt? You mean you can *see* me? You've got men in the building opposite? The Continental building? Are there guns pointed at me?' and he's having a focking canary, roysh, and I'm just there going, 'REMOVE YOUR SHIRT, SIR!' and he's like, 'I'm removing it! I'm removing it!' and then I'm like, 'Now go and stand out front. A cor will come for you,' and I hang up, roysh, and I swear to God, me and Oisinn laughed so much I had to go back to my room and change my boxers.

I'm there, 'Why is it called the Dead Sea?' and I should have known better than to ask. Fionn goes, 'Because nothing can live in it. Every litre of water contains about 30 per cent salt and minerals. Water like that can't sustain aquatic life,' and Debra's like, 'It's also the lowest point on Earth,' and Fionn pushes his glasses up on his nose and goes, 'Three-hundred-and-ninety-four metres below sea level, to be precise,' and I'm looking at them, thinking they're like that Richard and focking Judy – one storts a sentence and the other finishes it. They're also, like, holding hands, which makes me want to spew.

I'm there, 'All I want to know is, will I definitely float?' and Fionn goes, 'You're Ross O'Carroll-Kelly, surely you can walk on the surface?' and he's all smug, roysh, just because *he's* the one who ended up scoring Debra, though as far as I'm concerned he's welcome to her. I go, 'All I'm saying is that you know I can't swim. JP, you remember Playa del Ingles, don't you?' but he just, like, ignores me. We're walking from the cor pork down to the beach at Ein Gedi and JP's, like, ten yords ahead of the rest of us, in a total strop.

Oisinn goes, 'I can't believe you focked his Bible out the hotel window, Ross,' and I'm like, 'It was for his own good.

All that focking Joseph and his Coat of Many Colours. It's not roysh. When was the last time he actually said anything?' and Oisinn goes, 'He said something this morning. At breakfast. I asked him what was going on with the whole silent buzz and he said, "There's a time for talking and a time for listening?" I told him we'd all be relieved when it was talking time again and he said, "I'll talk when I have something to say",' and I'm just there, 'Mad as a focking toothbrush.'

It sounds a bit gay, roysh, but it's unbelievably, like, peaceful down by the water. I whip off my threads and of course the two birds have to cop a sly look – it's difficult for them, I know, but they both made their choices – and I get into the water, roysh, up to my waist and suddenly it just, like, takes the legs from under me, roysh, and it's amazing but I'm just, like, floating on top of the water. The goys and the three birds all pile in then. At one point, Shifra turns around and goes, 'That's Jordan over there,' and I nearly have a focking hort attack, roysh, looking around going, 'WHERE? WHERE? WHERE?' and Fionn laughs and goes, 'She's talking about the *country*, Ross,' and of course everyone cracks up laughing, roysh, and the joke's on me again.

I sort of, like, work my way over to JP. I feel bad about focking his book out of the window of the hotel, but it's just my way of saying, basically, get with the programme. I go, 'Some night out you missed last night, JP. I ended up scoring this French bird. She could have been Angelina Jolie's sister. Did you see the scratches on my back?' and he just looks at me, roysh, and goes, '*The acts of the sinful nature are obvious: sexual immorality, impurity and debauchery; and envy; drunkenness, orgies, and the like. I warn you, as I did before, that those who live like this will not inherit the kingdom of God,'* and just as I'm about to tell him he's a freak he goes, 'Galatians, 5:19.'

Fehily takes ages to answer, but he's, like, delighted to hear from me. He goes, 'Hearing your voice is like a gift from God . . .' and I'm like, 'There's no time for that shit. We've got a major problem, and we are talking major here.' He's like, 'Well, you know the ethos of this school, my child. We have no *past* pupils. When you're part of a family, you're always part of that family. I told you you all on your last day at Castlerock that wherever you are in the world, and whatever trouble you're in, we will help you.'

I'm there, 'Well, me and in the goys are in basically Israel,' and he's like, 'Oh, the Land of the Risen Lord,' and I'm there, 'JP's freaked out. Keeps spouting on about debauchery and the kingdom of God and, like, quoting the Bible and shit?' and Fehily laughs, roysh, he *actually* laughs, and he goes, 'Young JP has found God?'

I'm there, calm as you like, 'Okay, what's the cure?' and he laughs again and goes, 'There *is* no cure, my child, except to take the medicine of God's will. I've seen this happen before. It can happen at any time. I was in my early twenties when I had *my* calling.'

I'm there, 'But he's not coming out on the lash with us. He's, like, hordly saying anything,' and Fehily goes, 'Now is the time for thought and reflection. He will talk when he has something to say,' and I'm thinking, That's exactly what *he* said.

*

We're on the road to the airport, roysh, and though I was a bit, I don't know, sceptical about coming here in the first place, I have to say, roysh, I had an amazing time, even just, like, learning about other cultures and shit? Last night – we're talking Easter Sunday – I ended up being with a Spanish bird. There's a big world out there and it's full of birds who want to be with Ross O'Carroll-Kelly.

Fionn and Oisinn are saying their last goodbyes to the birds in the cor. Debra's saying she wishes we'd had more time. She's like, 'I would have liked to take you to see the Mount of Olives,' and Fionn goes, 'Ross thought that was one of the EU food surpluses,' and everyone cracks up laughing, roysh, but quick as a flash I go, 'Fock you, Glasses Head,' to which he has no answer and in fact it shuts everyone up.

Fionn's got his video camera on his lap and I'm thinking he never focking stops, that goy, probably hoping to film a couple more, I don't know, temples before we get to the airport. He tells Debra he's coming back as soon as he finishes his PhD and he probably will, roysh, because, looking like that, he *has* to travel halfway around the world to get his rock and roll. Shifra, though, is getting her last look at Oisinn and she basically knows it.

So we're pegging it along, roysh, and Shifra all of a sudden looks in her rear-view and goes, 'Uh-oh! Police,' and Debra's like, 'What speed were you doing?' and Shifra's there, 'Well, I was well under. He flashed me, though. I should pull in,' and she does, roysh, and I'm looking out the back wondering how she knew it was the cops, roysh, because it's, like, an unmorked cor.

The next thing, roysh, these two goys get out and one of them's got a serious-looking piece, which he points into the back of the people-carrier after reefing open the door. I swear to God, roysh, every basic drop of blood in my body goes cold when he turns around and goes, 'Which one of you is Ross O'Carroll-Kelly?' and before I get a chance to think of something, the rest of them land me roysh in it by, like, pointing at me.

The goy's like, 'Can you get out of the car, please?' and I am seriously bricking it, roysh, because I just remembered fecking a towel and a pair of slippers from the hotel room – they're not even *for* me, they're a present for Sorcha – and I'm thinking it must have been a pretty expensive towel if the Feds are chasing us to the airport, and then suddenly I'm wondering, roysh, whether this is one of those countries where they, like, cut your focking Christian Andersens off for basically robbing shit.

I get out of the cor and put my hands above my head. He goes, 'Ross O'Carroll-Kelly, did you place a call to a gentleman in Boulder, Colorado, purporting to be an FBI agent?' and I swear to God, roysh, my focking bowels move. I'm there, 'An FBI *agent* . . . em . . .' trying to bluff him, roysh, but he turns around and goes, 'We have a recording of the conversation, Sir. It won't be difficult to match your voice pattern with the voice on the tape,' and I'm letting off focking trouser gas here like nobody's business.

He goes, 'Can we take a look in your luggage, Sir?' and he sort of, like, motions me around to the back of the van, where I open the door and hand him my bag, with the big Castlerock logo on the side, and he hands it to the other dude, who unzips it and has a look inside. He goes, 'My God! Come and look at this,' and I'm thinking, Okay, get your story straight. Tell them the towel is very similar to one you have at home and you took it without thinking, when all of a sudden, roysh, he reaches into my bag and pulls out a bomb.

We're talking A FOCKING BOMB!

The goy with the gun goes, 'Okay, on the floor,' and I just, like, totally lose it, roysh. I'm going, 'It's not mine. I swear. I've never seen it before on my life,' and I'm bawling my eyes out, roysh, and I'm like, 'All I took was one towel and a pair of slippers for basically Sorcha and that's only because I didn't have time to get anything in the gift shop,' and I'm shaking, roysh, and I'm there, 'Even the goys will tell you that it's not mine. I've never seen it before,' and I can feel my right leg suddenly get all hot, roysh, and wet as well, and I realize I've done a hit-and-miss in my trousers and it's, like, definitely going to show, roysh, because these are, like, beige chinos I'm wearing.

After, like, twenty seconds of this, roysh, I realize that I've got my eyes closed, waiting to be shot basically, and when I open them, Oisinn and Shifra and Debra and Fionn have got out of the van and they're all, like, standing there, cracking their holes laughing, and so are the two coppers, and Fionn – focking Fionn – is pointing the video camera at me and I'm like, 'What the *fock* are you doing?' and he's going, 'And . . . cut!'

I go, 'What's going on?' and Fionn's there, 'Don't worry, Ross, it's not a bomb. It's the inside of a radio with a couple of batteries stuck to it with brown tape,' and I look at the two cops, roysh, and Debra just goes, 'My brothers,' and I point at the gun and I go, 'I take it *that's* not real either,' and Fionn cracks up laughing and goes, '*Real?* How long did you think Fisher Price had been making machine-guns?'

I'm there, 'So this is it then, Fionn? This is you getting me back?' and he goes, 'No, I won't have got you back, Ross, until this little film is on the internet.'

I don't FOCKING believe it. What are the chances? I'm sitting beside the same two old biddies on the way back. I'm miserable and I reek of piss, so you could at least say we have something in common. Mrs Holt offers me a Murray Mint. It's got no wrapper and it's got, like, fluff on it from being in her pocket. I tell her no. And she doesn't even focking remember me from the way over. We're not even off the ground when she turns around and goes, 'Have you a devotion to Our Lady?'

5. Staring down the Barrel

They say that travel, like, broadens the mind, roysh, but it's amazing how quickly you fall back into old habits. I'm already back to the old haunts, we're talking Lillie's, we're talking Reynord's, we're talking the odd Friday night in Knackery-Doo and sometimes the odd Nurse's Night in Club M, where it's free in with hospital ID and the loving is easy.

I was actually in Lillie's this Saturday night, roysh, when I realized that Oisinn was roysh when he said that, as far as the old Dublin club scene goes, I've been over-fishing the waters. Not being big-headed or anything, roysh, but I counted eighteen birds in Lillie's who I've either nipped or thrown a bone to in the past year.

It was pretty much brought home to me when I went to throw the lips on this bird from Dalkey who's, like, the image of Ali Landry and who I'd put, like, twenty minutes of spadework into, only to have her push me away. I went, 'Hey, like Bobby Brown says, you might not ever get another try,' and she goes, 'HELLO? I think I can, like, live with that,' and I'm like, 'You're bluffing,' and she's there, 'Ross, you've been with pretty much every girl between the ages of eighteen and thirty in south Dublin,' and I'm like, 'Agreed.' She goes, 'Being with you used to be SUCH a status symbol for girls. But now it's the thing to be able to say you've *never* been with Ross O'Carroll-Kelly.'

It's probably true. Oisinn had warned me about the dangers of, as he put it, flooding the morket, but I was just too handsome to listen. So then I just went home, feeling this big empty hole in my chest where my hort used to be.

I'm in town, roysh, on the way into BTs, when who do I see coming out only that stupid focking wench, in other words my old dear, and thinking she hasn't seen me, roysh, I do a quick turnaround and stort cracking on to be really interested in this, like, lamp they've got in the window display. Turns out she *has* focking seen me, though – never misses anything, the stupid cow.

She's going, 'Ro-oss! Ro-oss! *Ro-oss!*' making a show of me in front of half of Grafton Street. I turn around and I'm like, 'Would you mind shouting a bit louder? There's one or two people up in Stephen's Green who didn't focking hear you,' but she just, like, ignores this and goes, 'I'm just in getting a few *things*. Lotions and potions. I've got my photo-shoot in the morning.'

I'm like, '*Whoa!* I thought I told you you weren't doing it!' and she actually has the cheek to turn around to me and go, 'Well, it's for a good cause,' and quick as a flash I'm like, 'Why don't you get people to sponsor you to leave your focking kit on. You're only going to make a fool of yourself, *and* me,' and she's like, 'I don't know. Sally seems to think I've a great body. Pert, is the word she used,' and I'm there, 'Why are you focking telling me that shit? Hey, TMI. TM focking I!'

I'd been, like, expecting the call for days. No one knows JP as well as I do, but when his old man rings, roysh, I don't know what to tell him. It's, like, I can't explain his behaviour. He's going, 'He's quit, Ross. He hasn't shown up for work for two weeks. The first day, I thought, Good for him, the little pisshead. Twelve o'clock, I phone him, he tells me he's found God and wants to quit, turn his back on a great career in property and leave me to run Hook, Lyon and Sinker on my own. What the hell happened over there?' and it's weird, roysh, but even though I can't actually see him, I know that as he's saying this he's, like, eyeing up one of the secretaries and scratching his town halls.

I'm there, 'I don't know. He storted asking me did I believe in God one day, then he bought a Bible and suddenly it was, like, Goodnight Vienna.' He goes, 'He's talking about joining the priesthood, you know that?' and I nearly, like, choke on my club sandwich. I'm there, 'JP? A *priest?* You're shitting me now,' and he's like, 'I wish I was. He told his mother and I last night. My son! A priest! I'll never be able to hold my head up in court again. Ross, talk to him, will you? You're the closest one to him,' and I go, 'I'll try. Not sure it'll do any good, though.'

So that night, roysh, I peg it out to Rathgor to have a word, roysh, and I have to say that the goy who, like, greets me at the door seems like the old JP. He goes, 'Ross, I want to apologize if I, like, freaked you and the goys out while we were away. I was having, shall we say, an experience,' and I'm like, 'You mean you're back online now? No more of this Holy Mary Mother of God bullshit?' and he's like, 'I'm apologizing for going weird on you, Ross. I'm not apologizing for receiving the gift of the Holy Spirit, which is what happened to me.'

I'm about to ask him, roysh, if there's any truth in this story about him joining the priesthood, but then I notice the bottle of Baileys on the table and my worst fears are confirmed. He goes, 'You heard I'm signing up, so to speak?' and I'm there, 'I don't *get* it. What's the angle?' and he's like, 'There *is* no angle, Ross, unless of course it's the love of the Risen Lord,' and I go, 'But you were focking coining it in working for your old man,' and I actually end up apologizing for my language to JP, of all people.

He goes, 'I sold houses, Ross. But all was not good with my own house,' and I'm like, 'Look at the sponds you were pulling in,' and he goes, *'People who want to get rich fall into temptation and a trap and into many foolish and harmful desires that plunge men into ruin and destruction. For the love of money is the root of all kinds of evil. Some people, eager for money, have wandered from the faith and pierced themselves with many griefs,'* and then he's like, 'Timothy, 6:9,' and I'm thinking, he SO has to be making this shit up.

I hit him with, 'So what's wrong with making shitloads of money?' and he goes, 'You know, PJ Wingate once said that "Give us this day our daily bread" is probably the most perfectly constructed and useful sentence ever set down in the English language,' and I'm like, 'Meaning?' and he's there, 'Meaning that none of us really needs anything more than that which nourishes us,' which is, like – *whoa!* – big-time deep.

He goes, 'You're a restless spirit, Ross. Just like I was,' and it's weird, roysh, because it's not like talking to JP at all, and it's not just because he's stopped saying shit like, 'Can we think in the box,' and 'It's a win-win situation from my POV,' and 'Let's have a quick mind-meld on this.' It's like the focker can see into my soul.

He goes, 'What's the one thing you want in your life roysh now, Ross?' and I go, 'Probably the new Porsche 911. In black,' but there's no bullshitting him, roysh. He goes, 'And that would make you happy for how long? What do you *really* want, Ross?' and I just find myself opening up to the dude. I'm like, 'Sorcha back,' and he goes, 'Love, in other words,' and I'm there, 'I suppose you could say that.'

He rubs his boat. I think he's actually growing a beard. He goes, 'Love. It doesn't cost what a Porsche 911 costs, does it? It's free. And it's yours, if you want it,' and I'm there, 'Sorcha hates my guts,' and he's like, 'That girl doesn't have it in her to hate,' and he's actually roysh. I go, 'But it'll be a long time before she forgives me.'

He puts his hand on my shoulder, but not in a funny way, and he goes, 'Have you prayed?' and I just, like, burst out laughing, roysh, I shouldn't I know, but it's, like, the most stupidest question anyone's ever asked me. I'm there, 'Sorry, JP, but what do *you* think?'

He goes, 'I can't claim to know all the answers, Ross. I'm only embarking on my journey. But I know that prayer is a powerful thing.' I'm there, 'I wouldn't even know what to say, what, like, words to use and shit?' He's like, 'John Bunyan once said—' and I'm there, 'Dude, I don't even know who half these goys are that you're mentioning,' and he gives this little chuckle, I suppose you'd have to call it a priestly chuckle, if that's an actual word, and he goes, 'John Bunyan was a seventeenth-century English preacher. I've been reading quite a bit about his life. "When you pray," he said, "rather let your hort be without words than your words without hort",' and though I'm not exactly the sharpest tool in the box, I actually understand what he's trying to say.

He goes, 'Go home and pray, Ross. Then go and be with your wife,' and I'm like, 'Are you going to be okay, as in here on your own?' and he nods, basically to say yes. As I get up to go, roysh, he puts his hand on my shoulder, leans close to me and goes, 'Will you have a Baileys?' and I tell him, no hord feelings, roysh, but I'm fine for Baileys, thanks very much.

In Trap Two in the jacks in Kiely's, on the back of the door, someone's written,
WWW.ROSS-PISS-PANTS.IE
and it's, like, pretty obvious, roysh, that Fionn's actually gone ahead and put the thing on the internet and I'm actually disappointed in him, roysh, because I thought he was, like, bigger than that.

I spend the best port of Friday night standing *outside* the Club of Love rather than *inside* for two reasons, roysh, the first being that the pen off the corpet is totally Pádraig since cigarettes were, like, banned, the second being that all the really hot and, it has to be said, fit-looking birds are all to be found outside the front door, huddled in little groups, sucking on the old oily rags, which is why the

Government ban has actually *encouraged* me to, like, take up smoking.

It's a great opening line as well, not that I need any help in that deportment, but now I just say, 'Won't be voting for that shower again,' even though I've never voted in my actual life. And of course the birds tend to go, 'I know, it's like, *Aaahhh!*' and then I'm going, 'I'm thinking of giving them up,' and there I am, roysh, not even knowing how to inhale the focking things.

I must be pretty tired, roysh, because after seven or eight Britneys I'm totally horrendufied and – possibly not the best idea I've ever had – I decide that now is the best time, we're talking basically midnight here, to go to see Sorcha and, like, tell her how I feel, as you do when you're hammered. The thing is, roysh, I know for a fact that she won't turn me away because she has this, like, mothering instinct that always takes over when I'm mullered and she wants to, like, mind me.

So my mind's made up, roysh, I hop into a Jo and tell the driver to take me to Chateâu Lalor on the Vico. I bell her from outside, put on the old Little Boy Drunk act and before I know it she's opening the front door and asking me – OH! MY! GOD! – what the *hell* I think I'm doing calling to her door at that hour of the morning. She goes, 'It's like, OH! MY! GOD!' She looks incredible. I'm there, 'I couldn't wait any longer, Sorcha, to tell you how I feel,' and she sort of, like, waves her hand in front of her nose and she goes, 'You're, like, *drunk?*' and I look at her, roysh, as if to say, of course I am, then I go, 'HELLO? It's, like, Friday night?'

She invites me in. She goes, 'I'll make you some coffee, then I'll call you a taxi,' and I'm there, 'Kool and the Gang,' and she's like, 'And keep your voice down. Dad's still up. You know what he'll do to you if he finds out you're here,' and I don't, roysh, but I can imagine. I'm there, 'What's he doing still up?' just making conversation more than anything, and she goes, 'He's working. You know he's representing Lauren's dad now?' and I'm there, 'As in Hennessy?' and she's like, 'He's going to the High Court tomorrow to try to get him bail pending his appeal,' and I'm thinking how happy I'd be for Lauren if he gets out of the clink, but how focking unbearable my old man is going to be if he does.

We're just, like, standing there, roysh, and there's the usual electricity between us. Sorcha's trying not to feel it though. She's there, 'Look, I'll put on the kettle,' and quick as a flash I go, 'It wouldn't suit you,' and for the first time, roysh, since the whole wedding fiasco I see her actually smile. I walk over to her at the sink as she's turning on the tap and I touch her orm and she storts, like, trembling, roysh, and I go, 'You can't deny there was something between us that day on the beach in Wicklow,' and she's there, '*Don't*, Ross,' and I'm like, 'We saved a baby seal. You can't say it wasn't special,' but she won't look me in the eye, because she knows if she did she wouldn't be able to trust herself.

She goes, 'I said a coffee, Ross, then you can go. Dad'll have a fit if . . .' and I'm there, 'Forget about your old man, Sorcha. This is about you. *Your* happiness. It's about . . . us,' and I reach for her hand, roysh, and she lets me hold it and then she plucks up the courage to basically look at me and suddenly I'm, like, staring into her eyes, like a mongoose hypnotizing a snake.

Her eyes are, like, filling up with tears and I'd have

nipped her there and then, roysh, if I wasn't so bursting for an Eartha Kitt. I'm there, 'Sorcha, I'm going to leave the room for five minutes to let you think about what you want,' obviously not wanting to spoil the moment by telling her I've got to drop off the shopping.

I go out into the hall, roysh, and I have to pass her old man's study on the way to the jacks and even though I try to be as quiet as I possibly can, roysh, he hears me and I get this, 'Ross, come in here,' and from the way he says it, roysh, I know I've no choice and I end up just going in and he's there at his desk in this, like, big oak-panelled room.

I go, 'Hello, Mr Lalor,' but he's in no mood for my bullshit. He's like, 'Sit down,' which I do and he opens up a drawer, I presume to get out the bottle of port that he keeps for special occasions, but all of a sudden, roysh, he's pulled out a focking gun – as in an *actual* revolver – and he's pointing it straight at me and suddenly, roysh, I don't need the toilet anymore and I'm thinking this is, like, two things I'm making a habit of: one, having guns pointed at me and two, I don't know, soiling myself. He cops it straight away, of course. He sort of, like, looks down, then turns up his nose and goes, 'I must remember to clean that chair. That'd be DNA evidence.'

I'm having, like, palpitations I suppose you'd have to call it. I'm there, 'You can't . . . you can't *kill me* . . .' and he's going, 'Don't you remember me telling you what would happen if you ever hurt my beautiful daughter again?' and I go, 'I thought that was just, like, a figure of speech. You can't just . . . kill somebody. I mean, there's gonna be, like, evidence,' and he reaches down with his other hand – the one that isn't holding a gun – and he puts a shovel up on

166

the desk, then a bottle of Mr Muscle Multi-Task. He's obviously thought this through.

He presses the gun against my forehead, roysh, and I close my eyes and wait for the bang. Then an amazing thing happens, I *actually* stort praying. I think about what JP said and I'm there going, 'Please, God, let me live. Oh my God, totally let me live,' and suddenly, roysh, I'm not afraid. It's not the drink, roysh, but this wave of, like, peacefulness comes over me and I'm, like, as calm as you like, thinking, Hey, what can you do, dude! If he pulls the trigger, he pulls the trigger.

And after, like, ten seconds of waiting to hear the bang, roysh, I open my eyes and I look into Sorcha's old man's eyes and I go, 'You're not going to shoot me, Mr Lalor. You know why? I'm the one person in this world who can make Sorcha truly happy. We saved a seal together. I'm not scared of you. Shoot me if you want. It won't alter – if that's the roysh word – the fact that I love your daughter and she loves me.'

We sit there for a few minutes, roysh, just sort of, like, staring at each other, then I get up and I walk to the door, still not 100 per cent certain I'm not going to get a piece of lead in the back. Nothing happens. I go down to the jacks and make a bit of an effort to, like, clean myself up, and it's at that moment, roysh, that I decide that no matter what I have to face – even if it's, like, more guns – I'm going to get my wife back.

But not tonight. Not with my trousers in this state. I end up climbing out of the toilet window and I head back out onto the Vico Road and start walking back in the direction of town.

*

167

My phone beeps. A text from a number I don't recognize. It's like, **Saw u piss ur pants. Funniest ting i ever saw** and it's, like, the tenth one I've got this weekend. And I'm there thinking, If you only saw me last night.

Sorcha asks me to meet her in the coffee shop in Habitat, roysh, and she tells me over a couple of skinny *lattés* that if her old man had actually pulled the trigger, what I'd have felt would have been nothing compared to the humiliation I put her through on her wedding day – 'of all days' – which I think is a bit of an exaggeration, roysh, but I let it go. I'm just there, 'I wouldn't have felt anything because I'd have been, like, dead and shit?' but she goes, 'That would have been too good for you,' and she takes a sip from her coffee and when she pulls the cup away she's got this cute little white Ronnie on her top lip.

I ask her how can she say that, roysh, *and* be a member of Amnesty International, which I have to say I'm pretty pleased with, and she goes, 'I know. I've thought about that, whether it makes me a hypocrite. I mean, I've been campaigning against the death penalty since, like, transition year. Maybe for the first time I was able to see the other side of the argument. It's, like, SUCH a terrible thing to say, but if he'd shot you, Ross, I'd have put on a pair of rubber gloves and helped him dispose of the body,' and I just nod, cracking on that I believe her. This girl is SO in love with me it's not funny.

She goes, 'I admire you, Ross. And believe it or not, Dad admires you,' and I'm like, 'As in *your* dad? I don't think admire is the word,' and she's there, 'Well, not so much *you* as what you did. To defy him like that, when he was pointing a gun at you . . . it was brave. And he said you told him you loved me.'

I go, 'I wasn't lying,' and she's there, 'That's what Dad said. He said, "I don't like the little maggot, but when he says he loves you he's telling the truth",' and I'm thinking, Who the fock's he calling a maggot? but I let it go.

I reach across the table and touch her hand and I'm like, 'Well, if you understand *that*, maybe there's still hope for us,' and the next thing I know, roysh – the worst timing in the focking world – my phone rings and I wouldn't usually answer it, except that it's, like, Ronan. It's a pretty bad line. He goes, 'Alreeeet, Rosser? Storrr-ee?' and I'm like, 'Kool and the Gang, Ronan. How the hell are you? Are you smoking there?' and he goes, 'Won't tell you a word of a lie, Rosser, I am. Ah, me nerves are shot to fooken ribbons,' and I'm like, 'Ronan, you're, like, *seven*,' but I'm basically laughing as I'm saying it.

Sorcha's mouthing the words, 'Tell . . . him . . . I . . . said . . . hi,' across the table and I go, 'Sorcha says hi,' and he's like, 'Is she coming to me Communion, is she? I was meaning to text her, but I've no credit,' and I'm there, 'Sorcha, would you like to come to Ronan's Communion?' and Sorcha goes, '*Oh my God*, I'd *love* to,' and I go, 'You heard that, Ronan?' and he's like, 'Ah, game ball, Rosser. So what's the story, are you two back together or wha'?' and I don't say anything, roysh, and Sorcha goes, 'What's he saying?' and I go, 'He asked are we back together?' and I swear to God, roysh, this, like, surge – if that's the roysh word – of total happiness passes through me when she goes, 'Yes, Ronan, we *are* back together,' and I end up just sitting there, staring at her across the table, with the phone up to my ear, not saying anything, and obviously

Ronan cops what's going on, roysh, because he goes, 'I'll leave you two love boords to it. Tell Sorcha I'll text her later.'

We just sit there, roysh, staring into each other's eyes, our *lattés* going cold, getting total filthies from people queuing for a table. Eventually, she takes off her scrunchy, shakes her hair loose, smooths it back, puts it back in the scrunchy and then pulls, like, four or five strands loose. I go, 'You don't *have* to come, you know. To the Communion,' but she's like, 'If we're going to be part of each other's lives again, then I want to be part of everything,' and I just, like, nod and I'm there, 'I should warn you, Ronan's family, they're very . . . working class.'

She goes, 'I have to admit, I know hordly anything about these types of people. They're different, aren't they? I mean, what do they eat?' and I laugh and I go, 'Anything as long as it's got focking curry sauce on it,' and she sort of, like, stares off into space and she's like, 'I can have a chat with Claire. She's from Bray. I suppose that's an underprivileged area. She could give me some tips.'

I ring JP. He sounds surprised to hear from me. He tells me none of the other goys have called him since . . . well, since . . . I'm surprised at them. He's still the same JP to me. I go, 'Are you going to be, like, talking to God at any stage today?' and he cracks his hole laughing. He's like, 'I'm *always* talking to Him, Ross. It's an open line. Not just for me, for everyone,' and I'm like, 'Oh, roysh. Look, can you, like, give Him a message from me?' and he goes, 'Why don't you give it to Him yourself?' and I go, 'Because I don't believe in Him,' and he's there, 'But you want me to give Him a message?' and I'm like, 'Yeah,' and he goes, 'Makes sense.'

I'm there, 'I prayed to Him and, well, what I prayed for basically came true. And I just want the dude to know that it hasn't gone unnoticed, that I appreciate it,' and he goes, '*You* tell Him, Ross. He'd love to hear from you, you know?' and I'm there, 'Even if I don't believe in Him?' and he goes, '*Even* if you don't believe in Him,' and I'm like, 'Kool *and* the Gang.'

Sorcha's in the house, like, ten seconds and already Tina's old man's in her ear, crapping on about nothing. He's there going, 'Can't woork out de jaysusin price of anthin since de yoo-ro came in, knowhorramean?' and I can see Sorcha's eyes, like, panning the kitchen, wanting to be let loose in here with the J. Edgar and a packet of Flash wipes. He's going, 'In my day, now, it was four-bob, tree shillings, two-and-six, half-a-crown and tuppenceha'penny-fardin – you knew where ye stood.'

He nods towards this, like, filthy-looking ormchair in the corner and he goes, 'Sit down dare, love,' and I can see this, like, fear flash across Sorcha's face and straight away I know what she's thinking. She's dressed to focking kill, in this, like, silver, sequined top – 'the Lanvin one that Scarlett Johansson's wearing in the new *Vogue*' – black trousers and a pink, fluffy cordigan, and she's wondering would it be rude to wipe the seat before she does, but in the end she sits down without wiping it because people's feelings actually matter more to Sorcha than how she looks.

Tina comes in then, roysh, and I have to say she's actually scrubbed up pretty well, even if all the sovs make her look like a Jimmy Saville tribute act. The two birds are introduced and a couple of times I catch them checking each other out on the sly, roysh, not being big-headed or anything but obviously thinking, I wonder what Ross saw/sees in her.

'Holy Jaysus, Rosser, you are one lucky fooker.' Ronan in the house. Tina goes, 'You're makin' your Foorst Holy Communyin today, Ronan, any chance of it bein' a day widout coorsin?' but he's like, 'Sorcha, you look . . . well, you're after taking me breath away,' and she goes all red, roysh, but she's delighted and she gets up and gives him a kiss on the cheek and goes, 'Hi, Ronan,' and he goes, 'Hey, Doll,' and he looks her up and down and he's there, 'Unbelievable,' then he turns to me and he goes, 'Jaysus, Rosser, I hope it stays well for you.'

So me, Sorcha and Ronan hit the church in my jammer, which I can't help but notice that someone has cleaned again while we were in the gaff and this time, by the looks of it, polished too. Outside the church it's, like, wall-to-wall CHV, we're talking denim minis, we're talking white stilettos, we're talking peach-coloured trouser suits with matching bags and hats. Of course, Sorcha stands out among that lot like a focking banana in a bunch of carrots and I overhear a few, 'Who the fook does she tink she is?' comments, which thankfully *she* doesn't.

One of the first things I notice, roysh, is that all the little girls look like they're from focking Loompaland, they're, like, tangerine, which – as anyone who's spent time hanging around the Orts block in UCD knows – is a sure sign that they've been on the sunbeds. Sorcha, whose tan came out of a tube this morning, turns around to me and goes, 'OH! MY! GOD! They're only *children*, Ross. Do their parents not realize how dangerous that is?' and I give her a look to tell her to keep her voice down because I wouldn't mind actually leaving here today with my kneecaps pretty much where nature put them.

It's, like, eleven o'clock already, roysh, and I don't know why we're all still standing around outside, freezing our nuts off, but Ronan says everyone's waiting to see Arrecife arrive and I ask him who Arrecife is, roysh, and he says her old man is the Eliminator and I ask him who the Eliminator is and he says he's a mate of the Viper and I'm there, 'Is he a criminal?' and Ronan goes, 'A shut mouth catches no flies.'

So all of a sudden, roysh – and I am NOT joking here – this focking horse-drawn carriage pulls up and out gets this goy, roysh, with the shortest neck I've ever seen, which *is* saying something considering I played rugby. He's obviously, like, a minder. He holds open the door and out comes a girl, who I presume is Arrecife, and she's, like, orange as well and she's wearing a dress that Sorcha reckons cost about three Ks. Then out gets the man himself, the Eliminator, and he's a seriously scary-looking dude, and you know from just looking at him, roysh, that he didn't have to go to the Credit Union for the bread for this. Then out gets what I presume is his wife and she's dressed like she's going to a focking movie premiere, even though you can tell, roysh, underneath it all, that she's still pure focking skobe.

Everyone just bursts into applause, roysh, as if this is, like *their* day and we're just on the guestlist. Ronan turns around to me and, out of the side of his mouth, goes, 'We had this Show and Tell week couple of months back. A few of the mudders and faaders came up to talk to us about what they did for a living. *He* came in to us. Didn't the fooken Special Branch bug the classroom. They'd fooken listeners in the room next door,' and I'm actually a bit worried, roysh, because he's looking at him in total awe and everyone's, like, shaking hands with the goy and telling him that Arrecife looks like a little angel and I swear to God, roysh, I am not making this up, he spots Ronan, gives him a little wink and goes, 'Howiya, Ro?'

Then, roysh, like a herd of focking sheep, we follow into the church behind them, but then all of a sudden we hear this, like, car horn blaring behind us and everyone spins around, roysh, and the horse is, like, rearing up, I suppose out of fright. A lot of people scream, which actually makes the horse worse. Sorcha puts her hands to her mouth and goes, '*Oh my God!*' more than once let's say.

Some other kid has arrived late, in a stretch limo, and the driver beeped the horn to say, basically, shift that focking horse's orse, I need to pork. So of course while the coach-driver is, like, calming the animal down, roysh, the Eliminator steps out of the crowd, with his minder beside him and when they see him coming, the limo-driver and whoever the fock they are in the back totally kack themselves.

The driver's like, 'Jaysus, I'm sorry . . . very sorry . . . didn't know it was you . . .' and he doesn't know it, roysh, but he's actually bowing and so are the parents of this little boy, who's crying now and doesn't want to get out of the cor. The Eliminator – or whatever his real name is – he's unbelievable, roysh, he puts his orm around the old man and old dear and tells them that everything's okay, then he reaches into the back of the cor and he picks up the little boy in his orms and, like, carries him into the church and everyone's, like, clapping and cheering.

Of course the limo-driver's following after him, roysh, still apologizing to him and the Eliminator's telling him that it's mustard, no damage done, let's not let it ruin the big day, but then I see him giving the man with no neck the nod, roysh, and when I turn around a few seconds later the goy's writing down the registration of the limo.

There's a bit of a bottleneck in the aisle while everyone's, like, finding their seats. Behind me, I hear one of Tina's friends – they're called Livia, Shadden, Marteeenah and 'Cinta – turn around to her and go, 'Much is he givin' ye a week?' obviously talking about me. Tina's there, 'Two hundrit,' and one of the other birds – I'm pretty sure it's Shadden – is there, '*Two hundrit?* Jaysus, what solicitor are you usin'?' and Tina goes, 'Didn't even need to,' and this must seriously impress them, roysh, because I can actually sense them checking me out and generally giving me the big-time mince pies.

Because I'm basically Ronan's old man, roysh, I have to actually leave the residents of Carrickstown and sit with him and Tina up at the front of the church and, to be honest, roysh, it's all pretty boring stuff and I'm not really sure what I should be doing, although Sorcha mentioned earlier that I should check whether he understands the real importance of making your Communion, so I turn around to him and I go, 'What are you going to do with the moolah?' and he reaches into the pocket of his denim jacket – I don't believe it, his focking lighter falls out – then he unfolds this sheet of paper and it's a picture of this, like, naked bird draped across a Harley. He goes, 'I'm getting *her* tattooed across me back. There's a place off Capel Street does them,' and I just ignore him, roysh, thinking he's just trying to wind me up, like he does.

Our Father, who Art in Heaven, blahdy blahdy blah. Everyone gets their bit of bread and before we know it the whole family, neighbours, relatives and basic hangers-on are all sitting in McDonald's, we're talking the one on O'Connell Street. Sorcha's doing her best to blend in, roysh, but there's, like, a couple of times I have to actually tell her to close her mouth. She already stunned the entire restaurant into silence asking for a decaf *latté* with cinnamon, not chocolate, and I don't even know if she's been this side of the Liffey before. At one point she squeezes my hand and tells me that she is SO going to get a direct debit with St Vincent de Paul when this is all over. She actually says the words, 'when this is all over,' like it's a hostage drama or something.

Anyway, roysh, where all this is going is that Tina and her family decide that they're all going to go off and get shit-faced for the day and they ask me and Sorcha if we'll take Ronan to the flicks for the afternoon and we're like, 'Kool and the Gang,' because Sorcha and Ronan are getting along like a Northsider and a batter burger salesman. So we hit the Savoy, roysh, and I grab three Wilsons for *Scooby Doo* and then I hit the can because, as usual, I need to drop a plop badly.

I'm in there maybe five minutes, roysh, and when I come back, Sorcha's standing there like a focking Toblerone, basically on her own, as in *no Ronan*, and I'm there, 'Where is he?' and she's like, 'You mean he's not with you? He said he was going to the toilet,' and I go, 'HELLO? I've just *left* the toilet? He's, like, not in there,' and Sorcha storts, like filling up, roysh, and I have to tell her that everything's going to be okay.

I'm there, 'Let's just *think*. Where would he go? Sorcha's

like, 'He *did* say he'd prefer to go and spend his money rather than go to the pictures,' and suddenly it hits me, roysh, and it's like, OH FOCK!

I grab Sorcha's hand, roysh, and we peg it across O'Connell Street, then down this other street which I think is called Henry Street and we're passing by all these cheap clothes shops and skobes selling sports socks and for the first time, roysh, I feel really protective of my son, like I'd basically deck anyone who tried to tattoo him. We ask for directions, then we turn left at the end of Mary Street and onto Capel Street, then down this little, like, laneway, roysh, and we see this door with the word TATTOO over it. I let go of Sorcha's hand and I take the steps two at a time and I can hear Ronan's voice inside, roysh, and I put my shoulder to the door, like I'm tackling Martin focking Johnson, and I just go, 'DON'T FOCKING TATTOO MY KID!' and there's, like, total silence in the place.

Ronan's standing there, leaning against the window, talking to, like, the tattooist, who's working away on some other dude's orm. When he sees me, Ronan cracks his hole laughing. He goes, 'You didn't really think I was getting one, did ye?' and I'm there, 'You can't just wander off like that,' and he's like, 'Had to see a mate of mine. Rosser, this is Buckets of Blood. Buckets of Blood, this is Rosser,' and the tattooist, who must be, like, eighteen or nineteen, goes, 'How's it goin', mate?' and I'm there, 'Wrecked, actually. I've just focking run here all the way from O'Connell Street,' and I'm wondering how a seven-year-old becomes friends with an eighteen-year-old and then I'm wondering why he's called Buckets of Blood.

'This is only a sideline for him,' Ronan goes as we're going back downstairs to Sorcha. 'His real job is debt-collection,' and I go, 'And you *owed* him money?' and he laughs and he's like, 'Nah, he owed *me*. He's not very good at debt-collecting. We call him Buckets of Blood, but sure, the blood is usually *his*,' and I laugh.

He goes, 'In anyhow, relax. I'm not getting a tattoo. Don't like them,' and then he turns to Sorcha and goes, 'I'm sorry for taking off like that. I must have given you a fright,' and she says it's fine and Ronan goes, 'So, what's it to be, then? Will we go and see *Scooby Doo*, or will we hit Grafton Street and see all the boords coming out of work?'

I'm in Lillie's, roysh, standing at the bor, getting my round in, when behind me I hear someone going, '*Pssssss...*' making basically a pissing sound. When I turn around, roysh, it stops and I'm, like, eyeballing everyone, basically saying, whatever, don't push it, but then when I turn back to the bor, roysh, it storts again, it's like, '*Pssssss...*'

Emer's giving Chloë a seriously hord time for eating a blueberry muffin three days ago. Even Sorcha's, like, throwing her eyes up to heaven and she and Amie with an ie head off for a Jack Palance. I'm bored out of my tree waiting for Christian to come back from the bor.

Emer's there, 'I'm just saying, you were wondering why your Dolce e Gabbana jeans wouldn't close and I'm just telling you,' and Chloë's going, 'But *how* was it eighteen points?' and Emer's like, 'HELLO? I worked it out from the nutritional information on the packet,' and Chloë's there, 'It couldn't have been eighteen, is all I'm saying. It's only, like, bread,' and Emer's giving it, '*Oh my God*, I told

178

you I worked it out, Chloë,' and Chloë's like, 'You must have, like, worked it out wrong then,' and Emer goes, 'HELLO? *Who* was it who took grinds and still failed Pass maths?' and that's, like, game, set and match.

Christian arrives back with the Britneys. I'm giving the serious mince pies to this blondie bird who's, like, a ringer for Tanya Robinson and Sorcha cops it, roysh, from down on the dance-floor, and the next thing she's nodding to Amie with an ie to head back over to where we're standing, roysh, and she stands in front of me, with her orms around my waist, basically to show everyone that I'm her property, and every now and then she looks over her shoulder to give Tanya Robinson filthies.

Christian hands her a vodka and Diet 7-Up, fair focks to him. Emer turns around to me and goes, '*Oh my God*, I heard JP's totally flipped out,' and I'm there, 'What do you mean, flipped out? He's just gone mad into God,' and then Chloë goes, 'Oh, yeah, like he *needs* to be praying? He's loaded, Ross,' and Emer's there, 'Yeah, I heard he's had a total breakdown. It's like, OH! MY! GOD!' and Chloë's like, 'I heard that, too. I heard it was like, *Aaahhh*. And I heard that from Wendy, who's, like, in the Institute with a girl who lives two doors down from his parents.'

And I just lose it, roysh, listening to them talking about one of my best friends like that. I go, 'And I'm *focking* telling you that he hasn't had a breakdown. He's into God, not focking, I don't know, devil worship,' and Sorcha just, like, squeezes my hand, roysh, to tell me I'm making a tit of myself, people are basically staring, and Emer and Chloë look me up and down and, like, turn away as if to say, we rest our case.

Emer goes, '*Oh my God*, there's that girl who used to be

in Crunch with us,' and Chloë's like, 'OH! MY! GOD! I can't *believe* she thinks that skirt fits her,' and Emer goes, 'She is SO not going to the gym anymore, that's for sure. I heard she piled it on when she went on the pill.'

'Ronan's worried about you,' Sorcha goes to me the other night. I flush the jacks and head back into the room. She's sitting on the edge of the bed. I'm there, 'Worried? How so, Babes?' She goes, 'What he says is right, Ross, it's not normal, you living in this place,' and she, like, looks around the room. I'm there, 'It's the focking Berkeley Court,' and she goes, 'Yes and it's very nice, Ross, but as your actual *home?* It's like, *Oh my God!*'

I'm looking for my Dubes. I'm SO going to have to tidy this place. Sorcha's not going to let it go, though. She's like, 'Stability, Ross, that's what Ronan thinks you need,' and I go, 'He would never have heard of a word like stability,' and she hands me her phone, roysh, and shows me this text message and it's like: **Worried about d rosser lad, needs 2 get his shit 2 gethr n get the 2 of u a gaff. Needs stability. Girls lik u don't cum around evry day – don't ever let him 4 get dat.**

Anyway, roysh, I don't bother arguing anymore because Ronan – wherever he got his brains from – is basically roysh, we do need a gaff. So I end up doing the whole responsible bread-winning husband bit, roysh, I give her a few hundred sheets to drop into Rococo and Blue Eriu, while I hit Foxrock to ask Wank Features to give me the money to buy a house.

The first words that come out of his mouth when he opens the door, roysh, aren't, 'Hey, how are you?' or 'I'm sorry for being a focking tool all my life,' but, 'I have a *big* surprise for you, Kicker.' I'm there, 'Well, it better be half-a-million squids because I need to buy a gaff,' and he laughs and goes, 'Better than that, Ross. Come on, it's in the study,' and I walk ahead of him, roysh, and just as I'm about to push open the door, he puts his hands over my eyes and goes, 'Get ready for the surprise of a lifetime,' and sort of, like, edges me into the study, roysh, does a bit of a focking drum-roll routine, then whips his hands away and Hennessy's sitting there, knocking back the old man's cognac, like he'd never been away.

He goes, 'How are you, Ross?' and I'm like, 'When did you get out?' and he's there, 'Last night. Pending my appeal, of course,' and I go, 'I take it you'll be heading back to Rio pretty soon then?' The old man's like, 'Why on Earth would he do that? The man's as innocent as the day is long,' and Hennessy goes, 'And I had to surrender my passport anyway.'

Knob Head is like, 'It's a good job you arrived when you did. I was in the middle of telling Hennessy a story,' and he actually goes back to telling it. He's there, 'So I told the young service girl: "Call the police, if you think it'll do any good," and that's just what she did. So this chap arrives – straight out of Templemore, Hennessy, still wet behind the ears, cabbage and potatoes and so forth – and he tells me to put out my cigar. So I fixed him with a look and I said, "I provide almost two hundred people in this town with a living. I think you'll find that entitles me to a glass or two of cognac and big cigar on a Friday evening." Then he said it again: "Put out your cigar!" I said, "Who won the Second World War, can you tell me? It's just I think I may have misheard the result."'

Hennessy goes, 'What station did he take you to?' and the old man goes, 'Donnybrook. So I know something of what you went through during your incarceration, quote-unquote,' and then he turns to me and goes, 'Hennessy's going to become my election agent, Ross,' and I go, 'I couldn't give two focks if he's going to become a secret agent, I need half-a-million squids and it's not a focking joke,' and of course he makes a big deal out of it, roysh, letting the cigar hang out of his mouth, like it's a big shock.

I go, 'There's a problem?' and he's like, 'Afraid there is, Ross. Standing in the local elections is going to eat up a lot of my spare cash. Those posters aren't cheap. Your Ray Burkes and your Padraig Flynns would tell the likes of Kerrigan that, if he ever bothered to ask them. Have you talked to the bank, Ross, about a mortgage? That's how people generally pay for houses, over the course of a working life,' and I go, 'How the fock am I going to pay a mortgage? I don't even have a job,' and he just, like, stares at me, roysh, and I swear to God, he *actually* thinks I should get one.

I go, 'If it came out that your son had fathered a child with a skanger? And that you had paid off the child's mother so she'd never dorken your door? If the papers were to find that out, what would it do to your election chances?' and he looks at me in total shock, and we're talking totally. He goes, 'Damn it, Hennessy, he's right. *A grandchild?* In one of those wretched sink estates? It's not going to go down well with the voters of Dun Laoghaire-Rathdown, thank you very much.'

Hennessy's, like, swilling his brandy around in his glass, going, 'I don't know, Charles. There's are a lot of poor people out there and, for better or worse, they have votes. We might be able to use this kid. Show you appeal to all sorts. Us *and* them,' and the old man goes, 'I think you've had more than enough cognac for one afternoon, Hennessy. I've no interest in appealing to *them*. My only appeal to *them* is to leave my car alone, stop breeding like bacteria and move their wretched Christmas funfair somewhere more appropriate. Actually, write some of these down, Hennessy. Head the page, "Policies," and use a capital P. No, make it *all* capitals.'

I go, 'I'm getting bored here. All I have to do is ring One F. His mates in *The Stor* are bound to be interested in your . . . murky past,' and he's there, 'He's got me by the short and curlies, Hennessy, quote-unquote, pardon the French for their sins against wine-making. It's checkmate and there's not a bullet in my gun, to mix a metaphor, exclamation mark.'

I go, 'I'm going to leave you two orseholes to your sad little lives. Oh, by the way, me and Sorcha are back together – that's why I need a gaff. Those new ones in Blackrock are supposed to be nice. I'll let you know the damage. And by the way, you're a dickhead.'

I'm in town, roysh, basically mooching around, checking out the scenario, when all of a sudden my phone rings and I know without even looking at it, roysh, that it's Sorcha, because Christian downloaded the 'Darth Vader Morching Theme' for me and lashed it on my phone and that's what plays now when she rings. I'm there, 'Y'ello?' and she's like, 'Ross, where are you?' and I go, 'Er, Grafton Street?' and she's like, 'Oh. Do you fancy calling into the shop?'

and she sounds sort of, like, worried about something, so I tell her I'll be around in, like, five minutes.

When I get there, roysh, the shop's empty and she gives me this, like, huge hug, which is a bit OTT, considering I only saw her last night. I'm there, 'What's wrong, Babes?' and she goes, 'Erika's coming in. She's, like, SO pissed off about us getting back together and I just know she's going to be a total bitch to me. Please, Ross, I need you here for, like, moral support,' and I'm there, 'Hey, it's Kool and the Gang, Babes,' and all of a sudden, roysh, I see Sorcha's eyes sort of, like, widen in, you'd have to say, terror and I know without even turning around, roysh, that *she* has walked into the shop.

She's like, 'Hi, Sorcha. Hi, Ross. Look at love's young dream. All back together and everything. No more secret children out there, I hope?' and I'm like, 'Er, no, there's no more,' and I hate myself for sounding so focking weedy. She goes, 'That coat in the window, Sorcha...' and Sorcha's like, 'The Alberta Ferretti? It's, like, chocolate brown?' and Erika's there, 'Yes,' and Sorcha comes out from behind the counter and goes, 'Yes, it's nine hundred euro,' and Erika's like, 'Sorry, you misunderstood me. I don't *want* it. I'm just telling you that patent leather is SO last year,' and Sorcha's like, 'Oh,' and Erika goes, 'Mind if I look around?' and she doesn't even, like, wait for an answer. She's already laden down with BT bags.

I turn to Sorcha and I'm like, 'Why do you let her get to you?' and she goes, 'Because she *knows* how to get under my skin, Ross. She SO knows it. Look at that top she's wearing,' and I'm there, 'What in particular am I looking at?' and she goes, 'It's a Chloë, cotton, geometric-print button-down. As in, Stella McCartney? She knows I'm trying to get my hands on her stuff for the shop. *That's* why she wore it.'

Erika's going around examining clothes like they're, I don't know, toxic waste or something, even though it's all, like, good gear, as in Whistles, Moschino, Donna Karan, and Joseph. She keeps, like, tutting and shaking her head. Then she goes, 'Those Prada rust suede-and-wool patchwork coats you have were SO nice when they were *in*,' and I'm looking at Sorcha, roysh, and her eyes are, like, filling up, but of course Erika never takes that as her cue that she's won.

She goes, 'I met your little novelty friend – what's her name? – Claire coming out of Blue Eriu. She never stops making the effort, you have to give it to her. She said you were going to be doing Love Kylie,' and she storts making a big show of looking around, even though she knows Sorcha hasn't got it in yet. Sorcha goes, 'I haven't actually finalized the deal yet. I've been pretty busy with my Amnesty commitments,' and Erika just, like, looks her up and down, roysh, and goes, 'You're a talker, Sorcha Lalor. A talker and a dreamer. Always were, always will be,' and Sorcha has to turn away, roysh, so Erika doesn't see her crying and I decide, roysh, that I'm not having anyone upset my, basically, wife like that.

I'm there, 'Erika, you are one sad person,' and she goes, 'Oh am I, Ross? And you're in a position to see that, are you?' and I'm there, 'Yeah, you're actually sad *and* lonely. Because you've no friends,' but it has absolutely no effect on her, roysh, she just goes, 'But I *do* have a fabulous new boyfriend. He's a show-jumper. He's one of the richest men in Ireland,' and she give us both this, like, totally fake smile and then she goes, 'I'll leave you two to your sham of a marriage,' and then she turns around and walks out of the shop.

Sorcha just, like, bursts into tears and collapses into my orms basically. I'm telling her she should know better than to listen to Erika, but she's bawling her eyes out, going, 'She's right, though, Ross. I have let things slip here. I had that petition to organize for that guy executed in Texas. I should be more on top of things. I didn't even know that patent leather was *out* this year. Imagine that! I am SO going to have to get my act together.'

I'm like, 'This shop is a lot to manage on your own, Sorcha. Would your old dear not let you, I don't know, take someone else on?' and she goes, 'I'm thinking of asking Aoife,' as in her friend. I'm there, 'Is she not in hospital?' and she goes, 'She's out now. And she's actually much better,' and I'm there, 'If it takes the pressure off you . . .' and she tells me that to cheer herself up she's going to take the duchess, powder-blue, linen drawstring dress by Joseph that's in the stockroom.

Of all the focking ATMs in this town . . . It's taking its focking time spitting out the money as well. I know it's them behind me, but I don't know if they've copped me yet. He's going, 'You *have* to go away for the summer,' and she's like, 'I'd be miserable,' and he's there, 'But, like, your friends are going, we're talking Emily, Kate, Harriet. It's, like, Montauk. Who *wouldn't* want to go?' and she's going, 'Me. I'd rather spend the summer with *you*.'

The machine finally coughs up the old folding green and I turn around, roysh, and try to keep my head down and slip into the Merrion Centre without them seeing my boat.

It's actually *her* who cops me. She's like, 'Huh, look who it is,' and what can I do but turn around, roysh, and go, 'Hey, Jessica. How's it going, Pikey?'

They don't answer me, roysh, just look me up and down for a few seconds and then Jessica, like, links his orm, presumably to give me the message that they're, like, back together and working things out, then they step forward and Pikey sticks his cord in the machine.

As I walk away, he's like, 'I saw you piss your pants,' and I stop, roysh, and I end up going, 'Sorry?' and he's there, 'On the internet. I saw you piss your pants. And cry like a little girl. It was *very* funny,' and I just, like, nod and walk away. I suppose he's entitled to his moment.

I'm flaked out on the bed, roysh, flicking through the channels and I come to this, like, documentary and I actually stort watching it – going through one of my intellectual phases – and it's all about this thing called the Oedipus Complex, roysh, which, according to this, I don't know, psychologist or psychiatrist or whatever, means that every goy basically wants to kill his old man and, like, marry his old dear. But I actually don't, roysh. I want to kill my old man *and* my old dear.

I don't know if they have a name for that, roysh, but I actually feel the urge pretty focking strongly half-an-hour later when my old dear has the basic focking cheek to ring me and go, 'Ross, it's wonderful news about you and Sorcha,' and I'm there, 'What focking business is it of yours?' and she's like, 'I *knew* it. I knew you two would come to your senses. I called into the shop to see her today. Oh, she's so happy about it, Ross.'

I'm there, 'Is that everything? I'm getting focking bored with this conversation,' and she goes, 'Oh, the photo shoot. You never asked me how it went,' and I'm like, 'That's because this focking calendar isn't happening,' and she goes, 'The photographer – he's a neighbour of Sally's – he really put me at my ease,' and I'm there, 'This is a focking mare. I can't believe I'm *actually* having this conversation,' and she goes, 'Sally thought my hair would look nicer up, to help emphasize my—' and I'm like, 'Don't even focking *think* about saying that word,' and I just cut her off, roysh, and ten seconds later my phone rings, but it's not her again, it's actually Sorcha.

She goes, 'What's wrong, Ross? You sound like you're hyperventilating,' and I'm there, 'This *focking* calendar. I swear to God, Sorcha . . .' and she goes, 'Oh, yeah. Your mum called into the shop today,' and I'm like, 'I'm actually going to be a focking laughing-stock if this thing happens,' but she goes, 'Why a laughing-stock? Your mother's a very attractive woman, Ross. You must have noticed,' and I'm like, 'Uuuh, *no?*' and she goes, 'She is, though. I hope I look that well when I'm her age. She was telling me she tied her hair up, so as to emphasize her—' and I'm there, 'I don't want to focking hear it. I swear to God, I seriously think I'm going to spew . . .'

She goes, 'You are, like, *totally* overreacting, Ross. It's like, OH! MY! GOD!' and I'm there, 'What, because I don't like the idea of blokes in, I don't know, factories and garages looking at my old dear and . . . *Ugh*, I don't even want to think about it,' and she goes, 'Well, I think it's about time you grew up. Anyway, do you mind if we cancel the cinema tonight?' and I'm there, 'Fine, why?' and she's like, 'Oh, I'm going to Finnegan's,' and I'm there, 'With who?' and she's like, 'Erika.'

So of course I'm there, '*Erika?* What is it, like, a clear-the-air thing?' and she goes, 'Clear the air? What are you talking about?' and I'm like, 'Well, that day in the shop . . . she was a total bitch to you,' and she goes, 'HELLO? She's still one of my best friends, Ross.'

6. Bricks and Mortar

Ryle's off with his RTÉ mates, roysh, knocking back glasses of – I kid you not – *white wine*, and me and the goys are just sitting there, roysh, saying how much the dude has changed. An hour into the evening, roysh, he finally decides to focking grace us with his company and the first thing he says is, 'What the fock did you goys do to my cousin?'

Oisinn goes, 'Hey, some of us went to Israel and managed not to come back as religious freaks,' which I actually think is a bit out of order, roysh, because it's only, like, God he's into. Ryle goes, 'But a priest?' and Oisinn's there, 'Yeah, we're still trying to work out what the angle is. I suppose the wedge is decent enough. Free cor. Free rent,' and of course I bring half of focking Kiely's to a standstill by going, 'Maybe it's, like, genuine?'

Ryle's like, 'Explain,' and I'm there, 'I'm just saying, that's all. Maybe the dude found God,' and Oisinn straight away, roysh, goes, 'Well, his kicking must have improved then because he couldn't find the focking *touchline* when he played for us,' which is horseshit, roysh, because the dude was an unbelievable fullback, but it's a decent line, roysh, and well worth a high-five.

Ryle sort of, like, waves his empty glass at me, hinting, I suppose, that he wants another, but I'm focked if I'm asking the borman for the shit he's drinking. I have a rep in this joint.

He looks at Oisinn and goes, 'Well, personally, I think he's flipped his lid. I mean take a look at this,' and he shows us this, like, text message. Actually, it's an unbelievable phone – he must be on some focking wedge. Anyway, roysh, apparently he texted JP earlier and asked did he fancy coming out tonight for a few scoops – scoops obviously being a focking joke in Ryle's case – and what he got back was: **Be careful that your heart is not weighed down with dissipation, drunkenness and the anxieties of life, for that day will close on you unexpectedly like a trap. Luke 21:34.** I mean, what can we do when Ryle shows it to us, roysh, only shake our heads. No one can say that kind of shit is roysh.

Oisinn asks me to come up to the bor with him and, like, help him carry his round back, and I guess it's because he wants a word on the QT. When we're up there, roysh, he gets the round in and I notice that his orm is burned. I ask him what the Jackanory is and he says there was another explosion in his old man's shed last week, roysh, he mixed two or three things in the wrong doses – Tonka bean, persimmon and Gaiac wood were mentioned – stuck a flame under it and ended up stripping two layers of skin off his orm.

'But,' he goes, 'that's what I wanted to tell you. The good news is, it's finished,' and I'm there, 'The *Eau d'Affluence?*' and he's like, 'They're paying me a million sheets for it, Ross,' and I'm there, 'Who?' and he goes, 'Hugo Boss. I told you a year ago they were interested in buying it from me,' and I'm like, 'Yeah, but I thought that was in the same way that Christian is writing the next three *Star Wars* movies and I'm going to be Ireland's next number ten,' in other words, total BS.

He goes, 'No, I've been sending samples over to New York as I've gone along. Anyway, they've sent over one of their reps,' and I sort of, like, raise my eyebrows, and he goes, 'Giselle Lewisohn. We're talking hot here, Ross. The spit of Rachel Bilson. Manhattanite. Trouser suit. Lips that could suck a focking snooker ball up twenty metres of Wavin pipe,' and I can't help myself, roysh, I end up going, 'Cool.'

But Oisinn's not a happy camper. He goes, 'That's what I wanted to talk to you about. You can wipe that look off your face, Ross. She's coming here, as in tonight, as in any minute now and I want you on your best behaviour.'

I'm there, 'Why the fock would you bring her here?' and he goes, 'She sort of, like, invited herself. Asked me what I was doing tonight, then said she'd come along too, have a drink, celebrate doing business. But she doesn't take shit, this bird. She's going back to New York to get the contracts drawn up. I don't want you ruining it by trying to cop off with her by commenting on her top tens.'

I'm actually a bit insulted. I'm there, 'I'm actually a bit insulted, Oisinn. How come none of the other goys are getting this lecture?' and he goes, 'Do you want me to remind you of your previous in this area?' and I'm like, 'No need. Message understood,' and he goes, 'Cool. I mean, I can't promise I'm not going to make a move on her myself.'

We come back with the drinks and Ryle looks pretty

pissed off that there isn't one for him. He can ask focking George Hamilton or Wardy to get one in for him, if that's what he's into. He asks Oisinn what happened to his orm and Oisinn tells him about the explosion, then goes, 'A million sheets buys a hell of a lot of plastic surgery,' and Christian goes, 'You could actually get a mechanical one for that,' and as usual, roysh, it's a real, like, conversation-stopper. Everyone just, like, looks at him and he goes, 'Luke Skywalker got one, 2–1B fitted it,' and we all go, 'Oh, yeah, roysh,' because he's the last goy in the world whose feelings you'd want to hurt.

The next thing, roysh, who arrives over to us only JP's old man and fair focks to him, roysh, there's a lounge bird behind him carrying a tray of drinks with a full round on it, even one for Ryle, who I suppose *is* his nephew. He goes, 'Hello there, chaps. No sign of himself tonight, no?' and I'm there, 'He said he was staying in to do some reading and, like, meditation,' and he's like, 'Meditation? Yeah, I'd one myself before I left the house, but it's done nothing to lessen my drive,' and his eyes sort of, like, sweep the old battle-cruiser and fix on this bird who's just walked in the door and I know straight away from Oisinn's descrip-tion that it's this Giselle bird. And you can imagine Oisinn's face, roysh, when the goy turns around and shouts at her, '*Whoa!* Sit on my face and I'll guess your weight!' as she's looking around, trying to pick Oisinn out.

He ducks out of the way, roysh, because obviously he doesn't want her knowing that came from his group, and she doesn't actually see him and she turns left and storts looking around, but Kiely's is focking rammers tonight and it's pretty obvious, roysh, that it's going to take her a few minutes to find us.

JP's old man goes, 'Okay, you lot are JP's friends. I'm going to level with you. I couldn't give a shit if JP grew a beard, changed his name to Abraham and learned how to fart the chorus from 'How Great Thou Art' – as long as it doesn't cost me money,' and he all of a sudden spins around in my direction, roysh, and goes, 'WHAT DO I HATE LOSING?' and it's just, like, a natural instinct, roysh, from the days when I worked for him, but I automatically go, 'M.O.N.E.Y.' and he's like, 'AND WHAT DOES IT SPELL?' and I'm there, 'HAPPINESS!' and he goes, 'That's right. But right now, I'm not happy. I've lost my number one estate agent and it's costing me M.O.N.E.Y. – SLEEP!'

Fionn goes, 'Have you talked to him, told him how much Hook, Lyon and Sinker needs him?' and he's like, 'He said that what we do is unchristian. He said that to make false or exaggerated claims about houses was immoral. Can you believe that? The little shit who christened Tullamore, The Gateway to Dublin, is offering me lessons in morality. I said to him, "You found something you're good at. It paid for that apartment of yours, God damn it." Know what he said? "Better to be poor than a liar." It's Proverbs 19–22 apparently,' and I'm just there, like, shaking my head, wondering how anyone could treat their old man like that.

He goes, 'Okay, kids, the gloves are off. No rules anymore. Dirty is the name of the game. Your friend likes the broads, right?' and Oisinn's there, 'Understatement of the century,' and he goes, '*That* . . . is his Achilles' Heel. How's he going to get around the celibacy thing? Got a lot of strange desires that kid. Takes after his father. Should see some of the things his mother's found under his bed over the years. She nearly had to *phone* a priest for him one time.'

Oisinn's, like, looking around him, and it's pretty obvious he's kacking it that something's going to go wrong and I don't actually blame him.

I look at JP's old man and I go, 'So what are you *actually* saying?' and he's like, 'What I'm saying is that you guys know a lot of girls. And if you were to, shall we say, put temptation his way, remind him what he'd be missing if he goes through with this crazy idea, then let's just say that I'd be grateful.'

We all just, like, nod, roysh, but I'm the one who asks the question that's basically on the tip of our tongues. I'm like, '*How* grateful?' and he, like, stares me straight in the eye and goes, 'Ten thousand euro worth of grateful,' and we're all like, '*Ten focking Ks?*'

He goes, 'Tomorrow is the first of June. He starts in Maynooth the first week in October. You've got four months to stop this madness once and for all,' and just as he says it, roysh, this Giselle bird arrives over to us and I can see Oisinn, like, shaking her hand and just as he's turning around to introduce her to us, JP's old man looks at her and goes, 'You've got eyes like spanners,' and she's sharp this bird, she cops straight away that the goy's leering at her, and she's like, 'I beg your pardon,' because, like Oisinn said, roysh, she's an actual septic.

There's, like, total silence, roysh, and you could actually cut the tension with a knife and JP's old man goes, 'I said you've got eyes like spanners . . . every time I look at them, my nuts tighten.'

*

I'm in Café en Seine with Sorcha, roysh, having a bit of nosebag, sick to death as I am with the old room service in the Berkeley Court, when all of a sudden she jumps up, roysh, and says she's going to ask the borman to stick the old Savalas on, what with the old man being on the 'Six-One News', some shite they're doing about the independents running in the local election. I tell Sorcha we really should be hitting the road, but the next thing I know it's on, roysh, and up comes his ugly focking mug on the screen.

She goes, '*Oh* my God! I can't believe it's your dad. You must be, like, SO proud,' and I'm looking at him, roysh, and he's standing outside the Dorsh station in Dalkey, handing out leaflets, but only to people who look like they earn more than 50K a year. Then his stupid voice fills the place. He's going, 'Yes, I *am* an independent, but only because my policies are too broad and too . . . multifarious, quote-unquote, to cram into a short party title. If I did have to come up with a party name it would probably be something like, The Everyone Just Stop Dragging Up The Past With All These Tribunals And So Forth And Enough Of This Smoking Ban Nonsense And Fifteen Cents For A Plastic Bag Come On Get Real . . . Party. And that doesn't stand for anything before you try to work it out, Mr Charlie Bird, investigative reporter at large.'

It's, like, five minutes before the interviewer gets a question in. She's like, 'One of the central planks of your campaign is that we should draw a line under the various political and financial scandals of the 1970s, 1980s and 1990s . . .' and the old man goes, 'Yes and wind up these so-called tribunals. I think people are tired of answers and questions and questions and answers, who did this, who did that – who cares? Do you remember the seventies and eighties? Ireland was a miserable place to be, what with your recessions and what-not. People did what they had to do to stop from going under. Some of them salted a little bit of money away for a rainy day . . . in the Seychelles. Some of them forgot to tell my good friends in the Revenue Commissioners about the odd cheque. But we all survived, didn't we?'

And that's it. That's his focking message. Sorcha goes, 'Well, I can't say I agree with *everything* he said and I'm disappointed that the environment didn't figure as an issue, but he's certainly given me a few things to think about,' but the bloke behind me hits the nail bang on the head when he goes, 'Wanker.'

Me and Fionn are in the bor in the Berkeley Court going through a stack of old Mount Anville, Loreto Foxrock, Holy Child Killiney, Alexandra College and Loreto on the Green yearbooks, racking our brains, trying to come up with someone who JP has been basically dying to score all his life. I'm there, 'What about Emma Harms?' and Fionn's like, 'Now there's a name from the past,' and I go, 'Remember he started playing focking badminton on Tuesday and Thursday nights just to see her?' and Fionn's there, 'One small problem. I'm pretty sure the family moved to Canada,' and I'm there, 'Shame.'

I go, 'What about the girl two rows behind her. He had a thing for her as well,' and Fionn's there, 'Maria Twigger,' and I'm there, 'Twigger! Played hockey. Made the Leinster team. Didn't JP ask her to the debs?' and Fionn goes, 'Yeah and she'd no interest. Anyway, from what I hear she's all loved-up these days.' Maria was a total honey, like a young Nicola Roberts. I'm there, 'All loved-up, huh? Lucky goy,' and Fionn goes, '*Girl*,' and suddenly, roysh, a lot of shit falls into place. Me and Fionn just look at each other and at the same time go, '*Hockey!*'

I throw down Loreto Foxrock and pick up a book of Mounties. Fionn says we're like two cattle farmers looking through the herd register and I crack my hole laughing. It has to be said, roysh, me and Fionn have put the past behind us and we're getting on like a house on fire, which is how it should be with mates. Underneath it all, roysh, I think he respects me for being an unbelievable rugby player and for pulling the birds like Enrique Iglesias and I respect him for being into, I don't know, reading and writing and shit.

He nods at the borman and orders two more pints of Ken. I go, 'Fionn, can I say something to you?' and he's like, 'If it's about my diary, forget it. You don't have to apologize,' and I'm there, 'Of all the shitty things I've done in my life, I think that has to be the worst,' and he goes, 'It's all worked out for the best. Sorcha's fine about it now. And I'd never have had the confidence to put my poetry out there myself – now there's three different publishers interested in publishing my work. And before you ask, Ross, no, that doesn't entitle you to half my advance,' and it's like the goy's a focking mind-reader.

I go, 'But I'm glad we're, you know . . . I'm trying not to sound like a steamer here,' and he's there, 'Ross, we're not so dissimilar, you and I. For storters, we both love the same girl. We both see the same qualities in her. I think that makes us alroysh, don't you?' and I go, 'Yeah . . . okay, what about Medb Allen-Clark?' and he's like, 'As in the

Mountie? Hmmm. JP *was* mad about her, but as I remember it, she was in love with *you*,' and I hold up my hand and go, 'Guilty as charged,' hoping that didn't make me sound like a total Allied Irish Banker.

He goes, 'I've got Sarah Glenny. Holy Child,' and I'm there, 'Clarinet Sarah?' and he goes, 'Oboe. He was with her the night of the Junior Cert results.' I look at the picture. Doesn't ring any bells, but that night's a blur. I'm there, 'She looks a bit like Sienna Miller,' and Fionn goes, 'He was with her again a couple of years ago in Annabel's, but she had a boyfriend at the time. A Michael's boy,' and I'm there, 'Wanker,' and he goes, 'Agreed. I think our JP still carries a torch for her, though. I think Sarah's our girl.'

But there's, like, something not quite roysh about this. Getting involved in this kind of shit isn't Fionn's style, roysh, he's usually, like, the sensible one. 'Don't take this the wrong way,' I go, 'but why are you doing this?' He stops flicking through the Alex yearbook for 1999 and goes, 'Because I've a cousin who thought she'd been called. Eighteen years of age and she decided she wanted to be a nun. A year later she walked out of the convent. Went out with her old friends one night and realized the life she'd been missing.'

I actually *know* the cousin he's talking about – her name's Alison – and though I've never told him this, roysh, and not wanting to sound bigheaded or anything, *I* was the one who actually turned her around. She was one of those edge-of-the-bed plastic surgeons, roysh, who sat there for half-an-hour, roysh, agonizing, if that's the word, over what she was about to do, kept blabbering on about 'sins of the flesh' and I was like, 'Make your mind up, Babes. It's me, or God,' and, well, it was basically a walkover after that.

Fionn's there, 'I just want to know that JP's sure about what he's about to do. Alison thought she was sure. Then she gave it all up, apparently after one night with some idiot who didn't want to know her afterwards,' and I'm there thinking, No comment. He goes, 'JP's always been a bit spiritual, certainly more spiritual than the rest of us, which I suppose wouldn't be hard. Like all those gospel songs he knows. I've no doubt he *thinks* that something happened to him in Israel. I think it would be remiss of us, as his friends, not to make sure he knows what he's doing.'

Then he goes, 'So why are you doing it?' and I'm like, 'The money.'

I really don't know why I'm so nice to my old pair sometimes, what with them being orseholes and everything, but you have to make the effort, because they *are* my parents, which means they're basically, like, family. And it was in that basic spirit, roysh, that I pointed the old Golf GTI in the direction of Foxrock to check if the fockers were still alive, or was I going to have my inheritance – *ker-ching!* – coming to me sooner than I thought.

They *were* still alive, worst luck, although they might as well not have been for all the attention they gave me. The two of them were in the study – we're talking major borfarama here – sitting together, working on their stupid focking campaigns.

The old man goes, 'You'll have to forgive me if we seem a bit distracted tonight, Kicker. The local elections are only ten days away and I've decided to make these new bin charges a central plank of my campaign. I expect you've heard they're now proposing to charge for refuse collection by the weight rather than the bag. Now you can wipe that worried look off your face right now, Ross, because I'm going to get myself elected and then I'm going to make sure it never happens.'

I go, 'Sorry, this affects me *how?*' but he just goes, 'Sleep easy in your bed and tell young Sorcha the same. I'm going to make a speech at this protest meeting tonight that'll send shivers through the body politic. Remember that book of Churchill's greatest speeches that Hennessy bought me when I decided to run for public office?' and I just look at him, roysh, as if to say, you are some knob. He goes, 'Well, it's been an inspiration. Hitler charged for refuse collection by the weight as well, did you know that?' The old dear looks at him over the top of her glasses and then he goes, 'Well, I'm not entirely sure if that's true, but it's the kind of thing he would have done.'

The old dear – the stupid wagon – goes, 'Charles, will you pass me a sheet of your good writing paper, darling?' and I go, 'Oh, it speaks,' which she ignores, roysh, and goes, 'How's Sorcha?' and I'm like, 'How's *Sorcha?* Not, how am *I?* I could have been dead in that hotel for the last week for all you two would have known,' and without looking up, roysh, she goes, 'I'm sure Sorcha would have mentioned it to us if you were dead, Ross . . .' and her voice sort of, like, trails off.

There's no mention of that calendar, roysh, so I presume they took one look at her with her kit off, saw what a hound she was and went, 'We can't put that out – people will think we're ripping the piss.'

I go, 'What are you working on anyway, you stupid cow?' and she goes, 'Something for Angela,' who's her friend from, like, Sandymount. I'm there, 'Funderland? I hope they bring ten focking big wheels with them this year. Bring even more scum to the area.'

The old man goes, 'It's not Funderland that's occupying your mother's astute political mind right now, Ross. It's this new campaign of hers to have Ringsend designated Dublin 4E,' and she's like, 'Not that your father's been any help,' and he's there, 'Afraid it's outside my remit, darling. I'm as anti-Ringsend as the next man, but it comes under the auspices of the City Council. I'm running for Dun Laoghaire-Rathdown County Council, remember?'

She goes, 'But you can't *agree* with what's happening, Charles. These are some of the most desperately poor people in our society. The fallen. Many of them won't work. They claim multiple social welfare benefits under various . . . *aliases*, I believe they're called by the criminal classes. And yet they're entitled to say that these little Lego houses they bought for nothing are in Dublin 4. Is it any wonder Angela's upset?' and the old man goes, 'It's an injustice, there's no doubt about that. Dublin 4 – the very idea of it! Of course, when the floods come, it's *béal bocht* time: "Help us out, Bertie. We didn't have any home insurance because we spent all our money on stone-cladding and these fearful Lucky Streak lottery tickets," quote-unquote.'

The old dear's like, 'And yet when they sell these little . . . *hovels*, they call them D4. Charles, they *have* to be stopped,' and the old man's there, 'I'm all for redesignation, darling. Dublin 4E sounds good to me. I'm no friend of Ringsend. You mentioned the floods, I think you'll recall that I went on the record at the time describing them as not an act of God but rather the wrath of God. A couple of thousand years ago, Our Friend would have sent locusts and what-not to deal with these people. The exact words I used in the letter which, if you'll remember correctly, *The Irish Times* declined to publish.'

She's there, 'I still think there's something you could be doing, as part of your campaign,' and the old man turns to me and he goes, 'Wonderful tension, eh Ross? Like all the great political marriages. Teddy and Eleanor Roosevelt. Bill and Hillary Clinton . . . not that you'd compare me to that . . . moral eunuch. Oral sex and what-not. I said it to Hennessy this morning, it might happen in the Oval Office, I said, but I'm happy to report that the hallowed halls of Dun Laoghaire-Rathdown County Council shall be free from such moral depravity if I'm elected. And I don't think I'd be far wrong in saying that Clinton charged for refuse collection by the weight, too.'

The old dear goes, 'Oh, Ross, I forgot to say, Anita Roddick has agreed to write the foreword. I phoned Sorcha this morning and she's thrilled,' and I'm there, 'What fore-word? What are you bullshitting on about?' and she's like, 'For the calendar, of course. I doubt *she* knows much about these Ringsend people.'

I'm there, 'Get this through your thick skull – you will NOT be appearing in any focking calendar. Unless it's one for the dogs' and cats' home,' and she goes, 'Oh, I'm so excited about seeing the pictures. Sally rubbed this oil into my body so it made it look—' and I'm like, 'That's it, I am SO focking out of here.'

I've loved a lot of birds in my time, roysh, but I've never met one I understood. Get this, roysh, there I am in Sorcha's gaff the other night and we're, like, watching a flick, we're talking *Cool Hand Luke*, when all of a sudden Sorcha storts going on about what an OH! MY! GOD! total babe Paul Newman is. She's giving it, 'He's the kind of goy who, if I ever got a chance to be with him, I'd expect you to understand if I couldn't resist,' and not being the jealous type, roysh, I'm there, you know, '*What*ever!'

But she doesn't leave it at that, roysh. She thinks it would be SUCH a cool idea to each write out a list of the people we'd be allowed to basically score if we found ourselves in that position. I mean, she *actually* gives me a pen and a piece of paper and she's going, 'Come on, Ross. We'll both write out our wishlists,' and like a fool, I go along with it, in the spirit of things, of course.

So anyway, roysh, fifteen minutes later, she hands me her piece of paper and it's, like, the usual, we're talking Aidan Quinn, we're talking Brad Pitt (underlined), we're talking Matt Damon, we're talking Gabriel Byrne, we're talking George Clooney. Of course, I'm like, 'Kool and the Gang,' and I stort looking around for the remote, roysh, thinking of lashing on 'Big Brother', see if that bird's getting her top tens out again tonight. That's when I suddenly become aware of the fact that Sorcha's, like, staring at me, or *glaring* is more like it, giving me daggers basically.

She's looking down at my list, roysh, then she looks up at me and goes, 'These are all people we *know*, Ross,' and of course I see the signs, roysh, we're talking red alert here. I'm there, 'You said it was a bit of fun,' but she's going, 'Sophie. Emma. Antoinette. Leanne. Zoey. Ali,' basically reading them out, roysh, trying to make me feel, I don't know, ashamed I suppose. She's like, 'Erika? How could you write her down after all that happened? Aoife? Ross, she's one of my best friends. I've just given her a job in the shop . . . Who's Clíona?' and I'm like, 'Er, Aoife's old dear?' and she looks at me, roysh, like I'm vom on her new Jimmy Choos.

She goes, 'I meant, like, famous people we'd no chance of ever being with. Not . . . hang on. You've got about thirty names down here,' and of course I'm kacking myself in case she whips the page over and sees I've storted on the other side as well. *Erika's* old dear is actually on the other side.

Either I've obviously misunderstood the rules of the game, roysh, or she's got a starring role in a period costume drama at the moment, or maybe it's a bit of both. What I do know is that there's no talking to her when she's like this, so I'm pretty much moonwalking out the door at that stage, telling her that I'll give her a bell when she's not in a position to actually legally kill me.

I'm on the Stillorgan dualler, roysh, stuck behind some tool who's doing, like, thirty in the inside lane in this, like, Ford Primera, which has, like, a loudspeaker on top, roysh, and it's only after driving behind him for, like, five minutes that I cop that it's actually Knob Features and Hennessy and they're, like, canvassing. It's actually Hennessy who has the wheel and the old man's, like, talking into the mouthpiece, going, 'For too long the wealth-generating classes, of which I am a proud member, have been made to feel guilt for what happened in the past. A vote for Charles O'Carroll-Kelly is a vote for an end to all that.'

He's going, 'Ireland in the seventies and eighties was, inverted commas, the Albania of Western Europe. No one had any money. The sun never shone. Young people emigrated by the planeload. Despite the Depression, despite crippling taxes and an infrastructure that made us the laughing-stock of the world, some of us refused to give up on this country. I'm talking about captains of industry, such as myself and my good friend Hennessy here, whose willingness to tough out the recession, to take a punt on good old Ireland, brought about the economic miracle that is the Celtic Tiger, quote-unquote.'

He's there, 'I make no bones about it. I played a part in the birth of this beautiful animal. I'm not saying I'm its father, but I was certainly one of those who provided the . . . sperm. I think that's an analogy best not teased out, Hennessy. Suffice it to say, I played my part, as did many of you, enjoying your beautiful homes along this wonderful stretch of dual carriageway. Did we ask for anything in return? No. We asked for nothing. Although I wouldn't turn down a doctorate if anyone from Trinity College is listening. I know Sir Anthony has one. Michael, too.'

Then he goes, 'When economists were writing-off this country, some of us stuck it out. And our reward? To be hauled before these wretched tribunals. *Where did that forty thousand come from? Where did that fifty thousand go? How many times did you visit the Caymans in 1984?* That's what people like Hennessy and I have had to listen to. Our reward for believing in this wonderful country, for being clever and resourceful, for sticking around to pay exorbitant taxes, or at least some of them, for pulling this nation of ours up from its knees, is to be treated like common criminals. Senator Joe McCarthy, how are you!'

He's giving it, 'I've a message here today for you, Bertie. And I know you know me, Bertie. I've been bunging Fianna Fáil money for years. And my message is this – NO

MORE! No more sacrificial lambs. No more Ray Burkes! No more Liam Lawlors! No more Michael Lowrys! Good men. Honest men. *Hounded.* Let's stop the hounding! A vote for Charles O'Carroll-Kelly is a vote to stop the hounding!'

I go roysh up behind him and just, like, rear-end the focker with my bumper. He goes, 'Refuse collection is a topic I'm sure is dear to many of your—' and then he's like, 'Oh, good Lord . . . good Lord, Hennessy, we're under attack. They're trying to silence us. They want us dead . . .'

Sorcha doesn't even ring, roysh, just shows up at the hotel, I suppose you'd have to say unannounced, and, like, knocks on my door. And of course my face drops, not because I'm not pleased to see her but because, roysh, I'm just hoping she's not here for a bit of the other. I'd a Hand Solo this afternoon and another one, like, fifteen minutes ago and now I'm totally wankrupt.

I'm there, 'Hey, Babes,' and she goes, 'Greystones,' and I'm like, 'Sorry, have I missed a few lines of this conversation?' She's like, 'There's new houses being built in Greystones,' and she hands me this, like, prospectus, which *is* a word before you look it up and I know, roysh, because I worked in the property game.

I go, 'I'm not living in Greystones,' and she's like, 'What's wrong with Greystones?' and I'm there, 'It's in Wicklow,' and she goes, 'Only just,' and I'm like, 'Which makes it Bogsville in my eyes.'

She's like, 'It's *hordly* Bogsville, Ross. It's, like, one of the most beautiful villages in Ireland. The beach and the horbour are amazing. And it's, like, still in the 01 area. And

Chloë and Steve have bought one of these places,' we're talking Chloë as in her friend Chloë. She goes, 'They only got, like, one of the townhouses, but we could afford one of the four-beds. *Oh my God*, Ross, are you even listening to me?'

I'm there, 'No, because Greystones is, I don't know, too far away,' and she's like, 'Too far away from *where* exactly? You don't work,' which may or may not be a subtle dig. I'm there, 'I'm thinking of *you*, believe it or not. How are you going to get from there to Grafton Street every morning?' and she's like, 'HELLO? If I get up at five o'clock, I can beat the traffic,' and I'm there, 'I don't know, Sorcha. I was thinking more towards the Blackrock end of things. See, I've always been regarded as a Southside goy,' but then she just, like, puts her hand on my knee, roysh, and storts sort of, like, massaging the inside of my leg, going, 'Please, Ross. For me. Let's just have a look.'

I'm there, 'Er, I don't know, Sorcha,' and she carries on, going, 'Please. I'll be *very* nice to you,' but of course I'm sitting here with an empty Luger, roysh, and you never walk into a gunfight with nothing in the clip. So I jump up, roysh, and I'm there, 'Yeah, okay, let's do it,' and she's like, 'Whoa! Why the sudden change of hort?' and I go, 'Just that stuff you said about the 01 numbers. Sounds great. And if Chloë and Steve are living there . . . come on, let's have a look.'

She's like, 'I'll make an appointment tomorrow,' and I can tell from the way she's looking at me, roysh, that she's gagging for it. I'm there, 'No, let's go now,' and she goes, 'HELLO? It's eleven o'clock at night?' and I'm like, 'Well, we can see how they look in the dork.'

*

The night of the election count, me and the goys had it all planned, roysh, to meet for a few scoops in the Horse Show House, then all bail over to the RDS to see Dick Features – the CO'CK of Foxrock – get totally humiliated. But we ended up having one or two more than we originally planned, roysh, and by the time we got there the count had actually finished and I couldn't focking believe what I was seeing – we're talking the old man, roysh, being carried around shoulder-high, *actually* carried around by Hennessy and a bunch of tools he plays golf with, and at the top of his voice, roysh, he's going, 'THE PEOPLE HAVE SPOKEN! THE PEOPLE HAVE SPOKEN!'

I'm there, 'What's going down?' and Fionn's like, 'It appears your father has topped the poll,' and, slow as ever on the uptake, I end up going, 'Is that a good thing?' and Fionn's there, 'I expect it's going to be very interesting finding out. For better or for worse, though, your father has just been elected to Dun Laoghaire-Rathdown County Council.'

The dickhead climbs up onto the stage, roysh, where – I don't believe it – he's *actually* going to make a speech. The whole place falls silent. Someone – could be Hennessy – shouts, 'Keep it short, Charles,' and there's all this, like, laughter, then the old man goes, 'Keep it short, *Councillor*,' and the whole place goes ballistic, everyone, like, clapping and cheering and shit?

He goes, 'And just to forewarn you – I won't be keeping it short. For today I've been given a mandate to speak. I've been given a mandate to speak on behalf of a section of our society who have, until this moment, remained mute. Those who – like my old friend Raphael P. – believe it's time to draw a line in the sand. I want to send a message out – and I want to send it out loud and clear – to Mister Bertie Ahern, who was once proud to sit in Cabinet with our old friend. That message is simple: we've had enough of your inquiries!' and there's all this, like, applause and shouting.

He goes, '*Where did you get this cheque? Where did you get that cheque?* Let's just remember one thing. *We* created the wealth in this country. We are the brains behind the Celtic Tiger. And yet for nigh-on years now, we've been subjected to this . . . McCarthyite, quote-unquote, witch-hunt.'

He's there, 'My own campaign manager has suffered. Hennessy, my loyal friend despite losing quite a lot of money to me on the golf course over the years, had his name dragged through the mud. An innocent man, forced to flee to Rio de Janeiro to escape the Star Chamber down at Dublin Castle. If you can't hold bank accounts under twenty-eight different names in seventeen different countries, then somebody go and wake up Mr A. Hitler Esquire and tell him they've reversed the result of 1945 after consultation with the video referee.'

I look at the goys, roysh, but they're all like me, just standing there with their mouths open. He's there, 'Our preoccupation with these tribunals, quote-unquote, is distracting us from the real issues. For the poor, the unemployed, the disenfranchised, I have a message for you today and that message is: GET LOST! You've had your fifteen minutes of fame, oh you were good, we all enjoyed you, but you're last year's thing.'

He goes, 'I have a great many plans, some of which I've already discussed at length with the people who matter – the voters on the doorsteps. In office, I intend to put forward proposals to demolish two thousand local authority dwellings in the Dun Laoghaire-Rathdown area and move the people out to new townships in Dublin 24. The land – prime with a capital P – will be sold to private developers and the money used to fund a much-needed marina in Dun Laoghaire harbour.'

My phone beeps and it's, like, a text message from Ronan. It's like, **Ur old mans a tool** and I send him one back and it's like, **Hav sum rspct, tht wankers ur grndfther** and he's like, **I no, dont tel ne1** and I'm cracking my hole laughing at that.

The old man's using his moment in the spotlight to bring up every little thing that's ever pissed him off in his entire life. He mentions the time that someone porked across the driveway of the gaff, blocking him in, and how he ended up arriving late to Portmornock on the day he could have won the Captain's Prize. He mentions the time the old dear was dumped as chairperson of the Foxrock Combined Residents Association and the time a sub-editor spelt my name wrong in a photo caption in *The Irish Times*. He even has a word for the way the IRFU treated Gatty.

Then he goes, 'For the management of the RDS, thank you for affording me this platform today. But there the niceties end. You know me well and you know the way my wife and I feel about your wretched funfair – this so-called *Funderland* – an abomination, bringing trainloads of, pardon my French, riff-raff into this area. Outside the jurisdiction of Dun Laoghaire-Rathdown County Council you might be, but MARK MY WORDS, I will continue to be a thorn in your side.'

Then he's there, 'And lastly, to you, Bertie. I know you're watching. You will find me a formidable adversary. And you can cap up every one of those letters. The F, the O, the R and so forth. We've already crossed swords once, when you tried to lead Irish rugby out to some working-class wasteland. I beat you then. Keep It South Side. That was my simple message. Well? Where's your stadium now, Mister Dis, Dat, Dees and Dohs?'

Everyone claps, roysh, but the old man silences them with, like, a sweep of his hand. He goes, 'Bertie and I still have outstanding business. He has taken away my right to carry my shopping to my car in a plastic bag provided free of charge by the supermarket. And he has taken away my right to enjoy a cigar with a well-earned brandy in Fitz-william at the end of a hard week. Bertie, this is one councillor telling you that you've got one hell of a fight on your hands. Quote-unquote.'

The whole place just erupts. The goys are in total awe. Oisínn's the only one who can get a word out. He goes, 'God help us all!'

Must be pretty much a year since I've seen Aoife and I don't know what she was doing in the hospital, roysh, but she actually doesn't look much better. She's supposed to be eating again, but I don't see it, roysh, though she *is* in cracking form, going way OTT with the air-kisses and the hugs and the *Oh My God!*s when I call into the shop.

I'm there, 'Is Sorcha around?' and she goes, 'Lunch. Anyway, do NOT mention her name to me. I'm saying SO don't mention it,' and I'm like, 'What's the Jackanory?' and she goes, 'I know she's, like, your wife and everything, but she has SUCH an attitude problem. She is being, like, SUCH a bitch to me today. It's like, OH MY GOD!'

I'm like, 'Where's she gone for lunch?' and she's there, 'She won't even let me give out staff discounts, Ross. That's like, HELLO? No, actually, it's more like, *Duuuhhh!*' and I'm there, 'Should I come back in, like, half-an-hour?' and she goes, 'No, she should be back any . . . here she is now,' and I spin around and there she is, roysh, looking – I have to say, even though I know she's basically my wife and everything – but looking amazing. I forget sometimes what a total babe she is.

Sorcha air-kisses me and goes, 'Heard about your dad. He must be SO pleased,' and I'm there, 'I wouldn't know. I don't talk to the stupid penis,' and then she turns around to Aoife and she's like, 'Anything happen?' and Aoife goes, '*Oh my God*, yeah, remember that Coco tube top?' and Sorcha's like, 'What, the polyamide panelled one? I sold it yesterday,' and Aoife's there, 'No, the girl brought it back. Said it didn't fit. She got a bit snotty when I told her we only did credit notes.'

Sorcha goes, 'Do you want to go for your lunch now?' and Aoife's like, 'I think I'm going to go to that place that you went to. The chowder is supposed to be OH! MY! GOD! *amazing*,' and Sorcha goes, 'It is. It's like, *Oh my God!*' and Aoife goes, 'I won't be long, Sweetie,' and Sorcha gives her a big smile as she's going out the door and goes, 'Take as long as you like, Babes,' and when she's gone she's like, 'OH! MY! GOD! That girl is being SUCH a bitch today.'

I'm there, 'She still doesn't look the Mae West,' and she goes, 'She wore that Diane von Furstenburg dress I bought in, as in the red, wine and light blue, rayon-blend one with the ruched cowl-neck?' and of course I'm like, '*No way!*' cracking on that I actually *give* a shit. She goes, 'She says she didn't, but I know she did. She wore it to her cousin's engagement porty and, like, put it back thinking I wouldn't *actually* notice. There's, like, fake tan on the neck. HELLO? I think I *know* her colour.'

I go, 'I think I'm going to hit the road,' and she's like, 'Okay, Ross. I booked La Mer Zou for half-eight,' and I'm there, 'That's a big bottle of Kool-Aid from my point of view,' and as I get to the door of the shop she goes, '*Chowder!* She'll have what she always has – popcorn and a bottle of water while speed-walking up and down Grafton Street for an hour.'

Sorcha wants to head down to the bor for a quiet one, roysh, though to be honest I'd rather hit the scratcher early with Carol Vorderman's *Ten Steps to a Size Eight*, which I borrowed from JP ages ago and which he's not going to be needing where he's going. She's like, 'Ross, you can't *not* celebrate your birthday,' and she won't let it go, so I throw on the old Leinster jersey and we head downstairs in the lift.

Of course, I'm slower than a focking ninety-year-old in a Subaru Signet. The reason she was so John B. to get me downstairs was because she'd organized a surprise Russell for my birthday. I should have known when she turned up tonight dressed to the hilt and the hum of *Issey Miyake* strong enough to drop the Budweiser Clydesdales from fifty yords away.

We walk into the bor and it's just like, 'SURPRISE!' and everyone's there, roysh – we're talking Christian and Lauren, we're talking Oisinn, we're talking Fionn, we're talking . . . actually the rest of them are, like, Sorcha's friends, as in Erika, Aoife, Claire from Bray, of all places, Sophie, Chloë, Amie with an ie, but fair focks to her for, like, organizing it.

I turn around to her and I go, 'This is incredible. I don't know how to thank—' and then all of a sudden I'm just, like, staring across the other side of the bor and I'm like, 'Who the FOCK invited *them?* I can't focking stand those two,' and Sorcha goes, 'Ross, they're your parents,' and I'm there, 'So-called . . . just make sure they stay out of my way,' and I turn around and Oisinn hands me a pint of Ken.

There's no sign of JP and I'm thinking he's probably copped it's me who's been sending him copies of *Juggs*, *Penthouse* and *Gentleman's Companion* through the post, unanimously of course, if that's the actual word. I just wanted to remind him what he was missing, soften him up for the old sucker-punch. And then I'm thinking he actually *does* know it was me, roysh, because two days ago I got, like, a text message from him and it was like, **Everything in the world - the cravings of sinful man, the lust of his eyes and the boasting of what he has and does - comes not from the Father but from the world. John 2:16**, which I suppose is his way of saying he's on my case.

The pints are going down like a bagful of Ag. Science birds. Christian and Oisinn both ask me, roysh, whether I actually guessed what was going on tonight and I said of course I did, roysh, but I just, like, played along with it so as not to hurt Sorcha's feelings, because obviously I don't want the goys thinking I'm as thick as a can of tuna, although I suppose they do know me.

'Storreee?' I hear it from the other side of the bor. Sorcha goes, '*Ronan!*' and she runs over to him and pretty much squeezes the life out of him, all four-foot-nothing of him. He's going, 'Ah, howiya, Doll, give us a look at ya,' and he sort of, like, gives her the once-over, roysh, and goes, 'I swear to God, Sorcha, if I was ten years older, you'd be fighting me off . . .' and Sorcha's like, 'If you were ten years older, maybe I wouldn't,' and then she laughs and goes, 'Ronan, these are my friends,' and she sort of, like, waves her hand in the direction of the birds, who all go, 'Hey, Ronan,' all except Erika, who's got this, like, sneering look on her face, roysh, and I know she's about to say something totally focking awful, roysh, and I'm actually getting ready to jump in between them when Ronan turns around and goes, 'Erika, yeah?'

All of a sudden, roysh, there's, like, total silence. She's like, 'Er, yeah?' sort of, like, taken aback a bit. He goes, 'A face as beautiful as yours, I can understand you being scared to wrinkle it. But, see, if you smiled, you'd probably bring the roof of this hotel down,' and I swear to God, roysh, it's true, in the ten years I've known Erika, I've never actually seen her smile, not properly, not an actual happy smile, none of us has, until that very moment. It takes, like, twenty or thirty seconds, roysh, for the corners of her mouth to go all the way up, but they do, roysh, and it's un-focking-believable. I swear to God, roysh, there isn't a person in the battle-cruiser who can't say she's the most beautiful-looking bird they've ever seen. Ronan goes, 'There you are, boys, the sun's up,' and he turns back to Sorcha, who brings him over to us.

Fionn's going, 'I don't know what I've just witnessed. It's like the Aesop's fable – about the sun and the wind trying to get the man to take his coat off. Ross, he's . . . *unbelievable*,' and Christian's like, 'I think he could be the one referred to in the prophesy, the one to restore balance to the Force,' and when he arrives over he goes, 'What's the story, Rosser? Happy birthday, man,' and then he turns around to Fionn and goes, 'The brains, right?' and Fionn laughs and goes, 'That's me,' and then he turns to Oisinn and goes, 'The man who makes all that what-do-you-call-them?' and Oisinn's there, 'That's roysh. I notice you're a *Blue Stratos* man,' and Ronan goes, 'Ah, man and boy, Oisinn, man and boy,' and then he turns around to Christian and goes, 'And you're the wingman – Christian, right?' and Christian goes, 'You got it,' and Ronan's there, 'He takes some looking after, I'm sure. And the lovely Lauren . . .'

While this is going on, roysh, I notice the old pair have, like, retreated into the far corner, with their backs to us, bullshitting away to Hennessy, who's just arrived, and I'm thinking, If they don't want to know him, it's their loss, and then I look back at Erika and she's still smiling, roysh, like a dog who's just discovered a new trick, and all the other birds are just, like, staring at her, going, '*Ohmygodohmygodohmygod*,' with the occasional, 'OH! MY! GOD!' thrown in for good measure.

Ronan hands me a present. It's not wrapped, roysh, except in a Champion Sports bag. I open it and – I am not yanking your chain, roysh – it's an *actual* focking Celtic jersey, the old skobie tunic, and I turn around to him and I go, 'I don't know what to say,' and he's there, 'Get that faggoty rugby one off you. Have a butcher's at the back,' and I turn it around, roysh, and he's actually got the word ROSSER printed above the number six. I'm like, 'Ronan, it's . . . it's perfect.'

The next thing, roysh, one of the bormen comes over

to me and he goes, 'I'm very sorry, Sir, but we're not supposed to have children on the premises after . . .' and I'm there, 'He's not drinking – can he not just . . .' and Ronan goes, 'Can't stay in anyhow, Rosser. Buckets of Blood's out in the car. Told him to keep the engine ticking over, I'd only be a minute. I'll give you a bell,' and he gives me a wink and gives Sorcha a peck on the cheek and then he's out the door.

The old pair take this as their cue to, like, rejoin the porty. All of a sudden Knob Features and Hennessy are up at the bor beside me, bullshitting away to each other how these Chinese will work for nothing and Hennessy's going, 'Though not literally,' and the old man's like, 'Well, more's the pity.'

The old dear's talking – I cannot *actually* believe this – she's talking to Oisinn, who's going, 'There she is – heard you're going to be one of those Page Three stunners,' and sort of, like, laughs, pretending to be embarrassed basically, and goes, 'Oh, I wouldn't have anything worth looking at,' and I don't believe it, roysh, she's *actually* trying to flirt with one of my mates and I swear to God, roysh, I think I'm actually going to spew my ring. Of course, Oisinn's loving it and he's, like, ripping the piss on a major scale. He's got, like, his orm around her shoulder and he's going, 'You're a *very* attractive woman, Mrs O'Carroll-Kelly,' and she's sort of, like, giggling away like a schoolgirl and I can't actually take it anymore and I end up turning around and going, 'HAVE SOME FOCKING RESPECT FOR YOURSELF, YOU HOUND!' and then I turn around to the old man and I go, 'Is there a reason why you're hanging around like a bad focking smell?'

He's like, 'Well, there *is* actually. Okay, can we have a

bit of hush, everyone,' and he storts, like, tapping his Mont Blanc pen off his brandy glass, making a total tit out of himself and, far more importantly, me. He goes, 'I shall be brief. Since my election to political office, I have to use my voice a bit more sparingly,' and Hennessy's going, 'Shame! Shame!' and then Oisinn and Fionn join in, because they know I'm bulling.

He's like, 'Well, we all know why we're here – to celebrate the latest birthday of young Ross there. Fionnuala and I are very grateful that we have such a wonderful relationship with him. Non-stop talking and occasional joshing and so forth. We probably don't tell him enough that we're very proud of him. He's made a wonderful success of his marriage – eventually,' and there's a big, like, cheer. He goes, 'He's been successful at rugby and . . . well, lots of other things too, I'm sure. Now, Ross, we *do* have a little surprise for you, if you'd just like to follow me . . .'

He actually loves the attention. I follow him out of the bor, through the lobby and out into the cor pork, as does everyone else and . . . OH MY GOD! I cannot focking *believe* it, roysh, it's actually a cor. Not just *a* cor. We're talking the BMW Z4 here, as in the one that Pierce Brosnan tore the shit out of in *Goldeneye*, we're talking six-speed gearbox, we're talking speed-sensitive power-steering, we're talking cornering enhancement, we're talking sports seats, we're talking leather steering wheel, we're talking automatic soft-top.

The old man's going, 'Precision-engineering, Kicker . . .'

I don't know what to say. We're all, like, standing around outside the Berkeley Court, roysh, and I'm having basic palpitations looking at it, roysh, going, 'Th . . . Th . . . Th . . .' and the old dear turns to Sorcha and goes, 'What's happening to him?' and Sorcha's there, '*Oh! My! God!* I think he's *actually* trying to say thank you.'

I'm like, 'Tha . . . Tha . . . Tha . . .' and everyone's out on the road, roysh, giving it loads, going, 'Go on, Ross! Go on!' and I'm looking at the old man and I can feel my throat closing over and I'm like, 'Than . . . Than . . . Than . . . YOU'RE THE WORLD'S BIGGEST FOCKING TOOL,' and everyone sort of, like, groans, roysh, like when I missed that last-minute penalty in the Leinster Schools Cup final in 1998, and I sort of, like, collapse into Sorcha's orms and she's going, 'Don't worry, Babes. You did SO well.'

I look at my old man and I go, 'You're a focking dick-head,' and he's like, 'Quite right, Ross.'

Sarah Glenny *still* looks like Sienna Miller. The bird she's with looks like Eric Miller, but for ten grand, roysh, I'd be prepared to take a bullet, or at least give the impression that I'd take one. Daphne is its name – a complete and utter ditch-pig, if ever there was one – but I'm there giving it, 'I definitely know you. I never forget a face. Especially one as pretty as yours,' and I really don't know how I live with myself sometimes.

She goes, 'Have you met my friend, Sarah?' and she does the introductions, roysh, and Sarah's there, 'I already know you,' and I'm like, 'How?' and she goes, 'OH MY GOD, *everybody* knows Ross O'Carroll-Kelly,' and I look at Daphne and she seems to, like, consider this a good thing.

The music in Ron Black's is blasting. I go, 'I hope you don't mind me chatting-up your friend,' and Sarah goes, '*Oh my God*, no! Hey, you know JP Conroy, don't you?'

and I'm there, 'Just so happens he's one of my best friends,' and she's like, 'OH MY GOD! I kissed him the night of the Junior Cert results. *Oh my God*, SO embarrassing. And then I did the dirt on my boyfriend with him. How is he?' I'm there, 'He's Kool and the Gang. Single at the moment, as it happens,' and Sarah goes, 'Oh MY God! This is, like, SO embarrassing – I don't even know why I'm telling you – but I used to always say to my mum, "He's the goy I'm going to marry," and it's like, *Aaaggghhh!*' and Daphne goes, 'You actually *did* always says that. I was always like, *Oh* my God!'

I stand there listening to this shit for, like, twenty minutes, roysh, tanning the Ken of course because you need a seriously good anaesthetic for these two. Then it gets to the stage where I basically can't take it anymore so I basically make my pitch. I'm there, 'I'm actually staying in JP's tonight,' which is total bullshit, roysh. I go, 'Do you two fancy coming back with me for a few drinks. Might be a way for you to get *reacquainted*, if that's the roysh word, with the goy you're going to marry,' and Sarah sort of, like, flicks her hair, roysh, which she does a lot, and goes, 'OH MY GOD!' which she also does a lot, and before they have a chance to finish their vodka and cranberries, the three of us are in a Jo Maxi, pegging it out to JP's gaff, Sarah in the front constantly going, 'OH MY GOD! I cannot BELIEVE I'm *actually* doing this,' and me in the back with Daphne, who keeps whispering to me that she can't believe I find her attractive because most goys fancy Sarah and she, like, never gets a look-in. I'm just there, 'I find that very hord to believe,' trying to keep a straight face.

JP does NOT look a happy camper when he answers

the door. He's like, 'Ross, it's half-one in the morning,' and I'm there, 'You need to get a life. Look, I've brought you a focking carry-out,' and I just, like, flick my thumb in Sarah's direction, just so he knows he's not getting the dud. Daphne, it turns out, is even worse in the full light.

JP goes, 'Sarah! *Wow!* I haven't seen you since . . .' and she's like, 'I know,' and he's there, '*Wow!*' and I wonder when he storted saying *Wow!* instead of *Holy Fock!* He goes, 'You look great,' which is the first sign since we came back from Israel that there is actually still life in his trousers. He goes, 'And how's, em . . .' and she goes, 'Tadgh? *Oh my God*, we finished, like, ages ago. You know what Michael's goys are like,' and everyone just, like, nods.

I'm, like, scanning the gaff for evidence of how far this thing has gone. There's a book opened face-down on the coffee table and it's, like, *The Passion* by Geza Vermes and there's a focking humungous whack gone out of the Baileys, which now has a bottle of focking *Crème de Menthe* beside it for company. It's worse than I thought.

He goes, 'Girls, would you mind if I had a quiet word with Ross, in private?' and he sort of, like, grabs me by the orm, roysh, and pulls me into the kitchen and goes, 'What do you think you're doing, Ross?' and I go, 'When did you stort drinking *Crème de Menthe?*' and he goes, 'I asked you first.' I'm like, 'Are you focking slow on the uptake all of a sudden? That bird's gagging for you out there. And not the ugly one either.'

He just looks at me, roysh, and shakes his head, like he's all disappointed in me and shit, then he goes, '*Jesus was led by the Spirit into the desert to be tempted by the devil. After fasting forty days and forty nights, he was hungry. The tempter came to him and said, "If you are the Son of God, tell these stones to become bread"*,' and I'm like, 'Meaning?' and he goes, 'Ross, I thought you understood what I was doing. And why.'

He's actually good at focking guilt-tripping you, this goy, which will make him a huge hit in the priesthood. I'm there, 'JP, I thought you needed a bit of fun. You don't stort in Maynooth for another couple of months. There's nothing in the Bible to say you can't get your rock and roll between now and then,' and he shakes his head and goes, 'I've no interest, Ross. And I've no interest in that . . . *filth* you've been sending me either,' and I'm there, 'Oh, so you won't be wanting your Carol Vorderman DVD back then?' and he doesn't even flinch. He goes, 'I've promised myself to the Lord, that's the way it is.'

Fair focks to him, roysh, he goes back into the sitting-room and actually explains the situation – in other words God, etc. – to Sarah, who takes it pretty well, it has to be said. She's a bit embarrassed, roysh, and she storts, like, moonwalking her way towards the door, throwing out the odd, 'OH! MY! GOD!' on the way.

I'm looking at Daphne, roysh, she doesn't know what to do – does she leave with her friend, or does she stick around for the loving of a lifetime? – so straight away I just, like, relieve her of that little dilemma. I'm there, 'I hate long goodbyes,' and, being a nice goy, I slip her ten bills and I go, 'Get yourselves a Jo,' and it's all happened so fast, roysh, she doesn't know how to respond. She's standing there with her mouth open so I just go, 'Take the hint. Beat it,' and her eyes just, like, fill up with tears.

JP shows them both to the door, apologizing all the way, the sap that he is, while I pour myself a glass of *Crème de Menthe*, just to see what all the fuss is about. He comes back in and he goes, 'That was nasty, Ross, if you don't mind my saying so,' but I'm reading the label on the bottle, roysh, and I go, 'Focking hell, this shit is 50 per cent proof!'

We're sitting in my new cor, BMW Z4, outside this gaff on Newtownpork Avenue, roysh – we knocked back the one in Greystones – waiting to give it the old once-over. JP's old man finally arrives and he's, like, all apologies for being late, then he storts the tour. He goes, 'Although I know *you'd* do a better job than me,' and he's sort of, like, reminiscing I suppose you'd have to call it, about the time I worked for him as well and I'm wondering is he, like, dropping the hint that he wants me to come back now that he's, like, lost JP to God.

I ignore it and we stort following him around. He's going, 'It's a solid three-bed semi-d with adjoining garage extension situated on a highly regarded road in upmarket Blackrock, close to a range of top schools – including your own *alma mater* – shops, public transport and just five miles – a two-hour drive to you and I – from St Stephen's Green . . .' He's giving us the whole spiel, roysh, but I have to say his hort doesn't really seem to be in it. It's like he's going through the motions. Not only has his son and heir gone bonkers, but the word is that he's going to have to shell out some serious wedge to some secretary bird who's doing him for sexual harassment – supposedly he grabbed her orse and went, 'Is this seat taken?' and I'd say he actually definitely did do it, roysh, knowing him like I do and seeing the way he's copping an eyeful of Sorcha's rack every time he thinks I'm not looking.

Sorcha goes, 'I'm not being rude, Mr Conroy, but would you mind if I had a look around . . . without the commentary?' and JP's old man just, like, shrugs his shoulders and goes, 'Hey, you guys can see through my bullshit anyway. Feel free . . .' and he sort of, like, looks at me and nods in the direction of the kitchen and I follow him in there, roysh, leaving Sorcha to go exploring by herself.

He leans against the island and he goes, 'It's my birthday today, Ross. Know what he bought me?' and I'm like, 'Happy birthday . . . what?' and he's there, 'A gift voucher . . . for Veritas,' and I go, 'What kind of a sick . . .' and he's there, 'I've given up hope.'

I can hear Sorcha upstairs, admiring the back bedroom, which looks out onto a south-facing, landscaped rear garden offering total seclusion – it's amazing how that shit never leaves you. She's going, 'OH! MY! GOD! This can be Ronan's room when he sleeps over,' and I know she's already made her mind up on the gaff.

I'm there, 'I've tried everything. I've even sent him a few, shall we say, *exercise* magazines through the post,' and he goes, 'Hey, great minds . . . I thought of that too. It's just . . . well, you hear things. There's rumours doing the rounds,' and I'm there, 'Rumours?' and he's like, 'Ross, you're JP's friend. Remember, by telling the truth, you're helping him . . . is it true he's started drinking Baileys?' and I sort of, like, turn away. I can't look the dude in the eye. He goes, 'I thought so,' and even though it's probably in JP's best interests, roysh, I can't bring myself to tell him about the *Crème de Menthe* – no father needs to hear that about his son.

He goes, 'Can't you just, I don't know, stick a couple of Viagra in the bottle?' and I'm wondering why the fock I didn't think of something like that. I'm like, 'Where would I actually get Viagra?' and he goes, 'Here,' and pushes these two pills into my hand. He's like, 'That's the last of them,' and then he sort of, like, leans in close to me and goes, 'Seeing this broad tonight. Air-hostess. Tits like udders. Now I'm in serious danger of disappointing her,' and I'm thinking, He really *is* a perv.

I slip the pills into the Davy Crocket of my chinos and we go back out into the generously apportioned, skylight-lit hallway. Sorcha's coming down the stairs. She goes, '*Oh my God!* We *love* the house,' and I'm there thinking, What's this *we*, Paleface? when she turns around and goes, 'We'll take it,' and I'm there, 'Er, okay,' and that's how I end up agreeing to pay eight-hundred-and-twenty Ks for a house that I haven't even looked around.

Well, my old man's paying.

Ronan's out somewhere. Walking, by the sounds of it. He goes, 'Got me at a bad time, Rosser. I'm on me way up Henry Street. Get the cheap tobacco,' and though I used to think he said those things to, like, scare me, roysh, now I'm not so sure. I'm there, 'When are you off?' because Tina and this Anto she's going out with – he's actually called Decker – are taking him to Ibiza for two weeks and Tina's old pair are going as well. He goes, 'Seven o'clock tomorrow morning. Probably won't get to see you before you go, will I?' and it's nice, roysh, because he actually sounds disappointed.

I'm there, 'Not to worry, we'll do something together when you get back,' and he goes, 'Game ball. And no messin' around behind Sorcha's back while I'm away. I heard you left Reynard's with two a couple of weeks back. One was bet-down, I hear,' and I'm there, 'Nothing happened,' and he goes, 'I hope not. You know I'm not bluffin' when I tell you I'll find out, don't you?' and I'm there, 'Yeah, I know that. Hey, we bought a gaff. In Blackrock,' and he goes, 'That's good. Stability's what you need in your life, Rosser,' and in the background I hear him ask for six pouches of tobacco. Then he goes, 'I've got to go,' and I tell him to have a good time, roysh, and I'll see him in two weeks.

7. A Cheap Holiday

The old dear rings me – there's no focking fear in her, I can tell you that – and she goes, 'Your father and I wanted to invite you and Sorcha over for dinner on Friday night. We want to celebrate your new house, we're so pleased for you and Sorcha, Ross,' and I'm there, 'Why would we want to go to your house for dinner?' and she's like, 'Because it's borlotti bean, pancetta and rosemary risotto – Sorcha's favourite,' and I'm there, 'Excuse me while I spew.'

I'm there, 'Sorry, is there anything else?' and she goes, 'Oh, yes. I got the proofs back,' and I'm there, 'Proofs? What the fock do you mean, proofs?' and she's like, 'From the photo shoot. I think I know which one I'm going to choose. It's the one Sally likes as well. I'm leaning over the chair and my legs are—' and I'm like, 'I DON'T WANT TO FOCKING KNOW!' and I hang the fock up.

'Nothing's wrong.' That's what I tell Sorcha when she bells me on the Wolfe, but she knows me too well. She goes,

'You're not yourself. Anyone can see that,' and I'm there, 'It's this JP business, I suppose. I was talking to Fehily this morning and he didn't think there was much hope. Said JP had been, like, called and shit.'

Sorcha goes, 'It's not that either. Ross, you're missing him – why don't you just admit it?' and I'm like, 'Missing JP? That's benny talk,' and she's there, 'I'm talking about *Ronan*. It's okay for you to say it,' and she's basically spot-on. I've only known the little focker a few months, roysh, but he's grown on me in a major way.

Sorcha goes, 'He texted me this morning. He's missing you as well,' and I'm there, 'Really?' and she's like, 'In his own way. Only one more week, Ross,' and I go, 'I suppose,' and she's like, 'What are you doing?' and I go, 'Just sitting in my room, flicking through . . .' and I can't tell her it's *FHM*, roysh, in case she thinks I'm having an Allied Irish, so I just go, '. . . I don't know, *Newsweek*.'

She goes, 'Do you want company?' and I'm there, 'What about the shop?' and she's like, 'HELLO? I *think* Aoife can look after things for a couple of hours,' and I go, 'Yeah, that'd be nice then.'

The second she arrives she's, like, straight on my case, going, 'OH! MY! GOD! Will you *look* at this place! When was the last time you actually let them in to clean?' but I don't answer, roysh, and eventually she goes, 'I'm sorry, Ross. I'm, like, SO hord on you sometimes. Here,' and she hands me an envelope, roysh, and she goes, 'A present,' and I open it and it's, like, a flight to Ibiza.

She goes, 'It's just for the weekend,' and I'm like, 'When am I going?' looking for the date on the Wilson, roysh, and she's there, 'Your check-in is in an hour,' and I'm like, 'An hour? I can't . . . I've no, like, summer gear with me,' and she's there, 'You can buy it in duty-free,' and I tell her that I'm speechless and she tells me to hurry up because I'm already cutting it majorly fine.

The heat hits me straight away, roysh, as if someone's opened, I don't know, an oven door, even though it's, like, ten o'clock at night. I mosey through passport control, pick up what few threads I managed to throw together from the carousel, then go out through the arrivals gate and stort looking for Ronan. As usual, I hear him before I actually see him. He goes, 'Rosser, you steamer!' and he's, like, standing there in his Celtic jersey and not, I notice, the Leinster one I bought him for going away.

I don't know what to do at first, roysh, it feels a bit awkward, but in the end I go with it and give him a hug and when I pull away, roysh, he storts, like, dusting himself down and telling me he has a rep to live up to and that if I'm into that kind of thing, I should keep it to the rugby dressing-room.

I crack my hole laughing and I go, 'Are you having a good time?' and he's there, 'Ah, it's mustard, Rosser,' and I look around and realize for the first time that he's, like, here on his own. I go, 'Did you come to the airport by yourself?' and he's there, 'No, the others are in the bar.'

The bor? They let a focking seven-year-old saucepan wander around an airport on his own just because they can't say no to a drink? Ronan can tell I'm not a happy camper from the basic speed I'm walking. He runs up behind me, grabs me by the orm and goes, 'Stall the ball, will ya?' and I'm there, 'That shit's not on,' and he goes, 'ROSSER!' really loud, roysh, so loud that I actually stop, then he's like, 'You can't just march into our lives and start laying down the law, Rosser. You can't tell me Ma the right and wrong way to raise a kid. She hasn't done a bad job, y'know,' and listening to him talk, I know he's roysh, and I decide to say nothing.

'Did you change yisser money?' That's the first thing Tina's old man shouts at me when I walk into the bor. He's like, 'Ders a bayoo-ro de chonge out dare,' and he points outside, and I actually turn around, roysh, and I'm about to go back out when they all – we're talking Tina, her old pair and Decker, her Ken Acker of a boyfriend – crack their holes laughing. Tina goes, 'Don't *moyind* him, Ross. It's all yoo-ros over here, like in Oyerlind,' and I end up being made to feel like a total focking tool.

They're all hammered, of course. On the sauce all day, by the looks of it. Her old dear's off her face and she's practically asleep, sitting there on her low stool, red as a focking lobster, obviously having gone out in the sun with no cream on and barbecued the shit out of herself. Tina's the colour of milk and so is Decker, roysh, who's wearing the same Celtic jersey as Ronan and I feel this, like, sudden, I suppose you'd have to call it jealousy, roysh, that he'd rather wear what Decker wears than what I wear.

Decker goes, 'Are ye gettin' dem in or wha'?' which is basically Skobie for, 'Buy us all a drink,' which, like a fool, I do, roysh, the round being pint bottles of Bulmers for Tina and Decker, a Guinness for Tina's old man and a West Coast Cooler for her old dear, who wakes up when the drink's put in front of her. Ronan gets himself a Coke because, as he says himself, he doesn't want to get into rounds.

When I come back from the bor, Decker's looking inside Tina's mouth, presumably for any gold fillings he can rob

so he can buy, I don't know, hash and Aslan records. Tina closes her mouth and goes, 'Ask Ross,' and then she turns around to me, roysh, and she's like, 'Notice anyting diffordent 'bout me, do ye?' and I am SO tempted to say something really funny, roysh, except I can't actually think of anything, so I end up going, 'No,' and she sticks out her tongue, roysh, and she's actually got the focking thing pierced.

I'm a bit, like, squeamish about that kind of shit, roysh, and I have to, like, turn away, which Decker thinks is focking hilarious. Tina goes, 'I got it done today. It's killin' me but,' and her old man goes, 'Maybe you're not aposed to drink wirrit,' and Tina goes, 'Fook dat,' and of course that is also the funniest thing that anyone's ever said in the history of the world.

Ronan at least tries to make me feel, I don't know, comfortable, I suppose. He's like, 'Wait'll you see the apartment, Rosser. It's the fooken business,' and I'm about to tell him that I'm actually going to look for somewhere with a few more stors than they'd be used to, roysh, when all of a sudden my, like, conscience gets to me and I decide to stay in whatever Ballymun-on-Sea tower block their tour operator has dumped them in.

We finish our drinks and I'm, like, looking at my watch, thinking I wouldn't mind shooting off now and catching a few zeds because I'm, like, totally wrecked at this stage. Decker goes, 'Will we gerra Jo back to de gaff, or will we have anudder one?' and Tina and her old man laugh like it's the stupidest question they've ever heard. Decker turns around to me, like the focking skanger that he is, and he goes, 'Tink you'll find it's your round.'

*

Ten o'clock I hear noise coming from the kitchen, roysh, and I go out to find Tina's old man – Eddie's his name, if the tattoo on his left hand can be trusted – frying what looks vaguely like sausages, bacon and eggs, except they're floating in so much oil it reminds me of one of those Greenpeace newsletters Sorcha gets after some tanker has spilled shit all over the gaff, killing everything within, like, a 10-mile radius. He's like, 'Bitta brekky dare, son?' and I'm there, 'I'll, em, pass on that, if it's all the same,' and he goes, 'A woy-iz man. Sure de sausages ardent de sayim over hee-er. De bacon eeder.'

Ronan sticks his head in from the balcony, where he's smoking one of his famous rollies, and he goes, 'Moy Jaysus, what the fook are you wearin'?' and straight away I'm there, 'This jersey? It's, like, the New South Wales Waratahs,' and he shakes his head and tells me I'm some fooken tulip and he asks me do I know that.

I go, 'Sorcha texted me this morning. She's been on the internet. Said we should check out Aquamar. It's, like, a waterpork and shit?' and Ronan's like, 'Fooken deadly,' stubs out his cigarette, then goes, 'I'll go and ask me oul' dear,' and disappears into the next room.

Eddie's still working the pan, even though there's fock-all left to fry in it, roysh, everything's been, like, incinerated, if that's a word. The next thing, roysh, Tina comes out of the bedroom and goes to me, 'How are ye gettin' dare?' and I have to say, roysh, even though I thought I'd have a few problems with the language coming over here, I pre-sumed it would be when I was talking to the *actual* locals. I'm there, 'Sorry?' and Tina's like, 'HOW . . . ARE . . . YE . . . GETTIN' . . . DARE?' I go, 'Oh, I'm going to rent a cor. Sorcha checked it out for me. Said there's a place down the street.'

Decker comes out of the bedroom then, wearing a focking bogball jersey, we're talking Dublin. He goes, 'Do us a favour, whatever-you're-called. If you're taking him out, don't bring him back till late,' and Tina's there, 'What are ye sayin', Decker?' and Decker goes, 'I tought we'd check out dat new club. Get a few yokes into us,' and Tina goes, 'You don't moyind takin' um for de day, do ye?' and I'm about to go, Of course not, he's my focking son, isn't he? but in the end I just go, 'Of course not.'

I cop Ronan staring at Decker, then he disappears into his bedroom, roysh, and comes back, having changed out of his Celtic jersey into the Leinster one I bought him. Then we hit the road, roysh, and before we know it we're lead-footing it towards Playa d'en Bossa in a rented Seat Toledo, 1.9 litre, five-door with air-conditioning, with the Snoopster giving it loads on the CD player.

We're driving for, like, half-an-hour, roysh, when I notice that Ronan's pretty quiet, so I turn around to him and I go, 'You're not a fan of Decker's, are you?' and he sort of, like, shrugs his shoulders and goes, 'Just don't think he's good enough for me Ma,' and I am SO tempted to say that I think they're focking perfect for each other, but I end up biting my tongue and I can tell from Ronan that he doesn't want to talk about it anymore.

After a few more miles of road, he goes, 'So what's this place got, then?' and I'm there, 'Well, according to Sorcha, we're talking slides and rapids and all sorts of shit,' and Ronan goes, 'Happy days.'

So we go in, roysh, and all the various amusements keep him entertained for, like, twenty minutes, then he comes over to where I'm sitting, sipping an Americano, watching all the basically Spanish yummy-mummies mill about the place. I'm there, 'Are you, like, enjoying yourself?' and he goes, 'Ah yeah, but it's for *kids*, isn't it?' and he plonks himself down in the chair beside me, calls the waitress over and orders a double espresso for himself.

There's something on his mind. I can tell. I go, 'So, spit it out, Ronan,' and he just smiles at me as if to say that I'm basically a mind-reader. He goes, 'That school you went to, Rosser...' and I'm there, 'Castlerock?' and he's like, 'Yeah. Would they take me, would they?' I go, 'They have a junior school, yeah. It'd be a bit of a long trek for you in the mornings, wouldn't it?' and he goes, 'Right, I'm going to have to level with you. There's no other way to do this,' and he takes a long drag on his cigarette, knocks back his coffee in one mouthful, then goes, 'I've been kicked out of school, Rosser.' I'm there, 'Kicked out? As in, like, expelled? What for?' and he goes, 'Demanding money with menaces. Well, bullying, *they* called it,' and I'm like, 'And you want me to put your name down for my old school? That's what you're asking me, I presume?'

He's there, 'I swear to you, Rosser – not telling ye a word of a lie – I'll keep me nose clean,' and I go, 'What does your old dear think?' to avoid having to give him a straight answer. He's there, 'That's the problem. She knows fook-all about this. It'd kill her, see. She's not a great coper. That's why I try to make things easier for her,' and I'm like, 'So, you don't plan to tell her? That you've, like, changed schools and shit?' and he goes, 'Of course I'd tell her, but I'd crack on that I was big into rugby all of a sudden and I wanted to follow in your footsteps.'

He orders another double espresso while at the same time checking out the top tens on the waitress. I'm there, 'You have this all worked out, don't you? What about the fees? You know the junior school is, like, five grand a year?' and he taps the side of his nose and goes, 'Don't worry, I know where I can lay my hands on that kind of bread,' and I'm there, 'No focking way, Ronan,' having visions of him holding up a security van or something. I go, 'If you're accepted – and by no stretch of the imagination am I guaranteeing that you will be – I'll pay the fees. Deal?' and I'm thinking I'm on safe ground here, roysh, because there's a waiting list for Castlerock and you've got to have your kid's name on it before the midwife has even cut the focking cord.

Ronan goes, 'Game ball. Not a word to me oul' wan, 'member. It'd break her fooken heart,' then he knocks back his second double espresso and tells me he's going to have one last shot on the giant waterslide.

They're hammered, as usual. Don't get me wrong, roysh, I like my pop as much as the next man, but I don't think they've been sober for longer than ten minutes since I got here. It's, like, three o'clock on Sunday afternoon and we're all sitting outside the Fiddler's Elbow, roysh, and Tina and Decker are tanning the old Bulmers, while Tina's old dear is singing, '*Alice, Alice, who de fook is Alice . . .*' with three random birds at the next table, none of them easy on the eye. It's one of those nights you just *know* is going to end in karaoke.

Tina's old man is telling me that, 'Peepil tought Bang Bang was mad, but Ine tellin' ye he was as normal as you or I, clever is whoree was, made a bleedin' faar-chin ourra de too-erists, so he did.' I wink at Ronan, who's as happy as a dog with two mickeys since I told him I'd put a word in for him at Castlerock – he's actually smoking a lot less – and even though I know, roysh, that they'll tell him to take a focking hop, at least I can say I tried.

Eddie's going, 'Fortycoats was the sayim,' but I'm not really listening, roysh, I'm actually listening to Tina, who's telling Decker that her tongue is really sore where she got it, like, pierced and Decker says didn't he tell her not to gerrit bleedin' done, but you wouldn't listen, you stupid fooken slapper, which I don't think he should be saying in front of Ronan, or even actually Tina's old pair.

I'm about to say something, roysh, when all of a sudden Ronan gets up and says he has to go back to the aportment and I ask him does he want me to come with him, roysh, but he says he's mustard, which is Working Class for kosher, and he heads off, which is no bad thing, roysh, because it's a pretty bad atmos. There's, like, total silence, roysh, and Tina's trying to ignore Decker, but the goy's just, like, staring at the side of her face with pure focking hatred in his eyes.

Tina's old man tries to lighten the basic mood. He nods in the direction that Ronan went and he goes, 'Unbelievable dat wan, wha'?' and I'm there, 'Suppose he is, yeah,' and he's like, 'Years ahead of his time. You know, when he was foyiv, he bleedin' hot-wired me car, so he did.' I'm there, 'You're shitting me now?' and he goes, 'Not tellin' ye a woord of a loy, son. Hot-wired me car. Didn't get far ourra de droyivway now, but he started de fooken ting.'

I just like shake my head and I can't help but smile. He goes, 'I decided – I said it to ye, didn't I, Tina? – I said, "We're gonna have to givum a scay-er. De short, sharp shock treatment." So I took um down de stay-shun, see a mate a moyin what's a guard. Used to play ball wirrum.

Says I to um, "Lock um in de cells for an hour. Put de frighteners on um." So he did. Turned de key an' locked um up. After an hour he goes back into um and says he, "That's what happens to young fellas what gets in trouble wi' de law." An' says young Ronan to um, "I've nuttin to say to ye, Copper. I want me brief",' and we all crack our holes laughing, roysh, all except Decker, who goes, 'Should have fooken *left* him locked up,' and everyone's just, like, silent until about ten seconds later when he turns around to me and goes, 'Have ye a fooken problem gettin' yisser round in, have ye?' and even though it's not actually my round, roysh, I hit the bor anyway, I suppose just to get away from the situation.

I ask the borman for two more pint bottles, a bottle of Ken – except I have to say, like, the full name – a pint of Guinness and a Hierbas Ibicencas, which is what Tina's old dear has moved onto and it's probably best not to even ask. So the borman's putting the top on the Guinness, roysh, when all of a sudden Ronan's standing beside me and goes, 'What are you doing, Rosser?' and I'm there, 'Getting them in,' and he's like, 'You got the *last* round,' and I go, 'Look, Ronan, sometimes it's just easier to . . .' but he turns around to the borman and he goes, 'We're only going to be needing one of them Bulmers,' and he pushes one of the bottles back across the bor. Then he picks up half the round and he goes, 'He's a fooken bully, Rosser. Stand up for yisserself,' and we carry the drinks back over.

'Am I fooken black, am I?' That's what Decker goes when he realizes there's no drink for him. He's like, 'Am I fooken black, am I?' and I don't answer him roysh, I turn around and start listening to one of Eddie's Yoo-ro

Eigh-d-Eigh stories, cracking on that I haven't heard it before. So Decker just, like, shouts it then, roysh. He's like, 'ARE YOU LOOKIN' FOR A FOOKEN TUMP? I SAID, AM I FOOKEN BLACK, AM I?' and I don't know where it comes from, roysh, because I know it doesn't sound like me at all, but I turn around and I go, 'No, you're a focking skobie. If you want a drink, spend some of that focking dole money that you already ponce off the rest of us. Or are you keeping it to buy more focking sovvies, you social-security-sucking scumbag,' and everyone's jaw just, like, drops, including my own, it must be said.

Eventually, roysh, he gets it together and he goes, 'I'll fooken boorst ye for dat,' and he goes to stand up, roysh, but Ronan just, like, stands in front of me and goes, 'I don't tink so,' and Decker goes, 'Wha', are *you* gonna stop me, are ye?' and Ronan goes, 'Do ye want to find out?' and when he doesn't answer, roysh, Ronan goes, 'I've just been back to the apartment. I've packed your bags and put them in a taxi. It's waitin' for ye. You're on the eight o'clock flight. Your ticket's at the airport.'

Decker goes, 'Ask me bollicks,' and Ronan's there, 'You can go home tonight and sleep safe in your bed. Or you can go home another time and have a welcoming party waiting for you,' and suddenly, roysh, Decker's not so cocky. He just, like, stares at me, roysh, then at Ronan and then back at me. Then he goes, 'Fook yiz in anyway,' and he gets up and storms off.

Suddenly there's this, like, round of applause, roysh, and I wasn't actually aware that so many people were, like, listening in. Ronan looks at me with his eyebrows sort of, like, raised and goes, 'Social-security-sucking scumbag? Bit over-the-top that, wasn't it?' and then he laughs, roysh, and I do NOT believe it, roysh, but for the first time since I met him, he high-fives me, he *actually* high-fives me, and I'm thinking there might be hope for him yet.

I'm there, 'Where did you get the money? For, like, the flight and shit?' and he goes, 'Hope you don't mind, I rang Sorcha,' and I'm there, 'Sorcha? That was very, like, generous of her,' and he goes, 'Not really, she gave me your credit card number,' and I'm there, 'Oh, roysh.'

Tina's turned on the old waterworks and her old dear's, like, comforting her, roysh, telling her that he's not woort it and then she goes, 'Ye know what'd really cheer us all up?' and I know what's coming, roysh, even before she says the focking word.

I'm in the sack, roysh, half-awake, half-asleep and totally hammered, on the one hand looking forward to getting back to Sorcha, but on the other not wanting to say good-bye to Ronan again for another week. 'I Will Survive' is still, like, thumping around in my head. Tina must have sung it, like, six times. That and 'Beautiful'. *I am bayoorifil – no ma'er what dee say.* Even the manager was pissed off with her at the end. *Woords won't bring me dow-in.*

I'm drifting into a dream involving basically Holly Valance, Jessica Alba, Mischa Barton and a tub of Ben and Jerry's vanilla caramel fudge, we're talking the 500 ml one, when all of a sudden I'm woken up by Tina, who's come into my room, roysh, and is standing over the bed. She's totally focking mullered, of course.

I'm there, 'What's the Jackanory?' and she goes, 'Do ye not remember it, do ye not?' and I'm there, 'What are you, like, talking about? Remember what?' and she goes, 'Dis,' and as my eyes sort of, like, I suppose adjust to the light, I cop what she's talking about. She's wearing the nightdress – *that* nightdress – we're talking the one she was wearing the night I took her to heaven and back.

I go, 'Tina, it's late. You're hammered. Ronan's in the next room,' but she ignores me, roysh, sits on the edge of the bed and storts, like, running her hands up and down her legs. She has unbelievable pins, I think I mentioned. She goes, 'You're not gone all shy on me now, are ye?' and I'm there, 'I'm just saying, you're locked. You're also very focking fertile. Look where it got us last time,' trying to let her down gently.

She goes, 'So if I offered meself to ye now, you'd say no, is dat royt?' and even though she's not the Mae West, roysh, I'm totally, like, mesmerized, if that's the roysh word, by her legs. I can't stop looking at them. She goes, 'If I offered ye a nigh'a passion, dee answer'd be no, would it?' and I go, 'Tina, I'm pretty much a married man these days.'

All of a sudden, roysh, she whips back the covers and of course her eyes go straight to the old womb broom, which is on duty and we're talking big-time. She goes, 'You *look* interested to me,' and I go, 'That's not *for* you. It was actually for Mischa Barton,' and she's like, 'I'm shoo-er it was,' as she goes to, like, slip under the covers.

I'm there, 'Tina, this is SO not a good idea,' and as I say it, roysh, I can suddenly feel her fall like a dead weight on, like, my chest? I'm there, 'Tina? *Tina!*' and I sort of, like, push her off me, roysh, then lash the old light on. She's out for the focking count. Horrendufied, I presume.

The next thing I know the room is full of voices. Her old man and her old dear are, like, slapping her Brendan

Grace and, like, throwing water over her, trying to bring her round basically and Ronan's not saying anything, roysh, he's looking at me, standing there in my boxers, then at Tina in her nightdress, *that* nightdress, then back at me again, like he knows what was going on but he doesn't want to believe it.

Eddie goes, 'We better get ur to de hospital,' and I'm like, 'A hospital? Bit severe, no? She's just locked,' but Eddie's like, 'She's a stomach like a fooken goat, dat one. Drink a bleedin' docker under de table, so she would. Ders sometin wrong.'

The ambulance arrives, roysh, she's stretchered out of the gaff and her old pair get in the back with her, while me and Ronan follow them in the Seat Toledo. Ronan doesn't say a word the whole way there.

Of course by the time we arrive, they've already, like, discovered the problem. It was, like, the tongue ring. According to the doctor, roysh, she had a thing called metal-allergic contact dermatitis, which induced toxic shock. Don't look at me, roysh, I'm not a medical man, but what I got from that basically was that pretty much poison went into her blood and it was, like, lights out, Baby.

The four of us are sitting in the waiting-room while the doctors fix her up to some sort of drip or other. When Tina's old pair are, like, talking among themselves, Ronan turns to me and out of the corner of his mouth, roysh, he goes, 'What happened?' and I'm there, 'Nothing, Ronan. And we're talking totally,' and he's like, 'It wouldn't want to have.'

*

244

Fehily answers on the tenth ring. He goes, 'Sorry about that, my child. I'm trying to dig out one or two old 45s I thought I had of our old friend's speeches. What can I do for you?' and I go, 'If I had this *friend* who had a kid – now we're talking purely hypocritically here, if that's the roysh word – but if that *friend's* kid wanted to join Castlerock, as in the junior school, but he was, like, a bit on the old WC side of things, what would you say?'

He's there, 'WC, eh? Well, we're very full at the moment. There's a waiting list, you see. Has this *friend* of yours tried Terenure?' and I go, 'No, but I'll make sure and suggest it. Thanks, Father,' and he goes, '*Auf Wiederhoren,*' and I'm there, 'Yeah, whatever.'

I'm throwing the last of my shit into my bag, roysh, when the phone rings and I'm told that someone's down in reception looking for me and that someone is, like, JP's, old man. When I go down, roysh, he's chatting up the Keira Knightley one, telling her that her boyfriend's a very lucky goy and he hopes he knows it and she's sort of, like, blushing I suppose you'd have to call it.

I'm like, 'Let's get a drink,' and before we even get to the bor, roysh, we can see that the place is basically jammers. JP's old man goes, 'Bit busy for a Tuesday afternoon, isn't it?' and as we get closer, roysh, I can see that it's basically half the hotel staff and they're knocking back the drink, some of them totally mullered, even though it's only, like, four o'clock.

I'm there, 'Looks like some kind of staff porty,' and the second I walk through the door, roysh, everyone gives me this, like, big cheer and, like, raises their glasses to me. I think nothing of it, of course. I've always known how to handle my popularity and I just give them a little wave, then we find a table in the corner and I click my fingers at one of the lounge birds to get her attention.

I order a bottle of Ken and JP's old man orders a double Scotch and when the lounge bird comes back with the drinks, roysh, he goes, 'What's the party in aid of?' and she looks a bit, I don't know, embarrassed you'd have to say, then she sort of, like, nods in my general direction and goes, 'Well, Mr O'Carroll-Kelly is checking out of the hotel on Friday,' and I'm there, 'Bit of a poor show that, me not being invited to my own leaving porty?' and, after putting the drinks on the table, she looks over her shoulder sort of, like, awkwardly and goes, 'It's more of a . . . *celebration*,' and JP's old man cracks his hole laughing and gives her the change from a twenty as a tip, which actually puts me in bad form.

I'm there, 'What's all this about?' and he goes, 'What's it about? I want to know is that son of mine any closer to remembering why this precious God of his gave him a dick?' and I just, like, shake my head. He goes, 'What about the Viagra?' and I'm there, 'Well, I called around to his gaff. Said I wanted to borrow a couple of *Messenger* magazines . . .' He goes, 'And he wasn't suspicious?' and I'm like, 'He was at first. I just said I was passing Foxrock church, saw all these people coming out of, like, Mass and wanted to find out what all the fuss was about for myself. So he went into his bedroom and I sort of, like, broke up the tablets and dropped them into the Baileys.'

He sort of, like, shakes his head and goes, 'He's keeping them in his bedroom? Jesus, this is worse than I thought. Anything since?' and I'm there, 'I don't know. I mean, we're close but not *that* close. He certainly hasn't told me if anything's, like, stirred. But personally, Mr Conroy, I think he's a lost cause.'

He goes, 'I think you might be right,' and then he sits back in the chair, rubs his face, then grabs his Scotch, throws it back in one and then just sits there sort of, like, studying his empty glass. Then he snaps out of it and goes, 'I've tried reason. Called to see him yesterday. Tried to get him to see that just because he's found God doesn't mean he has to become a priest. I said, "What's wrong with being a Christian *and* working for your father?" Know what he says? "I *am* working for my Father." I said, "Not the father who paid eight grand a year to put you through school. Where was *He* then?" He told me not to blaspheme.'

I'm there, 'I think we've lost him to this crowd, whatever they're called,' and he goes, 'Roman Catholicism. I think you might be right. You know, his mother's over the moon. Thinks it's great. I had to tell her to stop telling her friends. Can't help but think there's still a chance of winning him back. Which is why I'm upping the bounty,' and I'm there, 'Upping it?' and he nods and goes, 'It's twenty, Ross. And tell those friends of yours. Twenty grand to get the boy back in the saddle.'

She looks at me, roysh, like she's just caught me in bed with her sister. Actually, that's a touchy subject. I'm there, 'I'm *going* to the closing, Sorcha, I told you. I've just got to shoot off afterwards, that's all,' and she goes, 'This was *supposed* to be our special day, Ross. *Oh my God*, we've bought a house. I *thought* we were going to go for dinner to celebrate,' and I go, 'But that was before the goys rang. Look, I said I'll be there when the cheque's handed over today and I will,' and she's just there – here it comes, roysh, it's been in the post for a while now – 'Don't bother. I'll get *Daddy* to come with me,' because she thinks that'll get a response from me, but I'm not scared of him anymore. She goes, 'I'll tell you what, you just do what *you* want to do,' to which I reply, 'Kool and the Congregation.'

She's not in the best of form this week, it has to be said. I think she realizes it was a mistake taking on Aoife. I tend to switch off when she's talking work, roysh, but from what I can gather, Aoife gave Oonagh, as in some nurse she knows from the hospital, fifty bills off a pair of Chanel cream and soft grey, shimmery, trim nylon, fold-over, mid-calf boots, even though she was told, roysh, that she wasn't allowed to offer staff discounts, and Sorcha is not a happy camper about it. There's no need to, like, take it out on me, though.

The goys are already in the M1 when I arrive later in the day. Oisinn looks unbelievably smug, and why wouldn't he? He ended up scoring that bird who came over from New York and he's got a million sheets on the way from Hugo Boss, meaning the goy's basically set up for life. I'm actually surprised he's even *interested* in JP's old man's money, but when I tell him that there's now twenty Ks on the table he sort of, like, whistles, roysh, and goes, 'This'll bring out the big game hunters.'

Fionn goes, 'Personally, I think we're wasting our time. I phoned him the other night and all he wanted to talk about was the Book of Ezekiel,' and Christian shakes his head, roysh, and goes, 'Madness,' which is focking hilarious coming from the goy who texted me this morning asking me who I think would win in a fight between Bossk and Chewbacca, as in a fair fight, we're talking no laser rifles, no bow-casters and definitely no interference from Chenlambec.

Oisinn goes, 'Just remember, impossible is nothing, goys,' and I go, 'Why are *you* interested? It's not like you need the shekels anymore,' and he goes, 'Even top international perfume designers have to earn a crust. Anyway, it's, like, easy money.' I'm there, '*Easy money?* Have you, like, *totally* lost the plot?' and he goes, 'Let's just say I've a plan,' and Christian goes, 'What kind of a plan?' and Oisinn's there, 'All in good time, my friends.'

So anyway, roysh, six or seven pints into the evening, my phone suddenly rings and it's, like, Sorcha and she's having a TOTAL knicker-fit, we're talking screaming, we're talking bawling, we're talking basically going totally ballistic, and it's definitely not the usual blob strop, roysh, because she had that last week. She's going, 'HELP ME ROSS! HELP! *AAAGGGHHH*! PLEASE COME, ROSS!' and I'm there, 'Where are you?' and she's like, 'IN BLACKROCK – WHERE THE FOCK DO YOU THINK? I just came to measure up and ... *AAAGGGHHH*!'

Of course, what else was I going to do except knock back the rest of my pint and peg it out to Blackrock as fast as the Jo would carry me and there she is, roysh, in the kitchen, standing on top of the island with a sweeping brush in her hand and her slap all over the gaff from crying. And she just, like, points to the middle of the floor and I look down and I cannot focking believe what I'm seeing with my own eyes, we're talking – get this, roysh – a focking snake, we're talking an actual snake, here – as in an *actual* snake? – in the middle of the kitchen floor and he's, like, looking straight at me, roysh, flicking his tongue in my general direction.

She's going, 'KILL IT, ROSS! KILL IT!' and I'm thinking, What happened to Save the Animals? Of course, without a thought for my own safety, I end up just, like, grabbing the sweeping brush and milling the focking thing. Five whacks and he's toast. I lash what's left of him into a bin-liner and throw it outside and when I get back in, roysh, Sorcha jumps down off the island and into my orms and from the way she looks at me, roysh, I feel like the best husband who ever lived.

Moving gaff is actually stressful enough, roysh, without any more, you'd have to say, complications. I've already dropped the John Rocha signature champagne flutes that Sorcha's old dear gave us as a house-warming present and I haven't seen the girl so upset since I told her – purely for the crack, roysh – that Fungi had been killed by Japanese whalers.

She pretty much bors me from carrying anything of value into the gaff, roysh, so there I am, bringing in my two Leinster rugby jerseys while she's struggling up the steps with the Waterford Crystal Hospitality Five-Arm Chandelier, when all of a sudden my phone rings and it's, like, Ronan. He goes, 'Good news, Rosser. I'm in,' and I'm like, 'In?' and he's there, 'Yeah, that school you went to. They've accepted me,' and I end up nearly dropping the phone.

I really expected more of Fehily, but it turns out, roysh, that Ronan skipped straight to the top of the waiting list because 1) my old man went to the school; 2) I don't know if I've mentioned it, but I captained them to their first Leinster Schools Senior Cup since the 1920s and was an all-round legend basically; and 3) Fehily hasn't actually focking met him.

Ronan goes, 'Got the letter last week. I'd have rung you, but I was busy. Problems with one or two of me investments, if you catch me drift,' and I'm there, 'So when do you stort?' and he's like, 'Started this mornin'. Orientation, they call it. Filled in a few fooken blanks for me, I can tell you that. It's no wonder you turned out like you did,' and I go, 'Excuse me?' while trying to hold in the laughter.

He goes, 'Ah, they're some shower of ponces out there, Rosser, so they are. Every sham in the place has two second names. Either that or they're called something Irish. Putty in the hand though,' and I'm there, 'Putty in the hand? Meaning?' and he's like, 'The other kids. Walked in there and I could sense the fear straight away. Suddenly there's a kid from the wrong soyid of town in among them. I walks straight up to this young fella – shiteing it, he was – and I says to him, "Who's your best man?" and he says, "Excuse me?" just like you do, Rosser. I says to him, "The best fighter in the class?" and he points out this little weedy fella – fooken Risteóir Ó Gallachór or some shite. So I walks straight up to this kid and I says, "Risteóir, there's a new face on the landing . . ."'

I'm there, 'Ronan, is that prison slang?' and he's like, 'It is, Rosser. Ah, you tend to pick it up in the circles I move in,' and I go, 'So, should I brace myself for a call from Father Fehily? Is that why you're ringing?' and he goes, 'No, you're sorted. There'll be no squealers. I'll rule this school with a reign of terror,' and I'm there, 'Ronan, me and you need to sit down and have a little chat. I presume your first day of actual school is next Monday?' and he goes, 'It is, yeah. But I've already got a new nickname. Overheard a couple of the other kids callin' me The General.'

Ten o'clock, roysh – I'm up ridiculously early – I'm wolfing down the old brekky when all of a sudden Sorcha sticks this piece of paper practically in my face, roysh, and goes, '*Look!*' and I take it off her and it's like, '**Lost: Slinky, a pet garter snake. If found, do not panic. Totally harmless. Contact Joanna**,' and then it has, like, a mobile number and an address, which is basically next door.

Sorcha goes, 'I found it in the letterbox. As in this morning?' and she's sort of, like, staring at me, expecting me to say something. Eventually, she goes, 'You need to go and tell this Joanna what happened,' and I look at her, roysh, like she's mad as a box of frogs. I'm there, 'I *do* hope you're ripping the piss,' but she's actually not.

I'm there, 'You want me to call in next door and go, "Hi, I'm your new neighbour. Oh, by the way, I've just battered your pet snake to death with a sweeping brush. And in case you want to give him a proper burial, his body's in our back gorden, wrapped in a focking black bin-liner"?'

Sorcha goes, 'Ross, you're lucky I'm still here after what you did to that snake. You *know* how I feel about cruelty to animals,' and I'm just there, 'But that's not what you said when—' and she's like, 'I don't *actually* want to hear it, Ross! OH MY GOD, why is sorry such a hord word for you? I'm asking you, Ross, to go next door and apologize . . .' and she just sort of, like, leaves it hanging like that and like a fool, roysh, I actually end up doing what I'm told.

As it turns out, roysh, I'm pretty happy I did at first, because Joanna turns out to be a little hottie, roysh, we're talking Nadine Coyle here, and from the very second she opens the door I can tell she likes what she's seeing. I'm wearing my black Ralph Lauren airtex, roysh, which shows off the old bod pretty well. I'm there, 'I'm Ross, your new neighbour,' giving it loads basically and she goes, 'Joanna,' and she shakes my hand and goes, 'Come in. Mum and Dad aren't here. I'm just here with my cousin,' and I'm like, 'I won't stay long. Just popped in with a bit of, em, bad news I suppose you'd have to call it.'

She goes, 'Oh? Well, come on, we're in the kitchen,' and she pushes open the kitchen door, roysh, and I don't believe it – we're talking, HOLY FOCK! – *what* are the focking chances? Her cousin only turns out to be Oreanna, as in the bird whose cat I killed, as in the bird whose dog I killed. And not surprisingly, when she sees me, roysh, she has a bit of a knicker-fit. She's going, 'OH MY GOD, no! *No!* Get him out of here, Joanna! *Get him out!*'

I don't want to come across here as some sort of, like, Hannibal Lecter dude, so I'll just explain, roysh, by way of, like, background, that both deaths were total accidents and we're talking *totally* here. I swung the old Golf GTI into her driveway in Greystones one night and ended up catching Simba a glancing blow with my front wheel. My only crime, I suppose, was not telling her, just popping his sorry bones into the boot of the cor with the intention of focking him in the Dargle on the way home. Of course, Oreanna whips open the boot to put her tennis gear in the next morning and sees Simba there doing an impression of a Gino Ginelli 14-inch ham and pineapple. As for the dog, the thing was humping my leg. I just, like, stood up, took four steps backwards and three to the side and then launched him – Rog-style – at the wall. How the fock was I to know that a) he had a weak hort and b) Oreanna was standing at the door watching the whole show?

Both times I was just, I suppose, unlucky, but Oreanna's not going to listen to reason. She's hysterical, roysh, and she's going, 'Where's Shasta? Where is she?' and she's, like, running around the kitchen, roysh, looking in cupboards and under tables and chairs. I turn to Joanna and I go, 'Who's Shasta?' and Oreanna goes, 'My new dog. You stay away from her!' and I'm there, 'Look, I think I better go,' and Joanna goes, 'I think it's probably best,' obviously still wanting me, but deciding there'll be other times. So I'm doing my usual moonwalk towards the door, roysh, when Joanna turns around and goes, 'Oh, you said you had some bad news,' and of course I'm there, 'Sorry?' trying to buy myself some time basically. She's like, 'You said you'd some news. It's not about Slinky, is it?' and I can't think of anything else to say, so I go, 'Basically.'

She's like, 'Is he . . .' and I can't do it to her, roysh, I can't bring myself to tell her that he's gates, so I end up going, 'I just wanted to tell you that I saw him. He somehow got into our house. He looked fine. Healthy, basically. And happy, if that's any consolation to you.' She's like, 'So what's the *bad* news? You said a few minutes ago that you'd *bad* news,' and I'm there, 'Did I?' and she goes, 'Yes. *Bad news, I suppose you'd have to call it* – that's what you said.'

So quick as a flash, roysh, I go, 'I just don't think Slinky's coming home,' and off to one side I can hear Oreanna going, 'NO! NO! NOT AGAIN!' and Joanna's like, 'Why do you think that?' and I go, 'He just seemed, like ... happy, with his, like, independence. He was excited about setting off on his own, at least that was the vibe I got from him,' and she's looking at me, roysh, like I'm off my focking cake.

Then Oreanna storts up, going, 'He killed him, Joanna! That's what he does. He kills animals! He's the goy I told you about, remember? He killed Simba and he killed Scooby! And I'm telling you he killed Slinky as well and he's come in here to – OH MY GOD! – *actually* gloat? OH MY GOD, I just hope he hasn't gotten to Shasta,' and I'm looking at Joanna, roysh, and it's pretty focking obvious from the way she's looking at me that she actually believes her.

I look at her and I go, 'Roysh, I am SO out of here,' and I head for the door. It's been a day of surprises – there's no focking doubt about that – but even so, roysh, I'm not ready for what's waiting for me when I open the door on my way out. Shasta – who turns out to be another Jack Russell – she's sitting there on the doorstep, roysh, wagging her tail, basically looking all focking delighted with herself. She's got something in her mouth as well and, of course, there's me, roysh, still trying to convince the birds that I'm, like, an animal lover.

I'm going, 'Hello, Shasta! Hello, I suppose, little dog! Is that a present for us? What have you got there?' and I sort of, like, get down on my hunkers and – OH FOCK! – I suddenly see what she has there. It's, like, a piece from a black, plastic bin-liner. And in front of her, there's Slinky, hard as a focking stick, with his head mashed in. Then the waterworks go on. The two birds stort bawling their eyes out and then Oreanna storts screaming, like she does.

I turn around and I go, 'Stupid idea for a pet anyway. A snake, for fock's sake!'

8. Consider the Lillie's

Oisinn sends me a text, roysh, and it's like, **Thnk of a way of getting JP into Kielys on sat night. Plans all n place.**

Saturday morning, roysh, I hit the old Fleck Republic to offer Ronan some, I suppose you'd have to say, fatherly advice about storting in Castlerock next week – we're talking don't bring a knife with you, don't get caught selling hash behind the boiler-house, that sort of thing.

Tina answers the door, not a bit embarrassed about what happened in Ibiza. She goes, 'Himself's out in the garden, havin' a smoke, ye know yerself,' and I swear to God, roysh, I'd actually fight for full custody except the contamination's gone too far. The kid's a skobe now, always will be and I have to accept it. My, I suppose, priority now is to make sure he doesn't disgrace the family name. The O'Carroll-Kellys have been going to Castlerock for over a hundred years and even though Ronan's second name is actually Masters, the school knows the score and the only reason he's there is because he's basically my kid.

Try to imagine my total surprise, roysh, when I walk out into the gorden to find Ronan puffing away while reading a book called *Rugby Made Easy*. I sneak up on him and I go, 'Finally showing an interest in the old gentlemen's game, I see,' and he goes, 'Ah, Rosser, me old segosha. I'm just reading the rules here. Trying to understand what makes you tick,' and he tips a long length of ash onto the ground, puts the cigarette in his mouth, roysh, then storts leafing through the book, looking for a particular page. He shows me a picture, which I think is Ireland against Romania. It's two packs anyway. He's like, 'What the fook is that, would ye mind tellin' me?' and I can't help but laugh. I'm there, 'It's called a scrum, Ronan,' and he goes, 'It's an excuse for you lot to see each other's arses up close.'

I'm trying not to laugh, roysh, but I end up just, like, cracking my hole. He flicks through the book again, then comes to a picture of some English player, roysh, shaping up to throw the ball into the lineout. He goes, 'And what do you call this dude?' and I'm there, 'He's a hooker,' and Ronan's just, like, shakes his head and goes, 'That's some kinky shit going on there. By the way, how's the gaff?'

I'm there, 'It's Kool and the Gang. We've, like, moved all our stuff in. It's just, like, unpacking now, then decorating. Sorcha has a lot of ideas for the place,' and he goes, 'Boot you out – that's the best idea in the world. I said that to her,' and I'm there, 'Thanks for that, Ronan. Look, can we be, I don't know, serious for a minute. I want to talk to you about school. I don't want to sound like my old man here, but being a student at Castlerock brings with it certain, like, responsibilities . . .'

He laughs as he's lighting up again. He goes, 'I think The Rosser's asking me not to do anything to disgrace the family name,' and I'm there, 'Exactly,' and he goes, 'You've some fooken Gregory, I'll say that for you. I had a chat with oul' Fehily. A gas character altogether. Told me some of the shit you got up to in your day. And your oul' lad. Fehily was in his class, y'know. Ah, don't worry, Rosser, I'm woyid,' and I'm like, 'Wide?' and he goes, 'Yeah, woyid. If you're good at rugby, you get away wi' moorder. You don't tink I'm readin' this buke because I suddenly fancy men, do ye?' and I just go, 'I suppose not.'

He drops his cigarette and puts it out with his foot and then he's like, 'I'll give you a bell later. Got to head. I'm playin' ball – a *real* man's game.'

Sorcha rings me and she goes, '*Oh my God*, that girl is SUCH a bitch,' and I'm like, 'Who?' and she's there, 'Aoife. You remember I told you I was keeping back that Donna Karan ecru cotton safari shirt until I got my pay-cheque?' and I'm there, 'Yeah,' obviously not having a focking clue what she's talking about and she goes, 'Well, she sold it. She *actually* went and sold it.'

I was the one who managed to, like, prise him out of his aportment is all I'm saying, roysh, but Oisinn's going on as if that's not a big deal in itself. He goes, 'And this entitles you to what exactly?' and I'm there, 'All I'm saying is that if this works, I'm entitled to half the money his old man put up, that's all,' but he doesn't answer, roysh, just slips his hand inside the pocket of his Henri Lloyd, whips out the bottle, gives it a shake and goes, 'This is going to be the easiest twenty Ks I've ever earned. JP better show.'

I'm there, 'He'll show. How does this shit work again?' and he sort of, like, throws his eyes up to heaven and goes, 'This *shit* just so happens to be nature's love potion, Ross. This here is pure Andtrostenol. It's a pheromone,' and he looks at me and he knows he's going to have to explain it to me again. He goes, 'Pheromones are naturally occurring bodily chemicals which are secreted when we sweat. They are colourless and odourless and yet they have a powerful effect on human behaviour, specifically sexual attraction and drive.'

These beers are going down well. I'm like, 'But if you can't actually smell them . . .' and Fionn throws in his two euro worth then. He's like, 'That's a good question. Pheromones are scents that we don't smell, as such. We detect them subliminally through a small receptor in the nose called the vomeronasal organ, which then sends a signal to the hypothalamus portion of the brain, stimulating sexual attraction,' and I'm just nodding, roysh, pretending I know what the fock he's talking about, like I used to at school.

Oisinn goes, 'Ross, have you ever met a woman and felt an unbelievably strong chemistry,' and I'm there, 'Every weekend, dude.' He's there, 'But that's just horniness; I'm talking about *chemistry*. Look at, say, Christian and Lauren,' and Christian suddenly brightens up. Oisinn goes, 'We're talking chemistry in its purest form. That's pheromones at work.'

Faye and Amie with an ie, as in, like, Sorcha's friends, arrive over. Faye's had the big-time hots for JP ever since they were, like, thirteen and in Irish college together, but they've never actually scored each other, roysh, although they nearly did at a porty in Oisinn's gaff one night, but JP was still technically going out with Frederika – as in, like, Russian and Byzantine Studies in UCD? – and Faye ended up drinking half a bottle of vodka and telling him that a fortune-teller told her that he was the man she was going to marry. I've been there once or twice myself – I mean, she looks like Lindsay Lohan – but she was only ever using me to get to JP, who she's basically in love with.

So the two birds come over and, like, air-kiss us all. Amie with an ie, who's looking pretty hot herself, tells Christian that they saw him and Lauren walking down Grafton Street last Sunday and they looked – OH! MY! GOD! – SO cute and Faye goes, 'OH MY GOD, it was like, *Aaawww!*' and Amie with an ie's there, 'No, it was more like, Oh *my* God!'

Oisinn is not a happy camper. He goes, 'Faye, you're wearing *Tommy Girl*,' and she's like, 'Oh my God, yeah,' and he's there, 'I *told* you not to wear anything,' and she's like, 'Go out wearing no perfume? That's like, OH! MY! GOD!' and he goes, 'I don't care what it is, Faye. I told you, perfume cancels out the effects of natural pheromones. Here,' and he hands her the bottle, roysh, and he goes, 'Wash that stuff off before you put this on, otherwise it won't work,' and the two birds disappear off to the bathroom. Amie with an ie's got the old Uggs on, roysh, and though I've never been an Ugger-Hugger myself, pins like hers would actually make me think again.

So JP arrives while they're gone, roysh, and God or no God, the goy's in cracking form. He's actually looking well and he's all, like, happy and shit and for the first time, roysh, I stort feeling guilty about my port in tonight. I'm there, 'So when are you storting in, like, Maynooth?' and he's like, 'Next week. Can't wait. I just feel like I've been morking time, even though I've been reading and thinking and praying. I'm afraid patience is the one fruit of the spirit the Lord is having difficulty persuading me to eat,' and we all just, like, nod, cracking on that we know what he's bullshitting on about, but it *is* amazing, roysh, because the goy has this, like, aura.

I turn around, roysh, probably trying to justify in my own mind what we're about to do, and I go, 'JP, I know you're really, like, happy and shit, but your old man's worried about you,' and quick as a flash, roysh, he's there, 'Ecclesiastes tells us, Ross, that to the man who pleases Him, God shall give wisdom, knowledge and happiness. To the sinner, He gives the task of gathering and storing up wealth, which is meaningless, a chasing after the wind,' and there's pretty much no answer to that.

He looks over my shoulder and he goes, 'I don't believe it. It's Faye Connolly. I haven't seen her for . . .' and the dude suddenly pushes past me, roysh, and, like, throws his orms around Faye, who's just come back from the can.

JP's, like, looking her up and down, roysh, going, 'So how *are* you? Did you finish in Portobello?' and she's like, 'OH MY GOD, that's, like, *ages* ago? I'm repeating the Blackhall exams. For the, like, tenth time? And what about you? How's your mum?' and he goes, 'Mum's great. I've got loads to tell you,' and he slips his orm around her shoulder, roysh, and sort of, like, ushers her over into a quiet corner and Oisinn goes, 'Easy. Money for jam.'

Christian tells me that Prince Xizor used powerful pheromones to seduce Princess Leia and I'm knocking back my pint, wondering what I should do with this information, when Amie with an ie turns around and hands Oisinn back

the bottle and goes, 'Here, it wouldn't fit in Faye's bag.'
Oisinn holds the bottle up, roysh, sees the massive whack
gone out of it and goes, '*Shit the bed!* Don't tell me she put
that much on her?' and Amie with an ie doesn't answer.
Oisinn's like, 'I told her on the phone – it's not focking
perfume,' and Amie with an ie goes, 'I told her that, but
she was just like, "He is SO not getting away this time,"
and I was like, "OH MY GOD!"'

All our heads turn in their direction. JP is, like, holding
her hand and talking to her really, like, seriously. Oisinn
goes, 'If she put that much on, I can't believe they've still
got their clothes on. Fionn, take a walk to the old TK
Maxx and see what you can hear when you're passing by.'
Fionn heads off, roysh, and he comes back five minutes
later and goes, 'I don't want to spoil the porty over here,
but he's telling her that he loves her but it's a different kind
of love from the love she feels for him. I heard Genesis
20:13 mentioned,' and Oisinn goes, 'Oh no. I *knew* I
shouldn't have focked around with the formula.'

Fionn goes, '*Focked around with the formula?* Oisinn, what's
in that bottle?' and Oisinn goes, 'Well, mostly Andtrostenol.
And ethanol obviously, as a base. And . . . well, I threw
some musk in as well,' and Fionn's there, 'Musk?' and
Oisinn's like, 'Extracted from the sexual organs of the civet
cat,' and Fionn goes, 'That must be why it's not working.'

We're all looking over, roysh, and Faye is, like, bawling
her eyes out and we're talking totally here, and JP's, like,
hugging her, roysh, trying to basically console her. They
stay like that for, like, twenty minutes, roysh, then he hands
her a tissue to clean up her boat, but her make-up's all over
the gaff, roysh, and she gets up and, like, runs to the jacks
and Amie with an ie gets up and, like, pegs it after her and

I'm looking at her orse disappearing into the distance, thinking I'd focking hop her in a New York minute.

JP arrives over and before any of us has a chance to say anything he goes, '*He who shares my bread has lifted up his heel against me,*' and it's obvious, roysh, that Faye has spilled the beans. None of us knows where to look. He goes, 'You know what that's from, don't you? Ross?' and I don't know why he's actually singling me out and I end up going, 'I suppose the Bible,' and he goes, '*While he was still speaking, a crowd came up and the man who was called Judas, one of the Twelve, was leading them. He approached Jesus to kiss him, but Jesus said to him, "You would betray the Son of Man with a kiss?"*' Ross, did you put Viagra in my Baileys?'

And Oisinn looks up and goes, '*Whoa!*' like he wishes he'd actually thought of it, then remembers himself and, like, looks down again. He's there, 'You'll be happy to know I spent a night without sleep, wrestling with my conscience,' and I'm there, 'And did you actually—' and he goes, 'No, I didn't, Ross. Let's just say it only strengthened my faith in the Lord.'

I'm there, 'Look, I'm sorry, dude,' and he goes, 'You're forgiven, Ross. You're all forgiven. The thirty pieces of silver my father offered must have been tempting,' and I pluck up the courage to go, 'It wasn't *just* the money. I don't know, bent and all as it sounds, we don't want to *lose* you,' and he sort of, like, puts his orm around my shoulder, roysh, but not in a gay way, and he goes, 'But, Ross, I'm *not* lost. I'm *found*. Can you not see that?' and I have my head down and I sort of, like, nod and I look up and the goys are sort of, like, nodding as well.

I'm there, 'But you can't still be our friend. Not when you become, like, a priest?' and he goes, 'Why not? You think priests don't have friends? *Jesus* had friends,' and Oisinn's like, 'But we're not going to have to, like, go to Mass and shit, are we?' and JP just, like, laughs and goes, 'Look, goys, I'm sorry if I haven't seemed myself since we got back from Israel and I'm sorry I haven't been around. But I thought about you goys all the time while I was reading. And I found this line. It's from the Book of Proverbs. I wrote it down and I stuck it on the mirror so I see it every morning when I shave and I remember how lucky I am. It says, *A friend loves at all times, and a brother is born for adversity . . . a man of many companions may come to ruin, but there is a friend who sticks closer than a brother.*'

I just automatically go, 'Amen,' because it seems like the roysh thing to say and Fionn's there, 'Don't forget us, JP,' and JP goes, 'How could I?' and the next thing, roysh, Faye and Amie with an ie come out of the can and Faye manages to hold it together until she passes where we're sitting and then she goes, 'I'll always love you . . . Father,' and she breaks down again and Amie with an ie has to help her out the door.

And that should have been that, roysh, except that just as I'm about to head up to the bor to get my round in, we hear what would probably have to be described as a ker-fuffle coming from outside and then all this, like, screaming, and it sounds like Faye and Amie with an ie. So we all peg it for the door, roysh, reef it open and pile out onto the road and I swear to God, roysh, when I saw what was outside I nearly had a hort attack on the spot.

Every dog within a 5-mile radius of Kiely's is outside the focking door, we're talking Alsatians, we're talking Dalmatians, we're talking basset hounds, we're talking huskies. Christian goes, 'God's set a plague of dogs on us for trying to tempt JP,' but Oisinn goes, 'Must be the musk of civet cat. She fairly slapped that stuff on.'

We're talking two hundred dogs here, all basically looking for their bit, with their doggy lipsticks sticking out. One – which Fionn later describes as a border collie – has Faye pinned up against the wall, roysh, and is attempting something I've only ever seen on the internet. And the traffic in Donnybrook is at a standstill because they're, like, everywhere, and all you can hear is dogs borking, cor horns blaring and Faye and Amie with an ie basically screaming their lungs out.

Oisinn goes, 'I suppose we'd better rescue them,' and as we wade through the queue, he turns around and goes, 'It's amazing. I haven't seen this many dogs since . . .' and at the same time, roysh, we all go, '. . . Fionn's twenty-first,' and out of the corner of my eye I can see that even JP's smiling.

Erika has a great Peter Pan after her two weeks in Martinique, roysh, and she's wearing *Be Delicious* by DKNY, which is doing serious shit to my hormones. She's there, 'I can't believe I *actually* let you talk me into having dinner with you,' and I go, 'You look great,' and she's like, 'Don't even *go* there, Ross. We both know how this one ends – you have too much to drink, you get delusions that you're *actually* in my class and then I slap your face,' and I'd kind of hoped she'd forgotten that night in the Ice Bor.

I'm like, 'I'd recommend the steak,' and she goes, 'Thank you, Jamie Oliver. I'll be having the Osso Bucco Milanese with pea and saffron risotto and gremolata, if it's all the same to you,' and I'm there, 'Hey, it's all Good in the

Hood, Babes,' and she shoots me this, like, total filthy and we're talking *total* as well.

She asks the waiter, roysh, for a bottle of Duckhorn Vineyard's Napa Valley Sauvignon Blanc and I have a sly look at the menu and it's, like eighty focking sheets, but I don't say anything. It's, like, worth it just to sit here looking at her.

She goes, 'How's Ronan?' and I swear to God, roysh, it's the only time in the whole meal that her face actually softens. I'm there, 'He's drinking the Kool-Aid, Babes. He's just storted in Castlerock,' and she goes, 'Tell him I said Hi.'

I'm there, 'Haven't seen you around. The word on the street is you're getting married,' and she just, like, shrugs her shoulders and goes, 'He's *asked* me. I've told him he'll have to wait for my answer.' I'm there, 'This is a new goy? I heard you kicked the last one to touch,' and then all of a sudden I'm like, '*Oh my God!* He's not Gick, is he?'

She's like, 'HELLO? He *happens* to be a Baron, actually,' and I sort of, like, nod, roysh, cracking on to know what a focking Baron is. She just, like, throws her eyes up to heaven and goes, 'He's a member of the British peerage, Ross. He's ninety-eighth in line to the throne. Owns half of Cambridgeshire,' and I'm there, 'Which makes it Kool and the Gang.'

My steak arrives. It's got, like, raw chillies on it and I pick them off. Erika looks at me like I'm handling nuclear waste. I'm there, 'So, he's worth a few squids, then? Nice pile of bricks as well, I'd imagine?' and she's like, 'A stately home on 500 acres. Thirty-five bedrooms. Twenty-five servants,' and I go, 'I wouldn't say you picked *him* up in the Club of Love.'

She storts playing with her Osso Bucco – and that's *not* rhyming slang – and she goes, 'I met him at the Mid-Summer Hunt Ball. Well, they *have* to come over here, you see, now that they've banned fox-hunting in Britain. Actually, I've got a petition I want you to sign.'

I'm there, 'A petition?' because it doesn't sound like her at all, roysh, because she used to, like, sneer at Sorcha when she used to collect signatures in College Green to try to have, like, angling declared a blood sport. I'm there, 'What's it about? Killing rabbits and shit?'

She goes, 'No, it's *actually* a protest at the way Tony Blair is attempting to criminalize the upper classes in Britain. The man doesn't understand his own country's history, tradition or culture,' and I'm there, 'Let me get this straight. You want me to, like, sign a petition that's actually *in favour* of, like, killing foxes and shit?' and she hands me a pen.

I'm there, 'But Sorcha wouldn't . . .' and she goes, 'Sorry, your wife does all your thinking for you now, does she? That's not the Ross I used to know,' and as she says it, roysh, I can feel a Pied à Terre boot rubbing the inside of my leg and suddenly I've got a focking truncheon on me that could beat Oisinn away from an all-day breakfast buffet.

I scribble my name on the petition and Erika gives me this, like, evil smile. She says she wants more wine, roysh, and she asks the waiter for a Fabrizio Bianchi Chardonnay Toscana, then she focks off to the can.

I'm sitting there for, like, ten minutes, roysh. There's a bird at the next table giving me the serious mince pies. Nice boat, but I'd say she's no stranger to a fish supper. Erika takes so long that I'm beginning to wonder whether she hopped out the focking window and went home.

She comes back with a big smile on her face, roysh, and I'm so focking slow that I actually think that I'm in with a shout here. The next thing, roysh, I get a focking text message from Sorcha, who thinks I'm at a Taize prayer meeting with JP tonight – I'm going to hell, I know – and it's like, **U bstrd. Cant blive u wer metin erka al alng. Cant blive u sined dat petition eder. Dont bothr comin hom. Stay in u parnts 2nite** and I look up at Erika in, like, total shock.

She goes, 'Close your mouth, Ross. You look like the chargrilled sea bass. I took a photograph of your signature and texted it to Sorcha,' and I'm there, 'Why would you do something like that?' and she goes, 'Oh, she just annoyed me in the Mandarin Lounge the other night. Made me sick to my stomach listening to Amie with an ie and Chloë and Aoife and that funny little Bray girl fawning all over her, just because she finally got that Love Kylie underwear in, like it's a big deal or something.'

I go, '*That's* why you rang me this morning? And *that's* why you dropped all those hints about this place, so I'd, like, ask you out?' but she's in, like, full flow now, going, 'I mean, I dropped in the fact that I might *actually* be getting married to one of the richest men in Britain and all they could talk about was that shop of hers. I was like, HELLO? Charles and Camilla might *actually* be coming to the wedding?'

I just, like, stand up, roysh, and I throw my napkin down on the table and I go, 'You know what, Erika? You're a total bitch,' and she's like, 'Sit down, Ross!' and I'm like, 'No, I won't. You know, Sorcha's eight times the person you'll ever be. No, actually, sixteen. No. No . . . er . . .' and Erika goes, 'Twenty-four, Ross . . . look, sit down. We both know I could be with you if I wanted to . . .' but I just drop two hundred sheets on the table and I go, 'Not this time . . . Princess. You know why you're such a bitch? Because you're lonely. You're one sad and lonely girl,' and probably for the first time in her life, roysh, she has no answer because she knows what I'm saying is basically true. I go, 'I wouldn't *be* you for all the money in the world,' and I storm out, roysh, stopping off on the way to drain the lizard.

Oh, a bit of advice, goys, if you have to have a hit-and-miss and you happen to have been handling chillies any time in the recent past, make sure you give your hands a good wash *before* you whip out the old schlong, just to save yourself a visit to the Blackrock Clinic.

Had the goys over, roysh, while Sorcha was out at this vegetarian cookery course she's doing – do NOT ask – and we're all there knocking back the tins, roysh, and Oisinn's there going, 'According to this survey I read about in the paper, 70 per cent of people from Tallaght have enjoyed sex in the shower,' and we're all there, wondering where this is headed, roysh, and then he goes, 'The other 30 per cent haven't been in the Joy yet,' and we all, like, crack our holes laughing and it's high-fives all round, until Fionn – focking Senator Windows Face – pipes up, roysh, and says there's something more important we should be talking about.

Quick as a flash, roysh, I go, 'More important than birds, Fionn? Oh yeah, I forgot, you're still a focking plastic surgeon at twenty-three,' and it's, like, cue high-fives all round and the dude's left there looking like someone's taken a focking Donald Trump in one of his Dubes, which I have on many occasions, as it happens.

He goes, 'I'm talking about the sale of Lillie's, goys. How would you like to own it?' to which there's, like, total silence. I'm like, 'As in the nightclub?' and Christian's there, 'Own it? What are you talking about?' and Fionn goes, 'It was withdrawn from auction yesterday. No bidder. They're looking for four million sheets. Said they'll probably sell it privately.'

I'm there, 'Four million bills? Where the fock are we gonna get that kind of money?' and Oisinn's like, 'Well, it's not a problem to me anymore. I'm minted. But the rest of you are all Trustifarians, aren't you? I'm sure you could all lay your hands on a couple of hundred Ks tomorrow,' and Fionn goes, 'And I'm sure we could all borrow two or three hundred more, between the banks and our parents.'

I go, 'So that's, like, four of us at, like, half-a-million each, which makes . . .' and Fionn goes, 'Five of us. JP's in,' and we all just, like, look at each other in total shock. I'm there, 'How the fock did you swing that?' and he goes, 'I don't know, to be honest. I told him about it and he just went into automatic – started talking about its prestige city-centre location, etcetera. I'm telling you, there's still some of the estate agent left in him. Between his trust fund and savings, he has half-a-million to throw in. Oh, on condition that there'll be no debauchery on the premises,' and Oisinn's like, 'You mean he wants us to change the basic character of the place?' and I swear to God, roysh, my hand is actually sore from high-fiving him today.

I'm there, 'Okay, that's five of us at, say, half-a-million each, which is . . .' and Christian, who I wouldn't have had down as a maths nerd, goes, 'Two-and-a-half million,' and I'm like, 'What about the rest?'

Fionn goes, 'You all remember One F, I take it?' and Oisinn's like, 'Working class. Big hair. Writes about rugby for *The Stor*. Mad into Vietnam. And Cher,' and Fionn's there, 'That's him. Met him on the Dorsh last week. Seems he'd like a bite of this particular biscuit. He's got two or three other parties interested. He wants us to join his consortium, goys. We're talking Echo and the Moneymen.'

Christian gets all, like, misty-eyed, roysh, and he storts going, 'Just think about it. The backbone of the old Castlerock Senior Cup team – proprietors of Lillie's Bordello,' and Oisinn's there, 'Every bird in this city is going to want to jump our basic bones,' and I'm like, 'For some of us, that's not a new experience.'

Oisinn goes, 'We are SO putting a Jacuzzi in the Library,' and I'm like, 'And we're SO getting Monica Bellucci to open it,' and there's a big cheer, roysh, but Fionn puts a dampener on it straight away. He's like, 'Let's not get carried away yet. It's not a done deal. I suggest we adjourn this meeting and go see what kind of funds we can put together.'

So off the goys go, roysh, listing famous birds who are going to be invited to the reopening – we're talking Estelle Warren, we're talking Jodi Albert, we're talking Laila Rouass, we're talking Eliza Dushku, we're *actually* talking Kate Beckinsale.

When they're gone, I check my watch. It's nearly ten o'clock. I flip open my mobile and I ring Knob Features. I'm there, 'I need half-a-million sheets. I want what's in my trust fund plus another 200K. You better think of some way of raising it. I'll be there in ten minutes. You dickhead,' and I hang up, roysh, and hit Foxrock.

He answers the door and straight away I'm like, 'Well?'

and he just, like, shakes his head, roysh, and goes, 'Haven't had a chance to think about it, Kicker. Haven't been able to think about very much at all. Your mother and I had the most awful experience tonight. Sally, of all people. Your mother and her have been friends for ten years. And Frank. I'm surprised at Richard. Have you five minutes to listen to your old dad?' and I'm thinking, I suppose I *could* put up with it if I get what I want at the end of it.

I go, 'This better be focking good,' and I follow him into the sitting-room and he's there, 'Well, you know they had a bit of a *soirée* tonight, pardon the French. Wanted to thank everyone for their help with this calendar they're bringing out. It was a lovely meal, Ross. Leek, blue cheese and rocket frittata, I believe. And drinks and so forth. Then, at the end of the night, Richard asked a few of us to stay back. Bit of a wink in his eye. Eduard and Lucy. Andrew and Grainne. The photographer chap and his wife . . .'

I'm there, 'Is there much more of this shit?' and he goes, 'Sally puts on some music. Think it might have been Ella. I'm still traumatized. Said she and Richard liked a bit of variety, if we knew what she meant,' and all of a sudden I cop what must have happened. I'm there, 'Don't tell me they're focking swingers?' cracking my hole laughing.

He goes, 'And you think your old dad isn't? I can get down – quote-unquote – with the best of them. I'm well capable of grooving, Ross, to say nothing of boogeying. That night your mother and I saw the Rocket Man and the Piano Man in Croke Field? It was after midnight when we got home.'

I'm there, 'Get to the focking juicy bit, will you?' and he goes, 'Well, as I said, Sally mentioned that they liked nothing more than a bit of variety in their lives. I said, "I'm hearing you, Sally. Every man and his dog knows I'm a fan of Mr S, but I wouldn't exactly shut off the radio if Mr Neil Diamond Esquire came on," and everybody laughed. God, I must have sounded so stupid now that I think about it.'

I'm there, 'Get to the point,' and he goes, 'Well, Richard put a bowl in the middle of the table. Naturally, I assumed Sally was going to serve some of her famous oyster rolls and quail's egg filo cups – and not a moment too soon either. It was a long time since dinner and your mother was feeling a bit faint. She's in bed now actually. I said, "Yes, I could use something to fill a hole." Laughter again.'

He goes, 'Then Eduard stands up, drops his car keys into the bowl and winks at Andrew. Grainne – she's the ladies' captain, for heaven's sake – she follows suit. Well, I never felt so disgusted and sickened in all my life when it finally dawned on your mother and I what we'd inadvertently stumbled into here,' and I'm there, 'Which was?' and he goes, 'Well, obviously some kind of car-swapping party. Richard's always had his eye on my Lexus.'

I just, like, crack up laughing in the tool's face. He really shouldn't be let out sometimes. He goes, 'And to think, I might have ended up with Eduard's Rover. The world and his mother knows the gearbox is banjaxed.'

I'm just, like, shaking my head. Never heard anything so funny in my life. I'm there, 'Half-a-million. Get it transferred into my account first thing in the morning,' and he's like, 'Absolutely,' and as I'm leaving I just go, 'You really are a dickhead.'

*

Fehily rings me, roysh, and it's, like, half-three in the after-noon and he goes, 'Hello, my child,' and I'm there, 'Hey, Father, what's the Jackanory?' and he goes, 'Ross, are you nearby?' and I'm there, 'Yeah, I'm actually in the Frascati Centre, pretty much chilling,' and he's like, 'Can you come up to the school. There's something I think you should see.'

So I go out, roysh, hop in the old Beamer, and I peg it up to the school and even from the front gate, roysh, I can see hundreds of people crowded around the rugby pitch and I take it for granted that that's where I'm headed. As I get closer, roysh, I can hear all this, like, cheering. I pork the cor and walk across and I swear to God, roysh, I actually think my eyes are playing tricks on me. The trials for the junior cup team are obviously on, roysh, and it's, like, the Probables against the Possibles and there in the middle of the pitch, with the ball tucked under his orm, daring people to tackle him, is Ronan, wearing, of all things, the Leinster jersey I bought him.

'Quite a sight, isn't it, child?' Fehily's standing beside me. He goes, 'I told him he was too young for the team. Those boys out there are fourteen, I told him. He went off, all disappointed with himself. The next thing I knew he charged onto the pitch, picked up the ball and, well, it's barely been out of his hands all afternoon. I suppose I should take him off, but, well, he's giving the rest of them something to think about.'

I stand there and watch in, like, total awe. He's, like, riding tackles, powering through forwards who are, like, twice the size of him, hitting ball-carriers like a focking locomotive. It's unbelievable. Of course he cops me then, roysh, and he goes, 'Rosser!' and I give the old thumbs-up and he sort of, like, throws his head in the direction of a ruck and goes, 'Piece of piss, this,' and then, like, dives into it.

All the other kids on the sideline are giving it, 'RO-NAN! RO-NAN! RO-NAN!' and Fehily turns to me and goes, 'I was fortunate enough to see the great Jack Kyle in action, you know. Saw Mike Gibson many times. Saw Tony O'Reilly, Brian O'Driscoll and yourself. That's what we're looking at here, Ross. He's going to be one of the greats.'

Sorcha's there, 'Who is it, Ross?' and I'm practically hanging out the window trying to see when the doorbell rings again. It's, like, some dude in a tin of fruit. I don't know anyone who wears one. I go, 'Must be a Jehovah's Witness,' and she's there, 'At, like – OH! MY! GOD! – midnight?' I'm there, 'Probably trying to get us when our defences are down. They've obviously heard about JP finding God and they think the rest of us are easy pickings. They'll soon get bored ringing,' but Sorcha goes, 'No, Ross. I am SO not listening to that for another twenty minutes. Get rid of them,' and she turns up the volume on the Savalas, roysh, as if to say, basically, conversation over.

So I end up having to peg it down the stairs in, it has to be said, roysh, a bit of a rage, I reef open the door and I go, 'I love chicks, meat and beer – you're wasting your focking time,' but the goy just, like, looks at me, roysh, like *I'm* the one with a screw loose. He goes, 'Ross, it's me,' and I'm looking at him, roysh, thinking the voice is very familiar. The penny drops. I'm like, 'One F?' and he goes, 'The one and only,' and I'm like, 'What's the story with the threads? And your hair. It's not . . . *big* anymore.'

He goes, 'We've got an important meeting tonight. I've been talking to the present proprietor of a certain premises in Adam Court, Grafton Street, Dublin 2 – you know which one,' and I'm like, 'Lillie's?' and he goes, 'Got it in one. I've managed to convince the owners that Echo and the Moneymen are serious about buying the place. We've been offered a viewing. As in tonight. I've got Fionn, Christian and Oisinn out in the jammer.'

I'm like, 'Are you serious?' and he goes, 'I'm as serious as the Mylai massacre. Now, quick – I've got to have the suit back to Black Tie by ten o'clock in the morning.'

I shout up the stairs to Sorcha, roysh, that I'm just nipping out to buy Lillie's and she goes, 'Dunnes in Cornelscourt is open. They've lovely ones there,' and it's obviously some sort of, like, communication breakdown, but I leave it.

Like he said, roysh, One F had already rounded up the rest of the goys, probably from Kiely's or the M1, judging by the hum off their breaths and the way they keep bursting into, like, choruses of, 'One F in Foley, there's only one F in Foley . . .' and it *is* true, roysh, the goy is a legend, even though he went to Blackrock and is a bit, I don't know, wacky.

We hit Lillie's and have the usual hassle trying to get past the bouncers. There's a bit of a debate going on as to whether Oisinn's black Skechers are runners or shoes – they've their work cut out, these bouncers, having to keep up with, like, fashion and shit – but eventually this dude arrives who turns out to be the estate agent selling the gaff and he calls them off us, roysh, and as we're heading in, Oisinn tells them that the second we buy the gaff their orses are SO sacked, and we're talking *totally* here.

The dude leads us up the stairs, roysh, and Christian's in my ear, telling me that if he has his way we'll be totally renovating the Library to make it look like the bor in Mos Eisley where Luke Skywalker and Obi Wan Kenobi recruited Han Solo and Chewbacca to take them to Alderaan.

The estate agent dude goes, 'I expect you'd like to be shown around,' and Oisinn – totally hammered – goes, 'Yeah, you can stort by showing us around five pints of Ken,' and One F ends up having to, like, rescue the situation by going, 'Tell us a bit about the property,' and the dude launches into what I straight away recognize as, like, fluent Estate Agentese. It's all, 'Apex of celebrity nightlife in Ireland . . . named after Lillie Langtry, Victorian court-esan and mistress of the Prince of Wales . . . tricked out in the livery of a high-class, nineteenth-century brothel . . . a nightclub of national and international renown . . . centrally located,' and blahdy blahdy blah.

He goes, 'Regular patrons include Mick Jagger, Bono, Julia Roberts, Bruce Springsteen, Prince, Van Morrison, The Corrs and Tom Jones,' and quick as a flash, roysh, I'm there, 'Julia Roberts and The Corrs are welcome. The rest are focking borred,' and I'm thinking I really should get Christian or one of the others to write down some of my one-liners when I'm in this kind of form.

One F plays a focking blinder, roysh. I can't believe he's still writing for that peasant paper. The estate agent goes, 'I take it you would intend for the club to continue attracting the glitterati?' and One F puts his orm around the dude's shoulder and goes, 'Not so much the glitterati as the clitterati. We're talking *fin de siècle* decadence, Baby, coming at you like a Chinese Type 59 main battletank.'

278

Ten minutes later, roysh, me, Fionn and One F are sitting in a corner of the Library bor with the estate agent, listening to Paul Harrington belt out 'Rock and Roll Kids' on the piano, while wrapping ourselves around a few pints of Gerard Adriaan H's finest. Christian's up at the bor, orm-wrestling with Damien Rice, while Oisinn's telling Robbie Keane, the Carter Twins and two dudes I know to see from 'Fair City' that there's a new name going up over the door and they're basically off the guestlist. I'm looking at this and I'm thinking, We've arrived.

The estate agent turns around and goes, 'An offer of four million will guarantee it,' and me, Fionn and One F just look at each other, roysh, smile and I go, 'We'll take it.'

9. One Plus One Plus One Plus . . .

It's, like lunchtime, roysh, and I'm in the old Margaret watching, of all things, the lunchtime 'Neighbours', looking at the lovely Libby with the humungous thrups, doing a bit of the old blanket welding, when all of a sudden I hear Sorcha's Rav 4 swing into the driveway and then the sound of her coming up the stairs.

She goes, '*Oh! My! God!* I cannot BELIEVE you're ACTUALLY still in bed?' and I'm like, 'I was actually thinking about getting up,' and then she's just there, '*Oh my God*, you're not going to believe what I just got a copy of?' and of course I stort getting a panic attack, thinking she's talking about the six-page spread on me and goys in the new *VIP*, we're talking, **The Darling Buds of Lillie's – Meet the New Owners of Dublin's Hottest Nightspot**. When the bird who interviewed us asked me if there was anyone special in my life, I probably shouldn't have said, 'No, I'm young, free and single and I just want to mingle,' but I just got a bit, like, carried away.

Turns out she hasn't seen it. She's, like, talking about something else. She's like, 'I got a copy of the Yummy-Mummy Calendar. Your mum is like, OH! MY! GOD!' and she has it in her hand, roysh, and she actually tries to show it to me.

I'm there going, 'I don't want to see it,' and she's like, 'Why not? She has an *amazing* body for a woman of fify-one. I wish I'd a pair of—' and I'm there, 'Sorcha, STOP, I'm going to focking vom,' and she looks at me, roysh, like I'm the one who's totally lost the plot and she goes, '*Oh my God*, Ross, I cannot BELIEVE you're ACTUALLY over-reacting like this. The way you're acting, Ross, it's like, *Aaahggghhh!*' and I'm there, 'I can live with that. Just – please – don't mention it again.'

She turns off the old Liza, which I take as a hint that it's time to get up. She's like, 'Anyway, Ross, you need to ring Ronan. He's in trouble,' and I sit straight up in the bed and I'm like, 'What kind of trouble?' and she's like, 'Look, he texted me. I promised I wouldn't say anything, but, well, he's in some kind of trouble in school. I think he's too scared to tell you himself,' and I'm there, 'Well, I don't blame him. It's the middle of November. He's only in the school a few weeks. This'll be drugs or some shit, I just focking know it.'

I pick up the Wolfe and ring his mobile and when he answers, roysh, I go, 'Okay, what the fock did you do?' and he's there, 'Stall the ball, Rosser, I'm in class,' and then he turns around – presumably to Horsman, as in his teacher – and goes, 'Better take this call, Sir. It's the Ross lad,' and when he's outside the door, he goes, 'Storee?' but I'm, like, too in shock to even remember why I rang. I go, 'Horsman's the biggest hord-orse in the school. Are you telling me he *lets* you take calls during class?' and he's there, 'Pete? Ah, sure Pete's game ball, Rosser. Play rugby in this school and you can do no wrong. Listen, Sorcha's obviously told you about this bullying shite. Load of me bollicks. I told her not to worry her pretty little head, but she's a darlin' boord, as me oul' grandda would say. There's nothing in it, Rosser. It's mustard.'

I'm there, 'You mean, you've been accused in the wrong?' and it's a good five minutes before he stops laughing. He's like, 'Good one, Rosser. Nah, truth be told, I slammed this kid in sixth class up agin the wall. Might have hit him a couple of slaps as well,' and I go, 'Sixth class? Ronan, you're in, like, second?' and he's there, 'They've all got to pay up, Rosser. It was Thursday. He was already a week in arrears.'

I'm there, 'You're running a focking protection racket?' and he laughs and goes, 'I'm only pulling your chain, Rosser. Look, I promised I'd keep me nose clean, didn't I? No, if you must know, he was picking on this other little kid, has a terrible bread-and-butter, takes twenty minutes to say hello, ye know yerself. I was doing me rounds at lunchtime, mooching around, seeing what was what and there was four of them, they had him in this classroom, up agin the wall, making him say things and laughing at him. I mean, that's not right, Rosser. So I goes in and I squares up to the main man – somethin' Swails – and I says, "Think you're a fooken hard man, do ye?"'

He goes, 'So he lets go of the kid and he laughs at me. So I turns around and I starts walkin' away from him and says he, "Shitter," but I had only turned around to lock the door, make sure none of them could escape when the slaps were being dealt out. Anyway, he was the only one I needed to sort out. The other three saw what I did to him and bottled it.'

I'm there, 'So why are you in trouble?' and he goes, 'Ah, same drill as in me last school. His oul' wan's coming up to the school this afternoon and Fehily wants you there too – make it look like the school actually gives two fooks.'

So I hit Castlerock, roysh, and the plan is that Fehily's meeting this Swails kid and his old dear first, with me and Ronan waiting outside, then we're going to be basically called in. I'm sitting there wondering to myself whether the old dear's, like, a yummy-mummy, when all of a sudden Ronan turns around and offers me a slug out of this hip-flask that he pulls from his pocket. I tell him no thanks, I'm not for whatever the fock he's got in there, but he takes a long drink from it and goes, 'Swear to Jaysus, this stuff's makin' me voice deeper. Fook knows what it's doin' to me liver.'

Five minutes pass and Fehily suddenly calls us in. Swails' old dear turns out to be far from a yummy-mummy, as it happens, she's actually a total focking swamp donkey. Then I cop her son. He must be, like, five-foot-eleven and I'm looking at Ronan, who must be, like, a foot smaller.

Fehily goes, 'Now, I've been trying to explain to Mrs Swails here that things can often be . . . misinterpreted,' and she does NOT look like a happy bunny, whatever's been said. Ronan goes, 'Like I said, Fadder, the kid had a dizzy spell. I grabbed him by the scruff of the neck to stop him from fallin' and hurtin' himself,' and the kid goes, 'That's *not* what happened and you know it,' and he's, like, whimpering like one of them spoiled little shits you see getting dragged around supermorkets, and I actually feel like hitting him a couple of slaps myself.

Fehily claps his hands together and goes, 'So, that's that then! Thank you for coming in, Mrs Swails,' but she's not leaving it there. She's a face on her like a well-slapped orse. She goes, 'It's because he plays rugby, isn't it? That's why you won't discipline him?' and Fehily doesn't answer, roysh, just turns his head towards the window, as if to say, like, meeting over.

She's like, 'Well, if that's your attitude, I'm taking Timmy out of the school,' and I'm thinking that if you want your kid to turn out to be a little shit, calling him Timmy's a good stort. She goes, 'You think rugby's that important? Well, let's see how the school orchestra survives without its best flautist,' and Fehily actually sniggers, roysh, and then she focks off and brings the beanpole with her.

Fehily goes, 'Well, Ronan, I think that went rather well,' and – I don't believe it, roysh – Ronan high-fives him across the desk and then, like, gets up to go. He's like, 'Gotta fly. Pete's startin' teachin' us German, Fadder. Don't want to miss it,' and Fehily goes, '*Auf Wiederschauen*, my child,' and when he's gone he turns around to me and he's like, 'A star of the future. And quite the chip off the old block . . .'

I'm in the gaff, roysh, flicking through a stack of Sorcha's *Now* magazines, actually looking for ideas for who to invite to the reopening of Lillie's on, like, Christmas Eve. I'm sprawled on the sofa and the old Savalas is on and it's, like, the news of all things and I'm looking at all the sad fockers bawling their eyes out because Bewley's is closing down.

Some dude's being interviewed and he's saying that you could a buy a cup of coffee and sit there with it all day, sometimes for two or three days, and I'm shouting, 'That's how the place went tits-up, you focking tosser,' and then I stort thinking how funny it would be, roysh, if the Feds arrived on the scene and, like, basically baton-charged all the old biddies and old forts, we're talking broken teeth and bits of focking Eccles cake scattered all over Grafton Street, and I stort, like, cracking my hole laughing, roysh, even though there's, like, no one else in the gaff, but then I stop when all of a sudden Sorcha's face fills the screen. She's on Grafton Street, roysh, which explains why she's not here making my focking dinner, and I'm wondering what her game is, roysh, because she hates Bewley's, she always cracks up when I say it's for boggers, septic tanks and coffin-dodgers.

The reporter bird's like, 'Not everyone at today's protest was sad to see the passing of an era,' and then you hear Sorcha going, 'I'm spokeswoman for the Campaign to Keep Bewley's Closed. What Grafton Street is crying out for is a Starbucks. We need white chocolate frappuccinos, tall skinny caramel macchiatos and pumpkin spice and eggnog mochas. What we don't need is menopausal women in French maid costumes serving sausages and beans from a *bain marie*.'

Fock me, roysh, I didn't even know anything *about* this campaign, and I'm thinking I really should listen to her a bit more. I can see, like, Chloë and Sophie and Claire from, like, Bray of all places, and Aoife, and I'm wondering what *her* objection is considering she hasn't let anything other than water, popcorn and Weight Watchers' soup pass her lips since she was, like, fourteen. She's next up. She's like, '*Oh my God*, Bewley's just, like, totally attracts the wrong type of people to Grafton Street. It's like, OH! MY! GOD!' and in the background I can hear Chloë go, 'She's SO right. It's like, *Aaaggghhh!*' and then Aoife goes, 'We *would* appeal to the Government, though, to make emergency provisions for all the down-and-outs and mental defectives who will be made homeless by the closure. Perhaps they could consider some form of, like, short-term detention, just to ensure a slow release of these people back into the community?' and I can hear Sorcha giving it, 'OH MY GOD! I don't agree with *that*,' and then it's like, 'Vivienne Traynor, RTÉ News, outside Bewley's on Grafton Street.'

I'm actually really proud of them, roysh, and, bent and all as I sound, I end up texting Sorcha and going, **Tought u wer gr8 on telE. Wen u comin home. Had no nosebag. I'm Hank** and then I add an **X** roysh, but then think better of it and, like, delete it.

No sooner have I sent the message, roysh, when all of a sudden Úna O'Hagan – I would, if you're asking, in a hortbeat – is going, 'Right-wing independent councillor Charles O'Carroll-Kelly was suspended from Dun Laoghaire-Rathdown County Council today for thirty days following derogatory comments he made about people on low income. The local politician, famous for his outspoken views, was asked to leave the chamber this afternoon after saying that the swarm of one hundred million pink locusts that arrived in the Canary Islands at the weekend was God's plague on Ireland's package-holiday classes.'

And I'm practically on the floor at this stage. I am seriously going to have to, like, wrap Sellotape around my waist to stop my focking sides from splitting. So they show these pictures of, like, Knob Features leaving the Town Hall in Dun Laoghaire, roysh, and the reporter's going, 'At this afternoon's engineering and traffic management meeting, Councillor O'Carroll-Kelly was asked four times by the Chairman to withdraw a comment that God had brought down his wrath on tens of thousands of socially disadvantaged people who, he said, had turned the holiday sunspot into a type of Finglas-on-Sea. He refused to withdraw the comment and was suspended from the chamber for thirty days. Leaving the meeting, he had this to say . . .'

And the camera just, like, focuses on him, roysh, and he goes, 'I'm telling you – it's justice, Old Testament style. The Lord's way of telling people on social welfare that they shouldn't be going on these, quote-unquote, package holidays. I make no apologies for saying it. Read your Sodom and Gomorrah.'

My wife and my old man. I'm thinking, Is it any wonder I'm focked up?

Ronan calls to the door with three of his, let's just say for the sake of argument, friends the other night, roysh, all of them about ten years older than him and they're called Whacker, Nudger and Gull and, of course, you don't need me to tell you that they're, like, totally CHV. I make no apologies for it, roysh, but I bring Ronan in and leave the three skobes out in the front gorden, where they just, like, stand around with their hoods up, smoking and making comments to any passer-by stupid enough to make eye contact with them.

Ronan's going, 'I'm looking for four, Rosser,' and I'm like, 'Ronan, it's out of the question,' but he's there, 'You're *supposed* to be me oul' lad, for Jaysus sakes. And you won't even do this one ting for me?' but he's, like, pissing into the wind if he thinks he can, like, tug at my hortstrings.

I go, 'Lillie's is no place for a seven-year-old on Christmas Eve night. Or any pub for that matter,' and he's there, 'Ah, that's a load of me bollicks, Rosser. Sure I've been drinking in the early houses this two year. I'm one of the faces down the docks,' and I go, 'Ronan, I know you only say those things for effect,' then I go to the fridge in the kitchen, roysh, and pour him a glass of Coke and when I put it in front of him he asks me if I have an oul' nip of something to go in it, which I ignore.

I go, 'I presume the *four* are for the cast of *The Commitments* out there. Ronan, would you not try and find some friends your own age?' and he goes, 'Friends? Nah, the boys are just working for me, Rosser. Need a bit of muscle around me right now. Some of me investments are the subject of, let's just say, hostile take-over bids.'

I'm thinking, Where the fock did he learn to talk like that? when all of a sudden, roysh, he's staring out the window and going, 'That doorty-looken doort boord's gonna break Sorcha's rosebush if he keeps doing that,' and he jumps up and thumps the window and then just points at Gull, or Whacker, or whichever one it was making shit of the roses and the goy just, like, stops immediately and sort of, like, puts his head down, all, like, ashamed and shit?

Ronan goes, 'I put that down to lack of education. Left school when he wasn't much older than meself. No social skills, has Gull. Bit tasty in a ruck but. And if you're wantin' any Tom fenced, he's your only man. No names, no pack-drill,' and then he sits down again and goes, 'So, who's going to this . . . party of yours?' and I'm there, 'No one, really. Gráinne Seoige. Sharon Ní Bheoláin. Caroline Morahan. Lisa Burke. Abi Titmus. Samantha Mumba. Rachel Stevens. Maybe Girls Aloud . . .'

He goes, 'Moy Jaysus, it's no wonder you don't want your saucepan hanging around. Let me level with you here, Rosser – I can do that, can I?' and I'm like, 'Of course,' trying to keep a straight face. He's there, 'I've no interest in going to your party and that's telling you the truth, although I'd fooken lash that Samantha Mumba wan out of it and I wouldn't need to be asked twice. The plan was to come here tonight and see how much you'd be prepared to pay me and the boys not to turn up on the night.'

He takes a sip of his Coke and, like, pulls his top lip back over his teeth, like he's just had a mouthful of, I don't know, whiskey or something. I'm there, 'Hang on, is this, like, blackmail?' and he goes, 'I prefer the word *security*, Rosser. You're paying for security of mind, my friend. For a relatively small outlay, you can enjoy your night, safe in the knowledge that no one from the wrong side of town will come within 500 yards of your club and cause a scene that might make the newspapers.'

I actually admire him, roysh, because he's thought the whole thing through. I'm there, 'And how much will this . . . *service* cost me?' and he whips an envelope out of his Davy Crocket and a pen from behind his ear and he storts doing these, like, calculations, I suppose you'd have to call them. He's going, 'Got my overheads to think of . . . staff costs . . . insurance . . . travel . . .' and then he crosses the last word out and goes, 'Actually, that car we arrived in tonight was robbed. Be unfair to charge you for that . . . so add them up . . . blahdy blah . . . carry your one . . . you're looking at a grand plus change.'

I'm there, 'Okay, fine,' and he looks at me funny, roysh, and he goes, 'The usual procedure, Rosser, is for you, the customer, to say you're not paying that, then for me to get Nudger in to remind you of the consequences of not having this kind of cover,' but I'm there, 'Ronan, a thousand sheets is fock-all to me. You can have it. I don't know what all this *Goodfellas* shit is about. When I want a grand off my old man, I just tell him I want a grand, call him a tosser, or a knob, or a dickhead and he ends up giving it to me,' and I pull out a wad of fifties, roysh, and peel off twenty and hand them to him.

He knocks back the rest of his Coke and goes, 'I was raised on the mean streets but. It's all I know.'

It's, like, three o'clock in the morning, roysh, and I can't sleep and I end up just, like, tossing for an hour – though not in that way – but it's no good, roysh, I just can't go off. So I get up, roysh, go downstairs and ring the old man. He answers all sort of, like, groggy, like he's been sleeping. I'm there, 'Wake up,' and he's like, 'Kicker? Is that you?' and I hear him turning to the old dear and going, 'It's Ross.' I'm there, 'Have I told you recently what a complete and utter penis you are?' and he goes, 'Er, twice this weekend. Once on Saturday morning when I gave you your allowance for the week and then again yesterday afternoon when I offered you the money to go on the Lions tour next year,' and I'm there, 'That's good. Don't want you forgetting,' and after that, roysh, I slept fine.

The bouncers have their instructions, roysh, and it's, like, no dogs, no riff-raff and no blokes who're likely to give me and the goys competition or take the spotlight off us on our, like, big night, which is why I can't believe it, roysh, when one of them bells me upstairs to tell me that Bono's outside. I'm in the Jacuzzi with, like, four birds and we're watching the CCTV footage of the front entrance on this, like, humungous, giant screen.

I go, 'Ask him who he is,' and I see the bouncer saying something and Bono looking at him like the dude's just done a Donald Trump in one of his rhythms. Then the goy goes into his mouthpiece, 'He says he's the lead singer with U2, Mr O'Carroll-Kelly,' and I'm there, 'Tell him I've never heard of them. Then tell him to fock off,' and me and the birds just, like, crack our holes laughing.

The queue outside is un-*focking*-believable. There's no doubt, roysh, that the All New Lillie's is *the* place to be this Christmas Eve, and I'm in my element, of course, giving it loads, playing God with people's social lives, deciding who gets in and who doesn't. I'm going, 'The one with the black hair and the slut wellies ... steer her in ... that's it ...' and it's like those sheepdog trials you see on the Liza, we're talking 'One Man and his Dog'. It's like, 'No, not the kipper with the trouser melons, her friend ... keep going ... easy does it.'

The next thing, roysh, who walks into the Library only Oisinn and One F. Oisinn, hands me a glass of something that looks like a urine sample and goes, 'It's my new invention. Try it,' and of course I splash a bit on my neck. He's like, 'It's a focking cocktail, Ross,' and I'm there, 'Oh, roysh,' and I take a sip and it's like, *Whoa!* and Oisinn goes, 'It's called A Slow Screw In A BMW Five Series. We're talking brandy, *Crème de Cacao*, goat's milk and diesel,' and I'm like, 'We'll make it the house special.'

Oisinn goes, 'Kool Plus Significant Others. You staying up here in The Library all night, Ross? It's, like, heaving downstairs, we're talking wall-to-wall Pavarotti,' and I'm like, 'Any sign of Bianca yet?' and Oisinn shakes his head sort of, like, sadly and goes, 'Probably doing the married thing. The goys are under strict instructions to let us know if she arrives. They're playing an actual blinder down there. They've just told Brian with an i McFadden to try Slapper-face Jacks,' and I crack my hole laughing.

I tell the birds they're going to have to excuse me, roysh, that there's babes downstairs wanting me to bring pleasure into their lives and I climb out of the tub and grab an old Jack Rowell to dry myself off. I can see the goys checking me out; not in a gay way, roysh, they're just, like, clocking my pecs and abs and obviously thinking, That goy could SO get on the Leinster team if he only pulled his finger out.

As I'm throwing the old threads on, one of the bouncers buzzes up again and he goes, 'There's a girl called Sorcha here. Says she's your wife. Shall I let her in?' and I turn around and I'm like, 'HELLO? Do you even *need* to ask that question?' and he goes, 'Er . . .' and I'm there, 'Tell her to *fock off!*'

The thing is, roysh, for some reason, Sorcha's stopped

putting out the last few weeks and I'm thinking I'm going to have to get it somewhere else, and I'm never going to be hotter than I am tonight.

Oisinn turns around to me and he's like, 'Ross, I know you don't want her cramping your style tonight, but that wasn't very festive,' and I go, 'I'm sorry, Oisinn, I just couldn't come up with a festive way of saying it,' and then, into my mouthpiece, roysh, I go, 'Actually, tell her there's no room at the inn,' which the bouncer actually does, roysh, he actually uses that focking phrase, and on the screen I can see Sorcha mouthing the words, '*Oh my God! Oh my God! Oh my God!*' while her friends – I can make out Chloë, Aoife and the lovely Erika – are just in total shock, like their Visas won't swipe in Nine West or something.

I tell the goys to come on and we head downstairs and there's this, like, big cheer when we arrive, roysh, three members of the Echo and the Moneymen consortium who now own the joint, and it's basically nice to see that everyone knows what side their bread is, like, buttered. Birds are coming at us from every angle, giving it loads, telling me I'm the man, it's a disgrace that Declan Kidney keeps ignoring me, blahdy blahdy blah, but I'm going around looking around for Christian, roysh, because I haven't, like, seen him all night.

Then I cop him, roysh, basically canoodling in the corner with Lauren, and as I get closer I can hear him telling her that Jawas has forty-three different terms for the word relationship and she's going, 'Forty-three? *Wow!*' and when Christian cops me he goes, 'Ross, you're here. Great. Look, we wanted you to be the first to know . . .' and I look at him, roysh, and I look at Lauren and she, like, holds up her left hand and she's wearing, like, a ring.

I fight the urge to go, 'YOU FOCKING SAP!' and instead I give it, 'That's incredible news,' and I kiss Lauren on both cheeks and give Christian a hug and I go, 'I have to say, roysh, having made the trip down the aisle myself, I can totally recommend it,' and of course in my Davy Crocket, roysh, the old Wolfe's ringing away and it's, like, 'Darth Vader's Morch', and I actually stort to feel a little bit, I don't know, guilty I suppose.

Lauren goes, 'So where's Sorcha tonight?' and I'm like, 'She's, em, I don't know, helping people. Homeless people. Homeless unmarried mothers. With Aids,' and Lauren says I'm lucky to have married someone with such a big hort.

Christian says he has something to ask me, roysh, and of course I'm expecting him to go, 'Do you think we could get Figrin D'an and the Mos Eisley Cantina band to play at the wedding?' but instead he goes, 'I want you to be my best man,' and I swear to God, roysh, I actually burst into tears, roysh, because what with that whole thing between me and his old dear – me knobbing her basically – I know how, like, awkward it's going to be for him having me as, like, his best man.

I tell them I'm, like, SO happy for them, which I am, roysh. I used to, like, worry about Christian, about whether he'd ever find someone on the same – I was going to say level, but I actually mean planet – and I order a large bottle of pop and it's great, roysh, just the three of us, sitting in the corner, basically toasting the future.

My phone beeps and it's, like, a text message. It's from, like, Sorcha, the defiant wench. It's like, **Wher r u? OMG d bouncrs wont let us in! Can u cum dwn?** and I just, like, delete it and head off to look for JP.

He's in cracking form, it has to be said. It's, like, the first time I've actually seen him since he storted in Maynooth and he seems really, I don't know, at peace or something. He's, like, chatting away to Caroline Morahan and Gráinne Seoige and they're having this, like, really deep discussion about whether Mel Gibson's take on *The Passion* portrayed the Jews in a fair light, all pretty interesting, I'm sure, if that's your basic vibe.

The unbelievable thing is, roysh, he's actually back on the Britneys. Have they no Baileys? That's what I go to him. I come up behind him and I'm like, 'Have they no Baileys, JP?' and when he turns around he doesn't look pleased to see me at all, roysh, he actually gives me a filthy and goes, 'Ross, I joined the consortium on the understanding that there'd be a chapel where patrons could go for a moment of quiet repose and perhaps speak to God,' and I'm thinking, The goy has *totally* flipped this time, and I have to think on my feet, roysh, and I end up going, 'We couldn't get planning permission for it.'

He stares at me, roysh, and he obviously knows it's a lie because I can't actually look him in the eye, but then all of a sudden he storts cracking his hole laughing and he goes, 'Ross, I'm yanking your chain,' and I'm like, 'Oh my God, you focking had me there, JP. That's if I can still call you that. I mean, you're not a priest yet, I take it?' and he goes, 'It's JP, Ross. And it'll always be JP to you and the goys.'

So all of a sudden we stort, I don't know, reminiscing I suppose you'd have to call it, about the time we borrowed his old man's cor, drove out to Terenure and totally wrecked the Gick's pitch, doing, like, wheelspins and handbrake turns all over it. Then we did Mary's and Blackrock on the way home. He's there, 'Happy days,' and I'm like, 'Are you happy now, dude?' and he goes, 'Unbelievably happy, Ross. It's a content I never thought I'd know,' and I just, like, raise my glass to him and I go, 'Hallelujah to that,' and he goes, 'Amen.'

He's like, 'Everyone's happy. Christian has Lauren. Oisinn's a millionaire, doing what he wants to do. Fionn seems really keen on that Debra – he's talking about going to a Kibbutz next year. Looks like things are working out for all of us. And you – you're happy, aren't you?' and I'm there, 'Pretty much. Hit me with some of that Bible shit. Some of that stuff you said to me before, it got me thinking . . .' and he goes, 'Ross, it was wrong for me to try to force my beliefs down your throat. It's an abuse of your friendship,' and I'm like, 'Come on, JP. Hit me with something. Give me a thought for the night.'

So he thinks, roysh, then he goes, 'Okay, Proverbs 5:15,' and I'm like, 'What one's that?' and he's there, '*Find joy with the wife you married in your youth, fair as a hind, graceful as a fawn. Let hers be the company you keep, hers the breasts that ever fill you with delight, hers the love that ever holds you captive.*'

I'm like, 'No, give me something else,' and he laughs and goes, 'Where *is* Sorcha tonight?' and I'm there, 'She's helping out with some, I don't know, homeless . . . one-legged . . . gay . . . junkie . . . refugees,' and he laughs because he knows that I'm basically ripping the piss.

I have to, like, excuse myself then, roysh, because out of the corner of my eye I see – I don't believe it, roysh, I don't *actually* focking believe it – Ronan's turned up and he's leaning up against the bor, eyeing up birds and drinking from his hipflask. I just, like, storm over to him and I go, 'How the *fock* did you get in?' and he's like, 'Storreee, Rosser? Didn't I tell you I was connected in this town?' and I go, 'I focking paid you good money to stay away.

What happened to that?' and he's like, 'There I was tonight, Rosser, looking forward to a nice night in front of the oul' box, when Sorcha rings. Said she was outside of here. Couldn't get past the bouncers. Said you weren't answering your mobile. Well, she knows I'm a man of influence – and I owed her a favour after Ibiza – so says I, "I'll be down. Gimme fifteen minutes, Doll".'

I'm like, 'Are you telling me she's actually *inside*?' and he goes, 'Of course. I know two of your lads on the door out there,' and I'm thinking, bang go my plans for a bit of extra-curricular tonight. Ronan goes, 'Do a disappearing act, will ye? I'm looking at boords and you're cramping me style,' but I've decided to make myself scarce anyway, roysh, before the storm arrives.

I manage to find Oisinn and Fionn, who're, like, huddled together in a corner, roysh, and they seem to be, like, studying something pretty closely. Oisinn sees me and goes, 'Have you seen it yet?' and of course I presume he's talking about Lauren's engagement ring, roysh, and I go, 'Yeah, great news, isn't it?' and Fionn goes, 'I thought you were against the idea,' and I'm like, 'What are you on about?' and – I swear to God, roysh, with absolutely no warning – Oisinn turns around and goes, '*This*,' and he holds it up, roysh, *it* being Miss October in the Yummy-Mummy 2005 calendar, in other words my old dear, the stupid focking weapon.

There's, like, no preparing yourself for a moment like that, roysh, basically seeing your old in the raw. I don't even want to focking describe what she looked like, but suffice to say, roysh, that Oisinn made sure I got a good eyeful for, like, five seconds before I managed to turn away. I'm like, '*Yeeeuuuggghhh*,' and I'm actually focking gagging, roysh, and Oisinn's going, 'You've got to be kidding, Ross. She's a stunner. Look at the size of those—' and I'm like, 'DON'T! I'm going to vom,' and Fionn's like, 'Better get used to hearing about it, Ross,' and Oisinn goes, 'Your old man's sending them to everyone as, like, Christmas presents. Oh, by the way, Sorcha's looking for you,' and I jump up and get the fock out of there.

Out of the corner of my eye I spot two of the blokes out of Westlife, roysh, the pair from Sligo, but I don't even have time to find out how the actual boggers managed to get in here tonight. I find a quiet spot in the corner, where I end up chatting to these two former Mounties, who are talking about the various ports of their bodies they're going to have botoxed when their SSIA money comes through. One of them might be called Iseult.

I stort giving it serious amounts of welly in the old chatting-up deportment, roysh, we're talking me at my knicker-loosening best, until this total dickhead called Donnacha, who happens to be a brother of one of the two birds, comes over and storts going, 'Hey, Ross, how the fock are you?' and I just, like, pretend not to know him, roysh, even though I do. He's actually a tosser, roysh, went to CBC Monkstown, was hooker on the S when we totally kicked their orses one year.

Actually, he was a total focking donkey, as I remember.

I'm just like, 'How the fock did *you* get in?' and he goes, 'I'm actually going out with Sorcha's friend, Claire,' presumably Claire as in Claire from Bray, of all places. I'm safe nowhere, roysh, because suddenly Claire's there and Erika's behind her, with that this-place-is-so-beneath-me look she seems to, like, wear permanently. When Erika sees me, she goes, 'Your *wife* is looking for you, Ross,' and I go,

'Well, I'm here amn't I?' and she goes, 'She has some joyous news for you,' and then she turns to Donnacha and she's like, 'So you're Claire's new . . . *boyfriend*. She tells us you're a barrister. My father knows Paddy McEntee. Which firm are you with?' and this is all news to me, roysh, because I always presumed Donnacha was like me – thick as a ditch basically.

The goy looks at Claire, roysh, then at Erika and he goes, 'Storbucks. Out in DCU,' and Erika just, like, screws up her face and goes, '*Storbucks?*' and then, looking all, like, delighted with herself, she goes, 'I thought you were a barrister?' and Donnacha goes, 'A *barista*! I'm a barista. As in, serving coffee?' and Claire's suddenly, like, pulling away from him, going, 'You said you were a barrister!' and he goes, 'Claire, I didn't. In fairness, the music was pretty loud in Rí Rá,' and Erika goes, '*Rí Rá!* Oh, Claire, he's just *perfect* for you,' and I can see Claire's eyes, roysh, just, like, welling up with, like, tears.

Erika goes, 'Don't start crying, Girl. You'll have that pan-stick make-up all over your face again,' showing basically no mercy and Claire turns around to Donnacha and goes, 'OH! MY! GOD! You've, like, *ruined* my Christmas. I can't believe you thought I'd *actually* want to be with someone who makes coffee for a living,' and off she focking storms to the jacks and behind me I hear Chloë go, 'OH! MY! GOD! That's like, *Aaahhh!*'

I'm about to peg it myself, roysh, before Sorcha gets here, but the next thing, roysh, who arrives over, only three of the biggest focking legends in the history of Irish rugby – we're talking Drico, Dorce and Shaggy, and Dorce says they met One F at a Russell earlier on and he told them to follow him on down and I'm like, 'Dorce, it's an honour to have you here. I worship at your altar, dude,' and what does he do, roysh, only high-fives me and tells me that he thinks I'm a legend too and he can't believe the IRFU have never given me a contract, which he doesn't have to say, roysh, especially given the number of times I wiped his eye with the ladies over the years.

Then I get chatting to the old Dricmeister himself about rugby and how I could be where he is today if I wasn't so into my scoops and getting my rock and roll, and I have to admit, roysh, I'm actually a bit in awe of the goy, though I'm pretty sure it's, like, mutual – two former schools rugby legends, living the dream, blahdy blahdy blah. So I'm just about to tell him, roysh, that I'm thinking of going back to playing rugby next year, maybe for, like, Greystones, when all of a sudden I get this, like, tap on the shoulder, roysh, and I spin around and who is it – OH FOCK! – only Sorcha.

I'm there, 'Hey, Babes. Thank God you got in. I was worried sick,' and she's like, 'OH MY GOD, Ross, *enough* already?! I've got something to tell you . . .' and I just go, 'Bit busy at the mo, Babes. I need to ask the bouncers to fock out those two boggers from Westlife,' and she goes, 'HELLO? I think this is slightly more important, Ross,' but everyone's watching and I SO don't want a scene.

So I go to walk away and I notice that Erika's suddenly up at the bor, roysh, and she's, like, chatting away to Ronan and he has his orm around her waist, the lucky focker, and I don't know what he's saying to her, roysh, but she's clearly loving it because she's, like, smiling again and then I see her turn around and give him, like, a peck on the lips and Ronan catches my eye and gives me the old thumbs-up.

Sorcha goes, 'HELLO? I *need* to talk to you, Ross,' but

I'm there, 'Later,' and she's like, 'Okay, I'll say it in front of everybody then . . . Ross, us two . . . are about to become three.'

And I just, like, freeze on the spot, roysh, because I think I know what she's hinting at. It's weird, roysh, might be all the champagne I knocked back with Samantha Mumba earlier, but everything's moving in, like, slow motion. I'm there, '*Oh my God*, I don't think I want to hear this,' and she goes, 'You *oh my God* better hear it, Ross,' and I look around me, roysh, and in that moment it all, like, suddenly hits me. JP couldn't have set it up better himself. I look at Erika and I go, 'A cow,' then I look at Donnacha and I'm like, 'A donkey,' then at Drico, Dorce and Shaggy and I'm there, 'Three focking kings.'

I see Fionn shaking his head. He goes, 'You goys didn't follow a stor to get here, did you?' and Drico nods his head over at One F and goes, 'No, we followed the goy from *The Stor*.'

This shit is, like, SO freaking me out. I go, 'What about the shepherds?' and Oisinn, who's suddenly arrived over, goes, 'The goys from Westlife – they're boggers, roysh? And we all know that boggers like to *look after* sheep.'

I point at Fionn and I go, 'Look, we even have a virgin.'

So Sorcha goes, 'Ross, I'm pregnant,' and probably the worst thing in the world that a basic husband can say at this point is, Oh, and I suppose it's mine? which is what I actually do say. I go, 'Oh, and I suppose it's mine?' which earns me a slap across the boat, followed by a Bacordi Breezer all over my new beige chinos.

Then Fionn – it would *have* to be Fionn – goes, 'The scene is complete. Look everyone, the child's father thinks he's God,' and of course everyone's just, like, cracking their holes laughing.

I'm just there, 'And a merry focking Christmas to you, too, orseholes.'